Vintages
and
Traditions

Smithsonian Series in Ethnographic Inquiry

William L. Merrill and Ivan Karp, Series Editors

Ethnography as fieldwork, analysis, and literary form is the distinguishing feature of modern anthropology. Guided by the assumption that anthropological theory and ethnography are inextricably linked, this series is devoted to exploring the ethnographic enterprise.

Advisory Board

AN ETHNOHISTORY OF SOUTHWEST FRENCH WINE COOPERATIVES

ROBERT C. ULIN

SMITHSONIAN INSTITUTION PRESS
Washington and London

Copy Editor: Peter Donovan
Production Editor: Jack Kirshbaum
Designer: Janice Wheeler

Library of Congress Cataloging-in-Publication Data
Ulin, Robert C. (Robert Charles), 1951–
    Vintages and traditions : an ethnohistory of southwest French wine
cooperatives / Robert C. Ulin.
        p.   cm.
    Includes bibliographical references and index.
    ISBN 1-56098-627-1 (cloth). — ISBN 1-56098-628-X (paper)
        1. Wine industry—France, Southwest.   2. Producer cooperatives—
France, Southwest.   3. Vintners—France, Southwest.   4. Ethnology—
France, Southwest.   I. Title.
    HD9382.7.S64U44   1996
    338.4'76632'009447—dc20   96-18749
                                                                                            CIP

British Library Cataloguing-in-Publication Data is available

Manufactured in the United States of America
03 02 01 00 99 98 97 96 5 4 3 2 1

Printed on recycled paper. ∞ The paper used in this publication meets the minimum
requirements of the American National Standard for Information Sciences—Permanence
of Paper for Printed Library Materials Z39.48-1984.

Cover illustration: Michel Besson of the St.-Estèphe cooperative performing the second
plowing to remove the soil from the feet of the plant. Photograph by Robert C. Ulin

For permission to reproduce illustrations appearing in this book, please correspond
directly with the author. All photographs were taken either by him or Inge Meffert.
The Smithsonian Institution Press does not retain reproduction rights for these
illustrations individually, or maintain a file of addresses for photo sources.

To the memory of my parents
Ruth and Alex
and especially for my wife
Inge

CONTENTS

ACKNOWLEDGMENTS

It seems only fitting that a book on wine cooperatives should acknowledge the contribution of informants not simply as individual suppliers of information but as coparticipants in this project. Most of what I have come to understand about wine cooperatives I owe to the winegrowers and administrators of the Sigoulès, Monbazillac, Pauillac, St.-Estèphe, Listrac, and Bégadan cooperatives and their marketing organizations. I am grateful for their intellectual challenge, patience, and trust in sharing with me what were often the personal details of their winegrowing lives. Without their assistance, it is unlikely that this book could have ever been written.

A special thanks goes to André Sabatier, who first welcomed me at the Centre d'Études et de Recherches d'Histoire institutionnelle et régionale (CERHIR) of the University of Bordeaux where I was a visiting scholar on two different occasions during my field research. Professor Sabatier's profound knowledge of rural French history and challenging intellect did much to set me on the right course. Professor Sabatier also made his office and personal library available to me. Moreover, the association with Professor Sabatier and CERHIR did much to legitimize my presence among winegrowers during the early stages of my research.

There are several French friends who have done much to support my research over the years. I thank Yvês and Martine Lebreton, the Agnès family, the residents of La Salle, and especially Malou LeCoq. Malou not only provided housing for me during my field research in Sigoulès but it was through her contacts that I was able to pursue field research in the Médoc.

I also express my gratitude to the Wenner-Gren Foundation for Anthropological Research for having confidence in my work on French wine cooperatives and most especially for funding my field research in 1984 and again in 1989. Likewise, a special acknowledgment goes to Allegheny College for granting me a paid leave in 1989 and for supporting my summer research in France as well.

There are numerous persons, colleagues and friends, who read parts of the original manuscript or in some cases its entirety. I thank, therefore, Jim McGlew, Jackie Litt, David Miller, Sherry Wellman, Michael Herzfeld, Andrew Strathern, Ivan Karp, and especially Len Helfgott who provided the most copious criticism. However, as the notion of authorship implies, I remain fully responsible for the arguments presented including whatever shortcomings that are present.

Daniel Goodwin, Director of the Smithsonian Institution Press, encouraged this project practically from its inception. Every year at the Anthropology meetings Daniel would inquire as to the progress of the research and expressed great interest in seeing the book come to fruition. This helped through the difficult times and so to him I owe a special gratitude. Likewise, I thank my production editor from the Smithsonian, Jack Kirshbaum, and my copyeditor, Peter Donovan, both of whom were an enormous help in transforming the manuscript into its polished version.

In order to present a number of different voices in this book, I have included material taken directly from interviews with informants. I thank Sheila Shinn who had the difficult task, more hermeneutic than technical, of transcribing tapes occasionally lacking in quality and often complicated by local dialect. Phil and Kathryn Wolfe read over and corrected my English translations of the French transcripts with the intention of preserving the colloquial nature of the original speech. To them I am likewise indebted. Finally, Brent Nordstrom solved the problem of how to generate computer maps of France and so is responsible for the maps showing southwest French wine cooperatives and the winegrowing regions of France.

Parts of this book have been published previously in the form of journal articles and so I would like to thank the following publishers for permission to reproduce them here. Chapter 1 on the theme of anthropology and history is taken in part from "The Current Tide in American Europeanist Anthropology" (*Anthropology Today*, December 1991) and "Critical Anthropology Twenty Years Later: Modernism and Postmodernism in Anthropology" (*Critique of Anthropology*, Volume 1, 1991). Chapter 2 is a longer version of "Invention and Representation as Cultural Capital in Southwest French Winegrowing History" (*American Anthropologist*, Volume 97, Number 3, 1995). Finally, parts of Chapter 3 are from "Cooperation or Cooptation: A Southwest French Wine Cooperative" (*Dialectical Anthropology*, Volume 13, 1988).

I save my final acknowledgment for my wife, Inge Meffert, who accompanied me throughout the second phase of my research in the Médoc and who has endured, along with our Yannick and Yolanda, the trials and tribulations associated with the writing of this book. Not only has her love and support brought me through more than one impasse, but her intelligence, honesty, and tireless critical readings of the manuscript have more than once forced me to rethink an argument and to avoid the caricatures that sometimes can mar ethnographic writing. To her I owe the greatest intellectual and personal debt and so it is to her that this book is dedicated.

INTRODUCTION

This book results from eleven years of research on southwest French wine cooperatives and their grower-members. As so often happens in selecting a research project, my initial encounter was fortuitous. While visiting one of the Dordogne's many historical sites in southwest France, I made the acquaintance of a French couple, Serge and Nicole, who were vacationing with their daughter and a friend. In what I came to discover was a typically French manner, they engaged me in a lively conversation, perhaps better stated as debate, about the United States, France, and the international political scene. Much to my surprise, they invited me to join them for a visit to Nicole's family in the nearby village of Sigoulès.

Shortly after arriving in the village, I was introduced to Nicole's parents, grandmother, and younger sister at the evening meal. The family owns a small grocery store that Nicole's mother runs and a farm that is managed by her father. In addition to raising cows on the farm, Nicole's father is a winegrower and a member of the local cooperative. Throughout the meal, he told stories of his life as a winegrower and shared just enough information about the local cooperative to stimulate my interest and especially my imagination. These stories brought to mind Marx's theory of commodity fetishism, and how often we focus on the product itself to the exclusion of knowing anything about the producers. As we shall see with Sigoulès wine, this is especially true when the commodity produced is regarded as relatively ordinary. At the time, I envisioned the cooperative in romantic terms, naively believing its collectivism to be anticapitalist and even a source of oppositional regional identity, a view that I would come to reject in due time. However, little did I realize that this initial encounter would come to engage so much of my thought and effort in the coming years.

WINEGROWERS AT THE MARGINS

The southwest French wine-cooperative movement is a comparatively recent phenomenon in French winegrowing history, which can be traced to Roman times. Though the first French wine cooperative was founded in the south in Languedoc at the dawn of the twentieth century, the movement in the southwest did not materialize until the middle to late 1930s following a series of crises widely acknowledged to be economic and political in nature. These first cooperatives, like those of today, sought to augment the competitiveness and independence of small growers vis à vis large producers and the dominant merchant houses of Bordeaux by vinifying and marketing their members' wines collectively. Although wine cooperatives facilitated collective production and marketing, they served an essentially pragmatic rather than political purpose in enabling small and medium-size proprietors to accommodate to changes in the capitalist production and marketing of wine.[1] Moreover, wine cooperatives offered growers and the French government a medium through which to control the quantity and quality of production, thus ameliorating the crises that ensued from overproduction and fraud.

The wine-cooperative movement also raises questions concerning the social construction of French winegrowing history and culture. In spite of the fact that there are currently more than one thousand wine cooperatives throughout France that in most cases produce a significant portion of regional production, very little has been written about the history and contemporary status of the wine-cooperative movement. With few exceptions, most notably Guichard and Roudié (1985) and Loubère, Sagnes, Frader, and Pech (1985), the major works by geographers, historians, and oenologists such as Roger Dion (1977), Marcel Lachiver (1988), and Emile Peynaud (1988) make only passing reference to cooperatives and then generally to note how they have improved the quality and competitiveness of small producers and thus have contributed to securing their livelihood. The principal focus of these works tends to be the large estates in elite winegrowing regions and especially those wines which are most renowned. The question remains as to why those cooperative winegrowers who are so important to French wine production have remained, in Eric Wolf's sense (1982), marginal to the writing of French winegrowing history.[2]

The above question is central to this historical ethnography in that I explore the interrelated political-economic and cultural processes through which the wine-cooperative movement has come to be marginalized in winegrowing literature and culture. Exploring the marginality of wine cooperatives historically reveals the cultural and class differentiation of winegrowers ensuing from the specifics of capital accumulation in southwest France. It also offers to open French winegrowing history to a multiplicity of narratives and readings which, in turn, raise the more general relation between representation and power.

THE FIELDWORK

With the relation between representation and power in mind, I arrived in France in the fall of 1984 to commence my fieldwork on southwest French wine cooperatives. I selected the village of Sigoulès and its cooperative as my field site for several reasons. Sigoulès is the cantonal seat for seventeen communes, the commune being the smallest administrative unit in France. Sigoulès thus houses the cadastral records that are important in documenting both the size and transfer of winegrowing properties. Most important, however, its location in the Dordogne or the Périgord and proximity to Bordeaux (90 kilometers) enabled me to focus on a winegrowing region that while having a long-standing historical connection to Bordeaux has nonetheless a reputation that generally falls considerably short of Bordeaux. Winegrowers from the vicinity of Sigoulès are thus largely ignored by wine experts and connoisseurs whose principal criterion of importance is the reputation for quality production. However, if we take size rather than quality alone

Winegrowing regions of France

as a criterion of significance, Sigoulès is far from marginal in that it is the second largest wine cooperative in southwest France. Finally, my contact in the village cannot be overemphasized in that it is nearly impossible to make much headway in rural France without the assistance of personal contacts and introductions.

The early phases of my research, like most fieldwork, proceeded very slowly. Apart from being somewhat unprepared for the temporal rhythm of the countryside, it took some time to acquire the patience to cope with canceled or postponed appointments and the all-too-common "I'll show you how that is done tomorrow." In the long run, I was rarely let down by informants, who explained with great patience the details of the cooperative and their lives as winegrowers. Moreover, there was

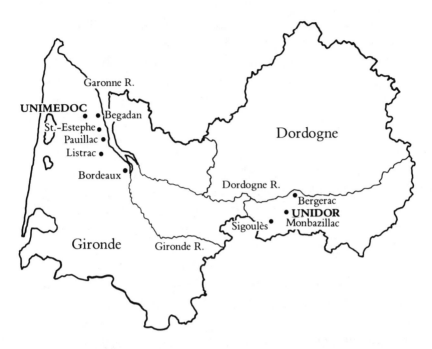

Wine cooperatives on which field research was conducted. UNIMEDOC and UNIDOR are marketing organizations.

much to be done in terms of archival work and my travels to the Bordeaux municipal library were frequent. Although I was led to believe that the departmental archives, located an hour's drive to the north in the city of Périgueux, contained very little of historical interest regarding the cooperative movement, I nonetheless spent considerable time perusing agricultural journals from the late 1920s and early 1930s. Every so often I was rewarded with an article that addressed the social conditions and political climate for small winegrowers in the period just preceding the founding of wine cooperatives.

I decided shortly after my arrival in southwest France that it was important to obtain ethnographic materials on a second wine cooperative so as to avoid reaching conclusions that were idiosyncratic. The nearest cooperative was Monbazillac, located a mere 9 kilometers from Sigoulès and just 3 kilometers from the important city of Bergerac. Monbazillac was a good choice for comparison because, unlike Sigoulès, the majority of its members pursued winegrowing on a full-time basis. Moreover, Monbazillac produced a renowned sweet white wine that considerably outdistanced the reputation of Sigoulès red, white, and even rosé wines.[3] Through the Sigoulès director, I was able to make contact with the director of Monbazillac as well as officials from an important marketing organization (UNIDOR) responsible for commercializing Dordogne cooperative wines. The director of Monbazillac facilitated, in turn, contacts with his member growers.

This first phase of fieldwork in the Dordogne lasted approximately one year. While I learned much about contemporary wine cooperatives and the early history of the wine-cooperative movement, I realized that my focus on cooperative growers to the near exclusion of elite growers and their wines may have hindered my efforts to draw closer to ethnographic materials seminal to understanding the wine-cooperative movement. That is, I recognized that the position occupied by wine cooperatives in the southwest French winegrowing framework and hierarchy was directly related to the long-term contact and relations between elite and generally small-scale growers. And so any foregrounding of the wine-cooperative movement must devote greater attention to how this relation has been constructed. I sensed this only partially when my Sigoulès informants so often asked me why I had come to study them when the famous Bordeaux vineyards were so close. I decided, therefore, that I would return to France at the first opportunity but this time to concentrate on southwest cooperatives in an esteemed winegrowing region.

With the exception of summer research of an exploratory nature, it was not until the spring of 1989 that I returned to southwest France to commence comparative field research on wine cooperatives. I selected the Médoc as a field site, located directly to the north of Bordeaux, because it is one of the most celebrated winegrowing regions in France, and unlike the Dordogne, has a significant number of cooperatives in proximity to famous château estates. I decided to focus my attention on the four Médoc cooperatives of Pauillac, Listrac, St.-Estèphe, and Bégadan as well as the marketing organization UNIMEDOC. I selected the first three cooperatives because of the celebrated reputation of their communal classifications and Bégadan because of its sizable membership and substantial vineyard hectarage cultivated (see Appendix) and the possibility that it offered a contrast to the others in carrying the more generic Médoc classification.[4] I telephoned the directors or in some cases presidents of these cooperatives to arrange initial interviews. Following these interviews, they agreed to introduce me to growers who fit the variable profile of age and gender that I had established for prospective informants. I was especially interested in interviewing older informants, because of their potential knowledge of the early history of their cooperatives, and female growers, because they were initially absent from my earlier study of Sigoulès and Monbazillac.[5] The cooperative administrators also agreed to familiarize me with all phases of cooperative work and to invite me to periodic festivals that were held to celebrate and promote local wines. These initial contacts were vital to meeting a wide range of cooperative winegrowers, officials from the collective marketing organization, and even independent growers and persons who were employed by the large château estates.

My research in the Médoc proceeded with relative ease compared to that in the Dordogne. I had a greater sense of what to expect from wine cooperatives and growers, and my overall knowledge of the wine-cooperative movement led me to pursue avenues of inquiry that were more focused. However, it did not take me long to realize that the systems of cultivating, vinifying, and marketing were nearly identical in the Dordogne and the Médoc and thus that the conclusions I had reached in my first study were essentially in need of only minor modifications. That is, at the formal level of organization and the mechanics of the cooperative system, there were few differences between wine cooperatives in the two regions of my research. This is, I believe, largely attributable to the legislation that established mandates for modernization and control of quantity and quality of production, institutionalized in a cooperative charter that is nearly uniform throughout the southwest. Nevertheless, my suspicion that I had overlooked important matters in my first study was borne out. My confirmation of the importance of elite wines to the formation of the southwest French winegrowing hierarchy and thus the subaltern status and identity of wine cooperatives more than justified my comparative research in the Médoc.

In fact, it was as a consequence of field research in the Médoc that I came to understand how important culture is, viewed as lived social interactions, the symbolic and the contested, to both the construction and reproduction of the political economy of winegrowing.[6] That is, differences in climate and soil can be invoked rhetorically to conceal the cultural and historical construction of class privilege or, in Roger Keesing's sense of mimesis (1992), subordinate populations can reproduce the very logic and hegemonic discourse of their privileged counterparts. The potential of subaltern populations to reproduce the conditions of their subordination through the product of their labor points to the cultural construction of commodities and commodity relations. This is not, however, to overlook, as the regional and global emphasis of the field research suggests, that political economy likewise limits the cultural representation of wine and winegrowers.

Although this book and the field research on which it is based have much in common with the global emphasis of recent ethnographies, it is somewhat distinct in focusing on institutions and their historical agents rather than the more common village and tribe. Moreover, I have departed from the anthropological convention of anonymity by using the actual names of wine cooperatives and their representative organizations. It would simply make no sense, for example, to compare the Pauillac cooperative to others in the Médoc or to Sigoulès in the Dordogne without knowing the history and associations of place that are so central to winegrowing. However, I have followed the convention of maintaining the anonymity of informants through the use of pseudonyms—to the disappointment of some, but not all, of my informants.

SYNOPSIS OF CHAPTERS

The book is organized so as to present early on much of the theoretical argument and historical background that I believe is central to a critical grasp of the contemporary wine cooperative and the problems it presently faces. The book commences with a more general first chapter that addresses the practical and theoretical relation between anthropology and history that has matured over the past twenty years. Special attention is given to the association between Geertz's interpretive anthropology in the form of "thick description" and what has become known as the "new cultural history." It is argued that although the interpretive perspective provides a highly textured, at times nearly sensory appreciation of daily life in a specific or local context, it often does so at the expense of the broader interregional, national, or international ties that link local and global domains dialectically. This chapter will be especially valuable to the general reader who may not be familiar with the interchange between anthropology and history. For the more specialized reader, this chapter sets the tone for my own treatment of historical themes throughout the work.

The second chapter qualifies Hobsbawm and Ranger's (1983) invention-of-tradition theme in order to challenge the assumption, common to much of the literature on French winegrowing, that the superior reputation of Médoc wines, not to mention the Bordeaux region as a whole, is attributable to an especially favorable climate and soil. This argument is deconstructed by showing that prior to the English occupation of southwest France from the twelfth to fifteenth centuries, and perhaps even as late as the dawn of the eighteenth century, it was actually the wines of the interior, with their reputedly less favorable climate and soil, that were regarded as superior in quality to those produced in the immediate vicinity of Bordeaux. The ascendancy of Bordeaux wines over those of the interior is thus, as I argue, largely inclusive of a social history that involves among other things the role of elites in shaping southwest French winegrowing legislation. This legislation obfuscated the recognition of wine as a social construct and the invention by elites of a winegrowing tradition that set the elite wines apart culturally from those of the peasant masses and small proprietors. Nonetheless, all growers of the Médoc, including the members of contemporary wine cooperatives, are able by virtue of a symbolic contiguity to make use of the region's considerable cultural capital in the marketing of their wines and thus have a commercial advantage not available to Dordogne cooperatives. Moreover, even though there is some degree of tension between the identities of small growers from the cooperatives and the elite owners of Médoc winegrowing estates, the opposition is largely couched in terms which are mimetic of the discourse and culture of elite winegrowing.

Chapters 3 and 4 trace the social history of winegrowing in southwest France with the end of identifying the multiple circumstances and processes that led to the founding of wine cooperatives in the early part of the twentieth century. Chapter 3 begins with the English occupation of southwest France from the twelfth to fifteenth centuries and its consequences for the ascendancy of the Bordeaux wine trade. However, the English occupation—while important commercially—did not essentially transform relations of production that were feudal. Rather it was the Religious Wars of the sixteenth and seventeenth centuries that indirectly precipitated social changes in the winegrowing sector by opening up new markets with northern Europe, by furthering a process of monocropping and an intensified division of labor, and by contributing to the ascendancy of a new class of bourgeois Protestant merchants who played an important role in cultivating the Bergerac wine trade and that of the interior in general.

Chapter 3 concludes with a discussion of the development of the *grands crus* and the social consequences of the infamous phylloxera blight. The development of the *grands crus* in the late seventeenth and eighteenth centuries was pursued by French growers in order to counter the flooding of French markets by cheaper foreign wines. However, its greater long-term consequence was to transform a mercantile capitalist wine trade into relations of production more identifiable as capitalist. The phylloxera blight which ravaged French vineyards at the end of the nineteenth century shattered a fragile accommodation between small producers and elites. Some large growers and merchant-proprietors turned to the production of high-yielding vine stocks, a type of production that was predominantly identified in southwest France with small peasant producers. The phylloxera blight, along with other maladies like mildew, reinforced the inequalities between classes of growers and thus helped set the stage for the appearance of wine cooperatives in the early twentieth century.

Chapter 4 addresses the political and economic climate in which the earliest cooperatives were founded. Contrary to the views of most scholars, I argue that political motives were intertwined with practical considerations in the founding of the earliest southwest French wine cooperatives. However, this is not to deny that wine cooperatives essentially provided an institutional framework whereby small growers could accommodate to the exigencies of the capitalist production and circulation of wine. Moreover, the cooperatives exemplify the desire of the

French government to modernize the viticultural sector and to control both the quantity and quality of production—a process that would eventually eliminate small growers who were unwilling to comply with the cooperative legislation.

Chapter 5 explains the cycle of labor that is characteristic of work both in the vineyards and at the cooperatives. It both addresses and elaborates the meaning of winegrowing work as articulated by cooperative growers themselves. I argue, moreover, that the historical rupture between viticulture, the cultivation of grape plants, and vinification, the processing of harvested grapes into wine, which is reproduced by the cooperatives, has done much to disempower the members of cooperatives. This is, however, shown to be consistent with the development of the capitalist division of labor.

Chapter 6 presents the cooperative organization as a potential vehicle for reproducing power and inequality at the cooperatives. The relation between the governance of the cooperative and its differential social-class composition is highlighted, as well as the seeming indifference of many growers to most cooperative issues with the exception of profitability.

Apart from vinifying members' grapes and monitoring the quality of wines produced, marketing is the primary activity that is vital to the success of cooperatives. Chapter 7 outlines both the strategies of marketing pursued by cooperatives individually as well as the institutions that exist for the exclusive purpose of marketing their wines collectively. This chapter not only analyzes the broader articulation of cooperatives with a world system of political economy but it also discusses and evaluates more local problems that have developed between individual cooperatives and the larger marketing organizations that commercialize cooperative wines.

Chapter 8 conveys the family stories of three winegrowers from the Pauillac, Listrac, and St.-Estèphe cooperatives. These stories bring us close to the daily concerns of cooperative winegrowers and raise such important issues as family succession and gender. The issue of gender is especially salient because there are a growing number of women who have assumed control of the family vineyards and thus are pursuing an occupation that is largely regarded in masculine terms.

The final chapter looks to the past history of winegrowing to grasp the present problems that cooperatives face—multinational corporations purchasing vineyards at vastly inflated prices, and the potential complications for marketing that are likely to ensue with the new liberalized trading regulations that are taking shape through the European Union. Although the challenge to small growers and their cooperatives is formidable in both cases, there is some hope on the part of cooperative administrators that the very strengths of collective production and marketing that enabled cooperatives to succeed in the past will enable them to forge new strategies that are well attuned to an increasingly concentrated and competitive international system of political economy.

The ethnohistorical account of southwest French wine cooperatives that follows should not be taken as exhaustive of the experience of all small-scale French winegrowers and French wine cooperatives. For example, the Languedoc region where the earliest wine cooperatives were founded and where cooperatives exist in large numbers today, stands out from Bordeaux and the southwest interior by virtue of the militancy of its growers. Likewise, the cultural construction of elite winegrowing history in Bordeaux, which strongly shaped the objectives and possibilities for southwest growers, is in some regards particular and therefore should not be regarded as simply identical to the history or current circumstances of France's other elite winegrowing regions. The Burgundy winegrowing region, for example, which is often regarded as the primary competitor to Bordeaux, does not have a history of château vineyards and thus has developed a system of classification and cultural representation that is distinct from what we find in Bordeaux. Nevertheless, the proximity and especially the shared history of the wines of the southwest French interior and those that have come to be celebrated in the immediate vicinity of Bordeaux and which serve collectively as the case study for this book point beyond wine as an object of consumption and to the more general theme of the historical struggle of real human agents in their political-economic and cultural self-formation. With this in mind, we turn our attention to this struggle and most immediately to the relation between anthropology and history.

ANTHROPOLOGY AND HISTORY |1|

The majority of southwest French wine cooperatives were founded in the mid to late 1930s following a worldwide economic crisis and a series of poor harvests that made it progressively more difficult for small-scale winegrowers to sell their harvested grapes and wines. Through the creation of cooperatives devoted to vinification and marketing, small growers were able to increase their competitiveness while gaining some independence from powerful Bordeaux marketing firms and their intermediaries. Many of these original cooperatives have grown in membership and volume of production, accounting nowadays for a large portion of regional production. However, because cooperatives produce wines of lesser reputation than those of the château estates and large independents, they are generally ignored in much of the literature on southwest French winegrowing. Consequently, wine cooperatives and their member-growers have been relegated largely to the margins of winegrowing history.

To draw cooperative winegrowers out of the shadows of history, it is imperative to show how the southwest French winegrowing past has come to shape a class-stratified and hierarchical winegrowing present. However, the opening of southwest French winegrowing history to other than the documentation of elites involves more than a simple chronology of events. It involves a process of mediation to uncover what is hidden or concealed in a differentiated past. This is a task that demands attention to both the commodification of wine historically, or its political economy, and the culturally formative process through which wine is represented as a mark of social or class distinction.

Pleading the case for a mediated history of wine cooperatives leaves, however, much to the imagination. There has been a vast increase in contemporary ethnographies that are cloaked in history and an equally large number of histories claiming to be ethnographic. Moreover, as Ortner argues, although the rapprochement of anthropology with history is positive, "it covers, rather than reveals, important distinctions. Insofar as history is being amalgamated with virtually every kind of anthropological work, it offers a pseudo-integration of the field which fails to address some of the deeper problems" (1984:159). It is thus important, as Ortner suggests, to establish some theoretical specificity to the relationship between anthropology and history. This chapter will therefore address, albeit selectively, the principal theoretical positions and points of tension that inform the recent interchange between anthropology and history and which, in turn, are important to the ethnohistorical account of wine cooperatives that unfolds in subsequent chapters.

THE PAST IN THE PRESENT

At this moment, as anthropologists of every ilk—structuralists, functionalists, hermeneutes, reflexivists, etc.—rush to declare themselves in favor of the study of history, the sturdy historiographic traditions of American anthropology have been forgotten. (Mintz 1987:176)

While the long-standing relationship between anthropology and history should be self-evident, the fragmentation and hegemony of intellectual inquiry and political practice, combined with a not-to-be-underemphasized appetite for novelty, has all too often resulted in scholars overlooking the continuities of current interests and modes of conceptualizing the *other* with those of the ancestors. By interests, I have in mind the political-economic and sociocultural processes that have shaped and that, in turn, are shaped by the discipline of anthropology. These interests are *knowledge constitutive* and thus have an ongoing historical significance in the practice of anthropology and how anthropologists construct their objects, or communicatively speaking, cosubjects of knowledge.[1] Therefore, I believe that the question of history *in* anthropology, both past and present, is related dialectically to the history *of* anthropology.

While I maintain that the history of anthropology has shaped anthropological uses of history, it is beyond the scope of this work to reconstruct this relation in any comprehensive sense. Suffice it to say that anthropologists have made noteworthy efforts, Talal Asad's (1973) and Dell Hymes's (1972) edited volumes being prime examples, toward disclosing the complicity between the early history of anthropology and European colonialism and now neocolonialism.[2] However, in spite of these efforts, many anthropologists still believe that this politically suspect past is simply an unfortunate legacy of our ancestors that has been left far behind with the embracing of scientific paradigms and the rejection of unilineal models of evolution that supported ideologically the "civilizing" mission of colonialism. That this view is naive and lacking historically, a condition by no means unique to anthropology, is supported by a number of recent works that focus on the issue of ethnographic and historical representation and the theoretical construction of the object-subject of knowledge.

The discipline of history, even more than anthropology, tended to uphold a positivistic outlook until surprisingly recently. Most historians maintained that conclusions arrived at through essentially archival research must rest upon "sound evidence" or "facts" (Cohn 1980, 1981). This perspective was challenged not only by a marxist-informed social history, E. P. Thompson being exemplary, but also through the theoretical alternative offered by the antihistorian's historian, Hayden White (1978). White, unlike Thompson, challenged the historical orthodoxy by examining the relationship between authority and the construction of historical narratives. Taking his lead from literary criticism, White maintained that arguments conveyed through historical writing rested necessarily upon the social construction of narratives that appealed, albeit unreflexively, to conventional rhetorical devices in order to appear authoritative. White identified four rhetorical styles or genres: tragedy, comedy, irony, and satire. For example, according to White, the power and hence authority of the marxist narrative comes from the rhetoric of tragedy—while celebrating labor and the original unity of the human subject, the narrative laments the fall of the working class at the hands of capitalist exploiters. The important point here, in spite of the ahistorical nature of White's neo-Kantian categories that ironically do not account for their own constitution historically, is that the authority of historical narratives, and one could just as easily add ethnographic, resides in rhetoric—that which is meant to persuade—rather than facts or evidence conceived to be independent of their social construction.

Though White's argument can be construed as challenging "realist" approaches to ethnographic and historical writing, a point also made by Marcus and Fischer (1986) and Clifford (1988), the perspectives represented by Edward Said (1978, 1989) and Johannes Fabian (1983) make a more direct association between representation and power. Said argues, for example, that occidental scholarship has presented the Orient in terms that largely accentuate its homogeneity and exoticism. This, he maintains, can even be discovered in authors such as Marx. Said's principal point is that there is a connection between the representation of the East as homogeneous and efforts to subject the East to Western hegemonic and civilizing processes.[3] While Said's position has been criticized for overlooking Eastern imperialism and for presenting the West in overly homogeneous terms (Ohnuki-Tierney 1990), it has also received much praise in anthropology and cultural studies. Said has been a principal illustrator of the exoticism of anthropology's other and in showing the relationship between this representation of the other and power.

Fabian, on the other hand, takes us directly to the heart of anthropology in his contention that the other has often been denied a temporality that would enable us to recognize indigenous societies as our contemporaries. Fabian approaches the question as to how anthropology constructs its cosubject of knowledge through a historical survey of European time reckoning. Beginning with Bossuet's universal history and the secularization of time, Fabian traces transformations in the concept of time through the eighteenth and nineteenth centuries and tries to show that there are continuities between this earlier time reckoning and the contemporary practice of anthropology.

Fabian argues that nineteenth-century evolutionary models took distance in space as a means of affirming distance in time in that the indigenous other was equated to humanity's dawn while Europeans were represented as quintessentially civilized. Although anthropologists have long rejected the sense of progress and linear development implicit in nineteenth-century evolutionary models, Fabian contends that the temporal distancing implicit in these early models has been maintained and reproduced through contemporary anthropology. This, believes Fabian, can be seen in the conceptual repertoire that divides primitive from civilized, rural from urban, and modern from traditional. That is to say that the above divisions or dualities serve to deny, as was the case with nineteenth-century evolutionary theory, a common temporal base to anthropologists and their informant others. Fabian maintains that unless anthropologists and informants share a contemporaneity, it is impossible to participate in social relations that are fully intersubjective and reciprocal. The denial of coevalness or temporal distancing serves in Foucault's sense as a technology of domination and, in turn, reinforces the commitment of anthropology to a noncontemporaneous other.[4] Fabian believes that the resolution of this problem is not so much epistemological as political in that anthropologists must strive to change the praxis and politics of anthropological research and writing.

The contributions of White, Said, and Fabian, although somewhat different in theoretical orientation and emphasis, can be taken collectively to support a view of ethnographic and historical research and writing as socially constituted and socially constituting. Although anthropologists spend the majority of their time with informants distant in space and historians with peoples and events distant in time, this, as the above comments imply, is a formality of little consequence to epistemology and power. Moreover, the perspectives of Said and Fabian suggest that the absence of subaltern populations from historical accounts is not benign oversight but is, as we shall see with respect to cooperative winegrowers in Chapter 2, a consequence of reproducing and even taking as natural their marginality within social relations of power.

While Said's and Fabian's insights are directly related to issues of representation and power, this by no means exhausts the continuity between past and present as it bears on the relationship between anthropology and history. As John Cole has argued (1977), and here he is close to Fabian, the colonial legacy of anthropology established "peoples without history" as the primary topic of social inquiry within a virtual framework that was circumscribed locally. That is, not only did anthropology become identified with the study of primitive and peasant societies of the Third World, but the theoretical perspective employed to study these societies in structural-functionalism emphasized the study of their institutions, customs, and social practices as timeless.[5] History became identified with literacy while the oral traditions of primitive cultures came to be regarded as mythological.[6] The independence movements of the 1960s shattered the theoretical hegemony of structural-functionalism. As a static and teleological model that regarded human society as continuous with nature, it was unable to account for social change.

Cole argues that although anthropologists began to shift their framework away from static systems to the evaluation of factors that promote or retard change, such a shift did little to transform the image of the single village or society as the unit of analysis nor did it do much to challenge the essentially static view of small-scale societies as represented by structural-functionalism and the colonial view of the other. Rather, the new emphasis on social change made use of the history of European modernization as a means of explaining Third World poverty and underdevelopment in technology, government, and social organization. Anthropologists employed a Eurocentric framework in attributing the blame for Third World underdevelopment to tradition or culture rather than a more broadly conceived world system of political economy. By a Eurocentric framework, Cole has in mind theories such as Lewis's "culture of poverty," Banfield's "amoral familism," Horton's "open and closed society," and Foster's "image of the limited good," to name just a few of the most influential. All of these frameworks imply, in one way or another, that if the Third World would remove the fetters of tradition and follow the European course of modernization, these presently impoverished and underdeveloped nations would enjoy the prosperity and enlightened social organization presently enjoyed by Europe and North America.

The relationship between anthropology and history discloses yet another side to hegemony when in fact, as Cole argues, European history serves as the model for development in societies conventionally studied by anthropologists. While it could be argued that more anthropologists now pay attention to global processes important to the societies they study, the dichotomy of tradition and modernity, as well as the fetish of the Third World other, still loom large in the discipline.

The dichotomy or opposition between tradition and modernity long predates the academic discipline of anthropology in that it can be traced to the intellectual heritage of the Anglo-French Enlightenment and the era of European colonial expansion. As Peter Gay among others has maintained (1968), the Enlightenment advanced the belief in the critical faculties of universal reason over the time-honored convictions of tradition. Moreover, the nineteenth-century reaction, in the form of Romanticism, to the apparent excesses of Enlightenment reason had the unintended consequence, as Gadamer has noted (1975), of casting beliefs held to be traditional as lacking in reason. While the nineteenth century may have lauded Romanticism, Europeans came to identify, albeit with some ambivalence, with the rationality and sense of progress invested in industrial capitalism.[7] Although I have necessarily simplified what is evidently quite complex, the imagery of tradition and a nostalgia for the past were extended simultaneously to the colonial frontier and the European countryside.

The Comaroffs have remarked, for example, that the civilizing mission and rationality of European colonialism and images of the colonial other had a profound impact on how Europeans saw their own peasantry and the working class (1992). Colonized peoples and European peasants and workers alike were regarded as rude and uncivilized, a view that contributed a moral imperative to plans for modernization in the European countryside. Likewise, the early wine-cooperative legislation mandated that low-interest loans would only be given to those peasant winegrowers who were willing to modernize their production. Those who chose to preserve the conventional methods of cultivating grapes and producing wine, an identity that was not distinct from the self-identity of traditional culture, were stigmatized and in the long run rendered extinct. However, there was some ambivalence expressed toward the inhabitants of the countryside as the reputed simplicity of primitive peoples and European peasants was also representative for Europeans of pastoral times long surpassed.[8]

While the tension between the traditional and modern may initially appear from the point of view of intellectual history as a theme internal to Europe, it was pushed by European statecraft and the globalization of European society and economy to apply dialeccically to the colonies and the peripheries of Europe itself. It should therefore come as no surprise, as Michael Herzfeld has argued (1987), that this dichotomy has been reproduced in most of contemporary scholarship and that it has greatly influenced the separate domains staked out by respective disciplines in the human and social sciences. This dichotomy can be recognized in sources ranging from Lévy-Bruhl and his concept of "prelogical mentality" (1965) to Lévi-Strauss's "hot and cold" societies (1963) to the Anglo-American rationality debates.[9] Anthropologists have come to be identified, therefore, with traditional societies and have invested a considerable part of their professional identities in preserving this association.[10] Moreover, the contrast between traditional and modern still upheld by much of contemporary anthropology has led to a view of tradition as inert, reified, and timeless.

John Cole's essay is one of a growing body of contemporary anthropological sources that challenge reified views of tradition and overly orthodox anthropological identities (1977). Cole's view, which is consistent with much of the neomarxist and invention-of-tradition literature,[11] is that what we often regard as tradition is a product of ongoing transformations in the world system of political economy. That is, Cole believes that there are no isolated societies as all peoples, no matter the size of the social unit, are tied into regional, national, and even international systems that profoundly influence their social development and reproduction. Consequently, the very expansive political, economic, and cultural forces that have contributed to the shaping of modernity have also contributed to what we take to be tradition. Tradition is, therefore, neither an arbitrary creation nor a continuity with a timeless past but rather a continually emerging, mediated relation between past and present, the local and the international.

The tendency in anthropology to identify tradition with what is time-honored and unchanging, and modernization with rationalization along Western lines, has reproduced, argued Cole, theoretically and politically the split between Third World societies and those of western Europe.

By associating the primitive and peasant other with tradition and the European with modernization, anthropologists reinforce the exoticism of the other to which, as I have remarked above, the discipline tenaciously clings. This, in turn, has provided a formidable obstacle to the development of a Europeanist anthropology and to regarding Europeans themselves as suitable cosubjects for anthropological research, a point which my winegrowing informants were quick to point out, believing that anthropologists were the scholarly caretakers of primitives and "stones and bones." Furthermore, the dichotomy between the traditional and the modern has led many scholars until recently to overlook the division of Europe itself into core and peripheral areas, and how the core areas have developed economically at the expense of the periphery. The wealth of industrial northern Italy compared to the impoverishment of the south is a case in point. Northern Italians often account for the underdevelopment of the south in cultural rather than political-economic and historical terms.

The primary challenge to reified areal orthodoxies that mystify the relation of the traditional to the modern has tended to come, although not exclusively, from the marxist arena and more specifically variations of world-systems theory with a principal focus that is global. Moreover, as Sidney Mintz (1985) and Jane Schneider (1978) have shown, theories with a global focus have proven to be especially important to the historical study of commodities such as sugar and cloth and will prove to be equally salient to the ethnographic and historical account of wine.

GLOBAL THEORIES—GLOBAL HISTORIES

Tim Unwin argues rightly, in an important work on the historical geography of viticulture (1991), that the vast majority of essays and books on the history and geography of wine are surprisingly lacking in theory. Unwin maintains that in spite of the influence of Braudel and the early Annales school, most of the literature on French winegrowing, with few exceptions, elaborates local cases of French history and geography and thus overlooks broader issues and themes. Unwin gives as an example the colloquium that was held in Bordeaux in 1977 and published in the following year in two volumes edited by Huetz de Lemps.

In his bibliographic conclusion to these volumes Huetz de Lemps lists 701 books and articles by French writers of which 470 are concerned specifically with France. Most are local or regional studies of viticulture in the period after the seventeenth century, and few address wider issues concerning the marketing, distribution or consumption of wine. . . . the individual papers stand largely as empirical examples of viticulture, vinification and the cultural landscape of the vine in past places. (Unwin 1991:4–5)

While the local, empirical focus to which Unwin refers may not come as a surprise to those familiar with the most recent products of the Annales school that emphasize *mentalité,* surely wine, as Unwin argues, has a story that tacks back and forth between the local and the transnational. This was confirmed in my own research on the southwest of France. Although there was an internal dynamic to the southwest of France since at least the twelfth century that established a hierarchy of wine and privilege, the international commerce in wine is noteworthy and had profound consequences on the local circulation and consumption of wine. English warships from the twelfth century on measured their size in terms of the volume of wine that they could transport. That a global or at the very least an interregional perspective is necessary to grasp the formation of French winegrowing history should be evident. On the other hand, what is implied theoretically by a global perspective is not univocal and is a source of debate among anthropologists, historians, and cultural theorists. At issue for most scholars, as we shall see, is what importance should be given to culture and human agency in the constitution of the social world.

Although Unwin appeals to a diverse group of theories in his own account of winegrowing history, including the Annales school and Anthony Giddens's theory of structuration,[12] it is the dependency theory of Andre Gunder Frank and the world-systems theory of Immanuel Wallerstein that have largely motivated anthropologists and historians of the Anglo-American tradition, against a background of marxist scholarship in all its versions, to raise research questions and issues of a more global nature. In short, Frank has argued that the economic development of the European center was linked directly to the under-development and economic dependency of the Latin American periphery (1969). The evidence for this, according to Frank, rests with the flow of capital from periphery to center as well as the creation of a landed bourgeoisie responsive to and shaped by European and North American interests. Wallerstein has made use of core and periphery to explain the origins and development of the modern world system (1974). Wallerstein shows that the growth of a European-centered world economic system followed from the exploitation of resources in the Americas and the expansion of European trade into Africa and Asia. Moreover, Wallerstein believes, amid great controversy, that the origins of the capitalist mode of production can be traced to the system of mercantilism of the fourteenth century.

Although heavily indebted to world-systems and dependency theories, social anthropologists in general have not accepted either of these theories in their orthodox version. Eric Wolf (1982) and Sidney Mintz (1985), for example, while accepting the general orientation of globalist theory, have been foremost in advancing the anthropological critique directed against Frank and Wallerstein. Wolf and Mintz have argued respectively that dependency and world-systems theories overlook the local dynamics of the periphery in that the periphery is theorized largely as a reflex of the core. Moreover, the overdetermination of the periphery by the core leads to a simplified view of human action as a conduit for global processes. Consequently, it becomes impossible from the perspective of Frank and Wallerstein to understand both local-level resistance and the degree to which people in the periphery produce and reproduce their own social existence.

Wolf's and Mintz's critiques of dependency and world-systems theory, although sensitive to local context, should not be understood atavistically as an endorsement of community or village studies. Rather, Wolf and Mintz maintain, like the Comaroffs (1992), that the relation of core to periphery should be conceived in dialectical terms and that the periphery, in turn, should be recognized as making, without necessarily implying symmetry, a measurable impact on the core. This theoretical perspective is splendidly illustrated through Mintz's discussion of the impact of sugar on modern life (1985). Sugar which was produced in the Caribbean periphery with labor that came mostly from Africa would come to play an important role, maintains Mintz, in the European core by provisioning and satiating farm and factory workers, thus reducing the cost of creating and reproducing the proletariat.

Wolf, like Mintz, makes use of a global approach in seeking to account for the historical and social dynamics by which Europe would assert its dominion (1982). Wolf commences with a survey of the world in the year 1400 that shows that European states of the period were only weakly organized and not very powerful. Europe would have to await the ascendancy of northern Italian mercantile centers such as Genoa and Venice before the tide would begin to turn. These centers would play an important role in funding the warfare carried on by European monarchs and in supplying the capital for European expansion abroad. Wolf is careful to point out, though, that it was not the circulation of commodities alone that launched Europe on its new destiny but rather gradual transformations in the social relations of production upon which the circulation of commodities depended. Wolf distinguishes in great detail the paths of development followed by the tribute-taking states of Portugal and Spain, precariously dependent on foreign capital, from those of France and England. In contrast to a world-systems approach, Wolf creates a historical narrative that seeks to tack back and forth between international political and economic processes and the small-scale populations that are normally the privileged subject of anthropological inquiry. In this way, he hopes to cast light on those people usually left in history's shadow.

Although both works are somewhat different in terms of historical scope, Wolf and Mintz base their historical accounts equally on the logic of political economy. Moreover, apart from linking broad historical connections to local dynamics, each author claims to address what he perceives to be the overemphasis in anthropology and cultural studies on the autonomy of culture. Mintz, for example, criticizes Geertz's notion of culture as "webs of significance" by arguing that the generation of meaning is always constrained and profoundly shaped by social-class relations—a factor which he believes to be apparent in the different historical experiences of sugar on the part of the upper and working classes. The view of culture as constrained by social class is given further support by Wolf in maintaining that it is modes of production specifically that condition human consciousness.

> Contrary to those who believe that Mind follows an independent course of its own, I would argue that ideology making does not arise in the confrontation of Naked Man thinking about Naked Nature; rather, it occurs within the determinate compass of a mode of production deployed to render nature amenable to human use. (Wolf 1982:388)

It is clear that the force of Wolf and Mintz's historical argumentation, as well as their discussion of power itself, comes from the assertion that labor establishes the context of human self-formation and transformation, a view of history making that aligns their position with a certain orthodoxy of the marxist tradition.[13]

While some anthropologists and historians may have reservations concerning Wolf's and Mintz's views on culture, their dialectical reformulation and application of globalist theory has generally brought them wide acclaim. However, one exception is Michael Taussig who, ironically, takes them to task for the very reasons that Wolf and Mintz criticize dependency and world-systems theory. Taussig argues that Wolf and Mintz fail in their respective celebrated works to tell us very much about actual micropopulations and their "lived experience" in spite of their claims to cast light on those normally left in the shadows of history (1987). Taussig believes, therefore, that the writing of history without reference to concrete subjects and their lived experience becomes, as he maintains with the works of Wolf and Mintz, a narrative that simply tells itself.

Taussig's critique of Wolf and Mintz resonates widely, albeit not uniformly or universally, with anthropologists and historians who have called for a greater appreciation of symbols and tropes in ethnographic and historical studies of social change.[14] Moreover, Taussig's critique is also illustrative of the theoretical chasm that divides orthodox versions of political economy from cultural approaches to understanding social life. This theoretical divide, as we shall see, is a significant tension in my own account of wine cooperatives as the history of wine since very early on has been linked profoundly to long-distance trade in the form of mercantile capitalism. However, as I argue in Chapter 2, the political economy of winegrowing does not exhaust its conceptual and practical significance. Wine has long been a commodity that is symbolically charged. Moreover, and this is the central theoretical and historical problematic, the establishment of a winegrowing hierarchy in the southwest of France arises from the convergence of processes that are inextricably political-economic, symbolic, and cultural in nature. Consequently, any narrative that seeks to construct and represent ethnographically and historically the past and present of wine cooperatives must bridge the very theoretical gulf that currently divides political economy from cultural theory in anthropology and history. With this in mind, we turn to the claim that culture and symbolism have been insufficiently addressed in ethnographic and historical studies of social change.

THE NEW CULTURAL HISTORY AS HISTORICAL ANTHROPOLOGY

The new cultural history does not constitute a school of thought or a unified body of theory. Moreover, the influences on those reputed to be practitioners are diverse, ranging from the cultural reformulation of the Annales school to the poststructuralism of Foucault, and perhaps most importantly, to the symbolic and interpretive anthropology of Clifford Geertz. However, without risking oversimplification, it can be argued that the new cultural historians share a common concern with elaborating the meaning of contextualized cultural practices rather than emphasizing broadly conceived relations between groups, classes, and institutions as did the older political and social historians. In the words of Lynn Hunt, "the accent in cultural history is on the close examination— of texts, of pictures, and of actions—and an open-mindedness to what those examinations reveal, rather than on elaboration of new master narratives or social theories to replace the materialist reductionism of marxism and the Annales school" (1989:22).

The emphasis on the meaning of cultural practices and the close examination of texts resonates, as will be apparent to most anthropologists, with the ethnographic model of "thick description" as formulated by Clifford Geertz. Geertz's numerous publications on the problematics of interpretation have become enormously influential among theoretically minded historians in general and the new cultural historians in particular. Geertz presents the task of the anthropologist in hermeneutic rather than scientific terms by arguing that ethnographic description is an interpretive exercise directed toward the detailed elaboration of locally constructed social meanings. Ethnographic description along Geertzian lines is not meant to "get into the heads" of informants but rather to give the audience to which it is directed a "distance near" impression of informants as they go about constructing and forging the significance of their daily lives.

The affinity between Geertz and the new cultural historians is not only based upon "thick description" but also on the analogy between social action and text. Following the lead of Paul Ricoeur (1971) and the writings of semioticians, Geertz maintains that social action is like a text in that the multiple meanings of social action or events are dependent upon their objectification in discourse just as the intentions of an author are dependent upon their fixation in writing.[15] Without their fixation in discourse or writing, events or the intentions of authors would have no duration. The analogy between social action or events and texts has enabled anthropologists and historians to bridge the gap between oral and written traditions and to realize, as argued earlier, that the task of interpretation which anthropologists face in the field and historians in the archives is essentially the same.

The best known and widely cited example across the disciplines of thick description is Geertz's essay in *The Interpretation of Cultures* on the Balinese cockfight. The essay begins with an interesting and highly compelling account of the Geertzes' invisibility to the Balinese at the early stages of their fieldwork. The ice is broken when the Geertzes decide to attend an illegal cockfight which ends up being raided by the police. Rather than present their credentials to the police, the Geertzes follow suit with the locals and flee. The description of the cockfight itself is seductive as the reader is drawn into a narrative resplendent with sensuous imagery and highly charged and elaborated symbols. The reader is left with the impression of having been there with the Geertzes—there is no division between subject and object here.

In terms of genre or style, this account is similar to Carlo Ginzburg's *The Cheese and the Worms,* Emmanuelle Le Roy Ladurie's *Montaillou,* and Robert Darnton's *The Great Cat Massacre,* to name just a few of the celebrated works in the new cultural history. Ginzburg's story of a sixteenth-century miller, like Geertz's work, is highly evocative and provides for the reader, as does Ladurie's portrayal of Albigensian heretics in the south of France, a sense of the "life world" or "lived experience" in distant times.[16] Moreover, Ladurie's emphasis on the culture or *mentalité* of Albigensian heretics can be regarded as a signif- icant reversal of the Annales-school prioritization of climate, biology, and demography (White 1978). Darnton's book is the most eclectic of the three in that as a series of essays it covers topics ranging from peasant tales, to readers' responses to Rousseau, to the story of the cat massacre itself. Moreover, Darnton's connection to interpretive anthropology is direct in that his book is based largely on a course that he taught with Geertz over a period of years at Princeton.[17] In all three cases, the readers of these works can imagine themselves as a miller, heretic, or apprentice in a Paris workshop during the late 1730s. If the rhetorical strategy of the new cultural history is to bridge for the reader the gap of time and space, to recover the meaning or lived experience of another era, then surely they are successful—or are they?

William Roseberry argues, in an essay entitled "Balinese Cockfights and the Seduction of Anthropology," that Geertz's interpretive meth- odology, and by extension popular or cultural history, mystifies culture through its analogy to text in that Geertz overlooks the differentiation of culture as a consequence of being insufficiently attentive to differential power. Moreover, Roseberry adds, in a manner consistent with Mintz's earlier comments, that Geertz fails to grasp culture as a material social process and so culture is regarded more as a product than a process of producing. Roseberry concludes therefore that:

The cockfight has gone through a process of creation that cannot be separated from Balinese history. Here we confront the major inadequacy of the text as a metaphor for culture. A text is written; it is not writing. To see culture as an ensemble of texts or an art form is to remove culture from the process of its creation. If culture is a text, it is not everyone's text. (1989:24)

Although Roseberry does admire Geertz's ethnographic talent and recognizes his importance against a background of positivism and vulgar
materialism, he believes, in short, that Geertz's account of the Balinese
cockfight fails to analyze this significant social ritual in the context of
Balinese state formation and furthermore does not take sufficient notice
of the class differentiation of Balinese society.

Much of the criticism that Roseberry addresses to Geertz can also be
applied to Ladurie and Ginzburg. For example, Renato Rosaldo, in an
essay that compares the narratives of anthropologist Evans-Pritchard
and historian Ladurie, concludes that the historian, unlike the anthropologist, does not give due attention throughout his book on Montaillou
to the conditions under which the text was produced (1986). At issue
here is the question of power and the authority of narrative as much of
Ladurie's book is based upon inquisitional records. Rosaldo claims:

In the body of his book Le Roy Ladurie cloaks himself with the borrowed
authority of ethnographic science. Indeed (as will be seen below) he even follows the ethnographer's tactic of confining to an introduction discussion of
the politics of domination that shaped the investigator's knowledge about the
people under study. Thus the historian's main text never returns to the opening discussion about how his document was produced. (1986:81)

Rosaldo goes on to criticize both Evans-Pritchard and Ladurie for em-
ploying a pastoral literary mode that in his view is quite distant from
French peasants of the late Middle Ages and modern-day Nilotic cattle
herders (1986:96). According to Rosaldo:

The use of the pastoral at once justifies and betrays the introductory efforts to
suppress the interplay of power and knowledge. Thus the narrators can enjoy
relations suffused with a tender courtesy that appears to transcend inequality
and domination. Yet the pastoral mode obliquely reveals inequalities in the
relations that produced ethnographic knowledge. (1986:97)

Rosaldo believes, therefore, that the rhetorical style employed by Ladurie, although very seductive, conceals the power relations through which
the text was produced.

Rosaldo's comments are equally applicable to Ginzburg's story of the sixteenth-century Italian miller, Menocchio. Ginzburg, like Ladurie, begins with a discussion of power which is then insufficiently thematized in the work as a whole. Moreover, Ginzburg seems to make little of the fact that Menocchio's account is taken from court records and that his narrative is most certainly coerced. Although Ginzburg concedes that Menocchio is an unusual character, he is employed by the author as a synecdoche for sixteenth-century peasant culture. In this case, the part does not substitute adequately for a peasant whole that itself is most certainly differentiated.

While Geertz's interpretive anthropology and the new cultural history seem, at least in some versions, to be insufficiently attuned to the differentiation of culture and power in the production of historical and ethnographic narratives, I believe, as Roseberry acknowledged, that their historical contribution to theory and ethnographic practice should not be overlooked or summarily dismissed.[18] Geertz has done much, for example, to refocus debate in anthropology on the concept of culture. Along with the cultural and social historians, he has drawn our attention to the importance of meaning and human agency in the formation of social life. This has, in turn, influenced innumerable ethnographies and cultural histories and surely has gone a long way toward countering efforts in the human and social sciences to reduce social life to objectified and law-like terms. However, as is the case with most social theories that depart from a phenomenological perspective, insufficient attention is directed toward the constraints on the constitution of meaning and the extralocal temporal processes that are interwoven in the texture of meaning.

HISTORY, STRUCTURE, AND EVENT

It is important to note, however, that Geertz's concept of "thick description" does not exhaust the influences on cultural history or historical anthropology as there are other cultural theoreticians within anthropology whose works are influential across the disciplines and who are concerned in a primary sense with cultural views of history and historical views of culture. Emiko Ohnuki-Tierney's recent volume (1990) serves as a case in point as does Marshall Sahlins's widely acclaimed *Islands of History* (1985). Although the essays in the Ohnuki-Tierney volume represent a number of different perspectives, there is a pronounced structural orientation.[19] These essays as a whole are significant in that they shift the focus from an autonomous, meaning-constructing actor to the dialectical relation between human action and the structure of culture. The structure of culture both enables human action through providing a shared framework of meaning and constrains human action through limiting the options and possibilities of individual actors—a position that has been advanced by Sherry Ortner in particular (1984, 1990).

Marshall Sahlins, likewise, has made an especially ambitious effort through a number of publications on the history of the Hawaiian Islands to reconcile what are widely regarded as opposed concepts in structure and human agency, or structure and event. It is, however, Sahlins's discussion of the arrival of Captain Cook in the Hawaiian Islands and the fate of the captain that has drawn the greatest attention. Sahlins remarks that the arrival of Cook corresponded with the ritual cycle of the god Lono and so Cook himself was taken by local commoners and chiefs alike for Lono. Consequently, Cook and his men were treated with the sort of accommodation, carnal details notwithstanding, that has made this encounter famous in the literature. However, while Cook's departure corresponded in good time with the end of the ritual cycle, his untimely return due to a disabled ship led to his death and consumption at the hands of the Hawaiians. Sahlins reconstructs this story, in part, to show the close association between myth and history and how myth can become history (or vice versa). Moreover, Sahlins is attentive to the articulation between local sociocultural processes and those associated with the world economic system. However, he argues against the grain of global theories that suggest that the impact of the capitalist system on preconquest Hawaii can be understood from the logic of the capitalist system. Sahlins shows how commodities that were brought to the Hawaiian Islands were recast locally and given new meaning within the context of the Hawaiian social and political system (1990).

Sahlins attempts to illustrate through his ethnographic and historical account of the Hawaiian Islands that history is culturally ordered and that culture is historically shaped. Moreover, Sahlins claims not to believe in the simple reproduction of the existing conceptual order as he argues that meanings are constantly reevaluated as they are enacted practically. By structure, Sahlins has in mind the cultural scheme or set of interrelated concepts and categories shared by a given population. As Aletta Biersack has remarked, "Sahlins moves from Braudel's geohistorical structure of the longue durée to structure as a category and thus from structural anthropology to historical anthropology" (1989:73). Sahlins's innovation comes from an effort to transform what is conventionally regarded as the virtuality of structure to a concept that can account dialectically for change while simultaneously preserving a place for human agency that is not focused, as in much of modern social theory, on the motives and interests of the lone individual.

The key theoretical move that enables Sahlins to reconcile structure and agency, or structure and event, is his concept of the *structure of the conjuncture*. By the structure of the conjuncture, he means "the practical realization of the cultural categories in a specific historical context, as expressed in the interested action of the historical agents, including the microsociology of their interaction" (1985:xiv). This conceptualization of history implies that agents are always historically contextual and that their interested action always arises from a shared cultural scheme. That is, cultural schemes become realized through historical agents that are themselves constrained and enabled by shared cultural understandings. Moreover, events only become historical to the degree to which they are appropriated through the cultural scheme. Events therefore have no significance outside of the cultural frame through which they are grasped. Sahlins maintains, like many of the contributors to the Ohnuki-Tierney volume, that there is no continuous identity to the cultural scheme as it is through acts of reference that the cultural categories obtain new functional values. As the cultural categories become "burdened with the world," their cultural meanings change. For Sahlins, changes in the relationships between cultural categories lead to changes in the structure (1985:138). The appeal, therefore, of this model as a theory of history is that through an emphasis on historical agents the structure is prevented from being inert and reified and yet the structure serves as a framework from which to inform the action of individuals and to bestow contextual significance on events as they unfold in the historical life of concrete populations.

In spite of the breadth and imagination of Sahlins's theory of history, especially the bold effort to integrate the local and the global and structure, event, and agency, the theory falters in ways reminiscent of Geertz's theory and reproduces some of the very problems that have been conventionally associated with structuralism. Roseberry argues, for example, that Sahlins is more concerned with conceptual schemes than he is with meaning and action (1989). Like Geertz, Sahlins fails to differentiate the conceptual schemes because he fails to differentiate the social actors in the Hawaiian Islands. Although we know that there are chiefs and commoners, culture is presented as if it were uniform throughout the population. It therefore becomes difficult to identify differential motives and intentions that potentially inform not only individual actions but the actions of groups as well. Consequently, as with most structural theories, the human agents of Sahlins's theory become mere conduits for the realization of preexisting conceptual schemes.

While there is little doubt that Sahlins tries to convey a more subtle and dialectical relation between local dynamics and that of the capitalist system, Roseberry also believes that Sahlins fails to tell us much about how contact with Western culture changed the society of the Hawaiian Islands. That is, Sahlins duplicates in reverse the very error for which world-systems theorists have been criticized by giving too much attention on the incorporation of Western contact into the existing conceptual categories of the population. I believe that Roseberry concludes correctly that practice has become for Sahlins a "theoretical category" and that culture has become "enacted" rather than "acted" (1989:10).

POLITICAL ECONOMY AND CULTURE:
A PROSPECTIVE INTEGRATION

Jürgen Habermas has assumed, perhaps more than any contemporary social theorist, the task of reconstructing historical materialism or political economy by addressing the problem of taking labor as a general theory of action. Beginning with his early *Knowledge and Human Interests* (1971) and continuing through more recent works (1984), Habermas has sought to show that the activity through which the human species forms itself, solves problems, and self-reflexively monitors its own action is dependent on a communicative framework which is distinctively broader than that implied in the marxist notion of production and reproduction through labor. Furthermore, Habermas argues that the logic of inquiry that follows from production is insufficient to serve the emancipatory interest of critical social theory. This is the case because emancipation not only involves understanding the genesis of exploitative social relations but, for Habermas, emancipation must also establish a means of reconnecting politics to a public life grounded in rational consensus.

Habermas's argument against taking labor as a general theory of action rests largely upon distinguishing the cognitive interest that informs labor from that of social interaction. Habermas asserts that the human species forms and reproduces itself through labor and interaction and that these activities are grounded in technical and practical cognitive interests respectively. Cognitive interests, furthermore, shape both actual and potential objects of knowledge and determine the "categories relevant to what we take to be knowledge, as well as the procedures for discovering and warranting knowledge claims" (Bernstein 1976:192). For Habermas, therefore, there is a direct connection between knowledge and formative social action.

While Habermas would agree with Marx and contemporary political economists that labor is the activity through which human populations transform the natural world to meet socially established needs, he would not agree that labor can also account for the reproduction of social relations. This is because Habermas believes that human labor is limited to a technical cognitive interest in that through labor human subjects constitute or objectify the natural world toward the end of technical control. From the point of view of the cognitive interest of labor, the natural world becomes an object of human appropriation and use. This is to be distinguished, argues Habermas, from social interaction upon which the reproduction and transformation of social relations are based.

Social interaction is informed by a practical cognitive interest in that it is characterized by norms of mutual expectation as embodied in symbolic, ordinary language communication. Social interaction is the arena, furthermore, in which knowledge claims are advanced and social and cultural identities negotiated and forged. As opposed to the technical rationality of labor, social interaction is informed by a communicative rationality which Habermas believes is oriented toward mutual understanding and mutual consensus. While it may be the case, as some critics of Habermas have argued, that technical and practical cognitive interests, and the rationalities of the systems of action that they avowedly inform, are intertwined in actual human practice and therefore can only be distinguished on the most abstract level, it is nonetheless his point to show that the logical reconstruction of symbolically mediated human activity in social interaction cannot proceed from meta-rules of actual and potential objectification and control.

Habermas maintains that all human activity, whether instrumental or communicative, is symbolically constituted. Consequently, although having a rationality oriented toward the objectification and control of the natural world to meet humanly established ends, the sociability of labor and its reproduction, such as in the social relations of production, are fundamentally dependent on a process of symbolic or communicative exchange. As Marx himself realized, in an observation redolent with cultural implications, it is the concept of a project prior to its execution that distinguishes human labor from the mere physical activity of a bee (1967, 1:178). The reconstruction of the social contexts under which all human action unfolds most follow, therefore, the logic of a hermeneutic science designed to mediate the density or opacity of symbolically constituted human action. A hermeneutic science (e.g. Gadamer 1975) postulates the process of understanding as a synthesis between the categories, assumptions, and expectations of the anthropologist or historian and those of the object-subject of inquiry. This process, furthermore, is ongoing and hence the knowledge that arises from the inquiry is subject to continual revision. The purpose of this hermeneutic science, which Habermas appropriates and raises to a critical theory of society, is not simply the elaboration of meaning along the lines of an interpretive anthropology, such as with Geertz and the new cultural historians sympathetic to "thick description," but rather the clarification of the contexts of mutual intelligibility and the social constraints to which action oriented toward mutual understanding is subject.

The fact that the instrumental process of labor is inadequate on its own to serve as a reconstructive science of symbolically mediated human action does not render labor's critical intent superfluous. To the contrary, a critical theory tied closely to the category of labor is important for grasping the social constraints to which symbolic exchanges are subject. This assertion is supported, as political economists and global theorists have shown, by the recognition that it has been ever-expanding capitalist markets and hegemonic political diplomacy informed by economic interests that have assumed a leading role in shaping and transforming social and political relations in the modern world. However, it is equally important to keep in mind, as Gramsci (1975) and more recently Thompson (1978) and Williams (1977) have reminded us, that social control, inequality, and the constraints of social interaction in general are not simply a function of the expropriation of surplus value or economic exploitation but perhaps, more important, of symbolically rooted cultural practices and their reproduction. According to these authors, there is a cultural or symbolic foundation of power even in what appear as merely economic imperatives.

While Habermas is by no means alone in proposing that human action is communicative, a view now widely held in the humanities and less so in the social sciences, he is one of very few contemporary scholars, as we have seen above, to apply this theory comprehensively to a reformulation of the marxist tradition. Although Jean Baudrillard, like Habermas, has criticized the productivist logic of marxism by arguing that it universalizes what is particular to the capitalist system and instrumentalizes and thus eclipses human action as symbolic, in the end he appears to reject marxism altogether (1975). However, as provocative as Baudrillard's analysis of capitalist culture is, he does not take us much beyond the formalism of semiotics. That is, for Baudrillard, not unlike Sahlins, the positioning of human actors in social and temporal space is replaced by the positioning or interrelation of signs within an ordered system. What is lost in the end is how the system itself is produced and under what sort of historical and social constraints. Moreover, as Bakhtin has argued, the emphasis on system or structure in formal views of language privileges uniformity and thus overlooks the plurality and discontinuities of competing or conflicting sublanguages or discourses—what he calls *heteroglossia*—that are present in all existing populations or speech communities (1986). Bakhtin's view thus confirms through language as discourse, and one could easily add culture (e.g. Williams 1977), the importance of considering the social location of concrete actors and the conditions that both divide and unify societies.

Habermas retains, to the contrary, in spite of the abstractness of his theory, a sense of the social world as constructed through the practical activity of human subjects. Moreover, these subjects are not presented as mere "enactors of the code" as Habermas believes in the capacity of human subjects to self-reflexively monitor and therefore modify the orientation and direction of their actions. The constraints on the activity of human subjects are not, for Habermas, structural but rather, like Bourdieu's concept of *habitus* (1977), built into the very communicative process through which subjects negotiate their identities and self-formation. This is a process that is historical to the core. With Habermas, therefore, we find a deliberate effort to preserve and restore the interest of political economy in both critique and emancipation, as well as a sensitivity to the changing historical character of capitalism.

Habermas's emphasis on human action as communicative is not meant to be methodologically prescriptive, nor is it a substitute for concrete ethnographic and historical analyses. To the contrary, Habermas has repeatedly acknowledged the importance of empirical inquiry, albeit as mediated by critical theory. However, his theory of communicative action forcefully addresses one of the principal objections, outlined earlier, of cultural theorists to a global political economy through reconceptualizing economic activity, especially its dependence on labor, in more fully cultural terms. In arguing that political economy can be conceptualized in cultural or communicative terms, Habermas does not mean to deny the potential for economic forces, whether in the form of class relations, local and national markets, or the global economy, to constrain and shape human interaction. However, economic activity, unless reified as the independent circulation of commodities, is based upon social relations and their reproduction and change over time. As Habermas reminds us, social relations are the arena in which individual and collective identities are formed and thus economic activity is invested with the same moral or cultural casting as human interaction in general.

It was my intention to craft a discussion of anthropology and history that was responsive to their social and political formation and character yet well attuned to the historical, cultural, and political textures of the southwest French wine-cooperative movement and French winegrowing history. Therefore, I limited my discussion to those theoretical alternatives and points of tension that I believe to be most germane to a critical account of the cooperative movement within a context that is both local and global. As I emphasized earlier, the wine-cooperative movement as an object of ethnographic and historical inquiry leads us in the directions of political economy and culture and therefore any discussion of this material must be prepared to theoretically integrate and analytically apply these seemingly distinct domains or fields of social inquiry and practice. This is no easy task as political economy and cultural theory are often couched in terms that are theoretically incommensurable. However, the prospect for working through this impasse rests, I believe, with taking a communicative view of social action. I argued, therefore, following Jürgen Habermas, that the emphasis on labor and, by extension, the mode of production in political economy, including its global versions, must be reconceptualized communicatively to account for the general symbolic nature of human action without, however, losing sight of the material and economic constraints of labor to which culture and human agency are historically subject.[20] This proposed reconceptualization is not so much definitive as suggestive to the ethnographic and historical analysis that follows.

INVENTION AS CULTURAL CAPITAL | 2

Wines produced in the immediate vicinity of Bordeaux have long enjoyed a worldwide reputation for superior quality. This reputation is attributed not only to the special attention given to the vinification and aging of wines but most especially to a climate and soil regarded by most experts as ideal for winegrowing. However, if we look to the more distant past, the fifteenth century and earlier, we discover that Bordeaux wines were not always highly regarded and in fact were held in less esteem than those produced in the interior.

I argue that Bordeaux's ascendancy to its current position follows conjointly from its political and economic history and from a process of invention that transforms culturally constructed criteria of authenticity and quality into ones that appear natural. Moreover, the relation between the economic privilege of Bordeaux, historically conceived, and the invention of the winegrowing tradition has provided elite growers in the Bordeaux region with what Pierre Bourdieu calls "cultural capital" (1984); that is, acquired resources that serve symbolically and practically to secure privileges, economic or otherwise, within differential fields of action and power. In turn, the possession of considerable cultural capital, as represented symbolically through an avowed connection to an aristocratic past, served elites both commercially and in constructing a winegrowing hierarchy that is regarded as authoritative.

Bordeaux's particular winegrowing history thus illustrates, as I asserted previously with respect to historical ethnography in general, the dialectical connection between political economy and invented tradition or culture. However, before we turn to the historical narrative of Bordeaux wines and cooperative winegrowers, it is imperative to address the theoretical and political implications of the invention theme, for I contend that power differentials between classes of winegrowers significantly silenced all but the elite growers and merchants in the invention of a hierarchical and hegemonic winegrowing tradition.

THE INVENTION OF TRADITION

The social sciences and humanities have long embraced a concept of tradition that emphasizes the generational transmission of time-honored customs, knowledge, and social practices. Such a concept implies that the younger generation accepts passively the cultural products of its ancestors and that cultural continuities are sustained and reproduced within insular social units. The embracing of a static concept of tradition has come to pass, in part, from the dominant influence of Enlightenment reason and its counterpart in the civilizing mission of colonialism and now neocolonialism. Enlightenment *philosophes* regarded tradition as opposed to reason and so indigenous or traditional peoples encountered through European colonialism were often seen as suspended in a timeless past and present and thereby moved by forces that they did not comprehend (Gadamer 1975; Fabian 1983). Moreover, the influence early on of scholars such as Durkheim and Weber did much to reify our understanding of tradition by contrasting its normative characteristics, or in the case of Weber the ideal type, to the logocentrism of modernity.

More recently, scholars from a wide range of disciplines have challenged the conventional wisdom on tradition. Hobsbawm and Ranger's volume, *The Invention of Tradition,* is one of a growing body of works that has sought to recast the concept of tradition in processual terms by focusing on the politics of identity and a sense of the past as imagined (1983).[1] The contributors to this volume illustrate through both ethnographic and historical case studies that the past does not exist independently of its social construction or mediation in the present. Rather, they argue that the invention of the past is largely motivated by the interested action, political or otherwise, of human subjects in the present. The kilt, for example, which is taken to be distinctive of Scottish national tradition, is shown by Trevor-Roper to be a modern invention that was bestowed on the Scottish Highlanders by an English Quaker industrialist (1983). It was only long after the union with England that the kilt became a symbol of Scottish identity and of resistance to the union. However, Richard Handler and Jocelyn Linnekin (1984) find fault with Hobsbawm, and those other scholars such as Edward Shils (1981) who maintain that "invented" tradition can be distinguished from that which is "authentic" or reputedly established as "real."

Handler and Linnekin together (1984), and each separately (Handler 1986, 1988; Linnekin 1983, 1991, 1992), have argued against objectivist views of history that conceive of the past as independent of the process through which it is known.[2] Moreover, Linnekin expands the conventional sense of objectivist as associated with positivism to include all perspectives, marxism notwithstanding, that distinguish an "authentic" from an "invented" past (1992). Although she has some reservations concerning the unlimited challenge to what she calls essentialist social-science concepts on the part of deconstruction, Linnekin prefers the decentering of postmodernism to the marxist critique of ideology because of its recognition of "complexity, difference and multiplicity" (1992:256).[3]

The postmodernist 'decentering' project is thus a more radical and a more fundamental challenge to the dominant social-science paradigm than Marxist or anticolonial analysis, for its target is not a particular authorship but the very premises of narrative authority and unitary point of view. (Linnekin 1992:257)

Handler and Linnekin appeal to Roy Wagner (1975) in arguing that tradition is merely a special case of the invention of culture. For Handler and Linnekin, tradition is a symbolic construction and therefore should not be viewed in terms of "boundedness, givenness or essence" (1984:273). Regarding tradition as bounded or as having an essence, as they believe to be the case with marxism, transforms what is a social and cultural entity into one that is natural. For Handler and Linnekin, tradition refers to "an interpretive process that embodies both continuity and discontinuity" (1984:273). Moreover, Handler and Linnekin show, through their respective field studies of Quebec and Hawaii, that scholars are likewise engaged in the construction of invented pasts and that these scholarly inventions or interpretations are often invoked at the local and national levels as authentic tradition. While they acknowledge the possibility that there are continuities between past and present, albeit as a product of interpretation, Handler and Linnekin's position can be regarded as a radicalization of the invention-of-tradition theme in that by rejecting authenticity as simply other than invented, they relativize and thus undermine the authority of all discourses concerning the past.

While Handler and Linnekin's concept of the past as a cultural construction is consistent with much recent literature in the social sciences and humanities that recognizes the significance of rhetoric to historical interpretation, there are a number of potentially serious epistemological and political issues that are generated through their version of the invention theme and most especially through Linnekin's appeal to postmodern social theory (Ulin 1991). Linnekin has argued, for example, that the invention of tradition implies that cultural construction is negotiated and that at the level of the nation-state this negotiation often takes the form of a strategic politics. While there is no doubt considerable contesting or negotiating of invented pasts when these are concerned with the formation of national identities and culture (e.g. see Herzfeld 1982, 1987; Lass 1988), Linnekin overemphasizes the independence of human subjects from the determinations and limitations of their past, as well as the capacity of individuals to come to terms with their tradition reflexively. Moreover, this problem is not avoided through an appeal on the parts of both Linnekin (1992) and Handler (1988) to Cohn's concept of objectification (1987:228–29), a process through which individuals (in the case of Cohn, the Western educated class of India) step back and consciously make their culture a "thing-like" object of reflection.

Gadamer has argued from the position of hermeneutics, and in what can be taken as opposition to Linnekin's postmodernism, that we come to terms with tradition, and one could add history, from already living in the midst of tradition (1975). This is not to say that Gadamer believes that it is impossible to view our past critically, even if this past takes, as Handler and Linnekin argue, a multiplicity of competing versions. Rather, our past in its plurivocity is fundamental to our identities and social beings. Gadamer therefore conceives of tradition ontologically and discusses its determinations in terms of what he calls "effective historical consciousness." Simply put, our immersion in a specific cultural and historical tradition prefigures our initial anticipations or understanding of our objects or cosubjects of knowledge. These anticipations or prejudgments are not dogmatically held as they are corrected through a dialectic of question and answer. That is, there is no escaping our past, even as an object of critical reflection, as our past serves as the inextricable context from which we both have a world and problematize our social being in its multiplicity. Contrary to Linnekin's view, Gadamer holds that there is no position outside tradition or history from which we can relativize tradition and thus challenge its authority.

Linnekin also argues that all perspectives that distinguish authentic from invented traditions are objectivist in a manner that allies them with essentialist and therefore positivistic social science. Although her point is well taken in terms of theories of history or social science that contend that facts exist independent of their social construction, her assertion that the objectivist position, even if distinguished by conservative and critical varieties, holds for the marxist tradition seems misconceived and insufficiently attentive to the Hegelian and phenomenological roots of marxism. Marx nowhere conceives of the natural world as an independent object and he is, furthermore, critical of philosophical positions that are merely contemplative and therefore lacking a vision of praxis.

Marx argues, to the contrary, that the human species forms itself through labor and that the natural world becomes an object of appropriation and transformation by virtue of human practical activity. Moreover, Marx never rejected outright the self-interpretations of human actors, as suggested by Handler and Linnekin in their embracing of Geertz's critique of the marxist concept of ideology (Geertz 1973). Rather, Marx believed that reality is incompletely manifested in what is immediate and visible and that self-interpretations are therefore in need of mediation in order to move from a naive to a critical view of the social world. Although Marx can be faulted, as I argued in Chapter 1, for an overly instrumental view of human action in his privileging of labor, he hardly falls prey to objectivism in any of its usual philosophical or practical senses.

While controversies concerning unorthodox interpretations of objectivism are likely to be limited to the academic arena, Handler and Linnekin's challenge to indigenous and/or scholarly claims to authenticity, and by extension visions of an authoritative past, raises issues of a more political nature. Linnekin is, however, clearly aware of the political complexity of challenges to indigenous claims to authenticity (1991), especially in nationalist contexts, as evidenced by her sensitivity to Maori outrage over Allan Hanson's contention that Maori tradition is invented. Linnekin believes, however, that Hanson's argument does not trivialize Maori culture, nor can it be construed as anti-Maori, as Hanson maintains that "inventions are common components in the ongoing development of authentic culture" (1989:899). Moreover, Linnekin argues that anthropologists have little control over how their works are publicly represented. The problem here is not with the past viewed as a social construction or invention, as I believe that there is much merit to this conception, but rather with the implications and consequences of relativizing and thus equating all discourses concerning the past. Such a move negates the potential of the past to command our attention and thus undermines the authority that is part of the political struggle for self-identity and autonomy.

When qualified to incorporate the inequality of social relations, however, the invention-of-tradition theme has much to contribute to our understanding of historical and cultural processes through viewing the past as socially constructed, polyphonic, and contested. This theme reinforces, furthermore, what Raymond Williams (1977) has identified as the selectivity of culture and Pierre Bourdieu (1984) as distinction. That is, Williams and Bourdieu propose that culture, like class, is positional and therefore responsive dialectically to historical and social conditions or fields of power. In like fashion, scholars sympathetic to the theoretical implications of political economy have been quick to point out, as we have seen through John Cole, that what is often regarded as "authentic" tradition is itself a product of global political and economic processes. This view of "authenticity" as produced applies not only to the relation between core and periphery, as in world-systems theory and its variants, but it is also replicated within the boundaries of individual nation-states. Moreover, the recognition that what we take to be "authentic" tradition is linked dialectically to the formative properties of a global system should serve as a reminder, if not a warning, that the invention of tradition, or for that matter the symbolic construction of culture, is not autonomous. To the contrary, social constraints such as class and gender limit not only what is invented but they also limit who does the inventing, a point that is insufficiently addressed by Handler and Linnekin in their distinction between authenticity and invention.

THE INVENTION OF THE FRENCH WINEGROWING TRADITION

I have qualified the theme of invention so as to frame a discussion of southwest French wines that emphasizes the inventiveness of the winegrowing tradition, yet recognizes as central the political and economic mediation of French winegrowing history. To claim, however, that invention has played any part at all in the establishment of a winegrowing hierarchy will no doubt strike some, especially the connoisseur, as heresy. After all, the very principle of connoisseurship implies not only a recognition of distinctiveness but an intuitive judgment of qualities thought to be objective. Moreover, a wealth of publications by oenologists, historians, and geographers emphasize the importance of climate, soil, age of plants, and even the *sous-sol* or subsoil as central to the production of quality wines.[4] Consider, for example, geographer René Pijassou's assessment of the importance of soil in a chapter devoted to geomorphology in his celebrated two-volume work on Médoc viticulture: "The vigor of the Mendelian dissection has allowed the subsoil, composed of gravel, limestone, or clay to become associated to some extent with the surface gravel; the diverse formulas (i.e. geomorphological) thus elaborated largely explain the hierarchy of *grands crus* in the Haut-Médoc" (1980:214). While there is no doubt some truth to the argument about climate and soil, the argument takes for granted the social construction of authenticity, quality, and taste and therefore tends to naturalize, a consequence not uncommon to cultural invention in general, the social and historical conditions that have long differentiated winegrowers.

The historical relation of Bordeaux wines to those produced in the nearby interior illustrates how socially produced differentiations can be constructed or invented as natural.[5] This is especially the case since it is, with few exceptions, favorable natural conditions that are invoked retrospectively by winegrowing experts and elites to explain why interior wines have been repeatedly denied the prestige of the Bordeaux classification. For example, winegrowers of the Bergerac region, located 90 kilometers to the east of Bordeaux, have sought several times in the last century to have their wines classified with those of Bordeaux, as they believed their wines to be equally good. However, in spite of the proximity of the two regions, the requests for a Bordeaux classification have always been denied to Bergerac winegrowers ostensibly for reasons of quality attributable to a less favorable climate and soil.[6]

While it is widely believed today that Bordeaux produces among the very best wines in the world, this has not always been the case. As Pijassou has noted, the wine exported from the Haut Pays of southwest France (Périgord, Agen, Toulouse, and Quercy) through the end of the twelfth century was considered more important than that produced in Bordeaux (1980:299). Bordeaux production rarely surpassed a meager 120,000 hectoliters yearly and much of this production was consumed locally by its thirty thousand inhabitants. According to Pijassou, the wine consumed in Bordeaux tended to be of the table variety as so-called distinctive wines were relatively unknown in the Middle Ages. Moreover, Guichard and Roudié remark that Bordeaux as a wine port lagged considerably behind La Rochelle in that the latter had developed a "veritable civilization" around the production of wine (1985:7).

The tide would eventually change as Bordeaux's reputation and influence as a winegrowing region profited immensely from the English occupation of the Aquitaine from the twelfth to fifteenth century. The stage was set for the occupation when Eleanor, Duchess of the Aquitaine, married Henry Plantagenêt, the heir to the English throne, in

1152. Henry became, in turn, the Duke of the Aquitaine and thus a vassal of the French king. However, the new duke's loyalty was to the throne which he was destined to inherit and hence he allied himself with the King of England in defeating the armies of the French king. According to Guichard and Roudié, the English conquest reduced the vast continental principality of southwest France to the Aquitaine or what essentially amounts to the present-day Department of the Gironde (1985:8–9).

The English made use, in short, of Bordeaux's access to the coast to establish commercial ties to northern Europe of such magnitude and significance that Bordeaux came to surpass La Rochelle as the leading French port with access to the Atlantic Ocean. The commerce in wine became so important that English vessels during the period of the occupation were rated by the volume of wine that they could transport (in *tonneaux* or 900-liter barrels). Due to the difficulty of land transport, wines coming from the interior by way of the Dordogne and Garonne rivers had little alternative but to pass through Bordeaux on their way to distant markets. The Bordeaux elite obtained from the English crown special protective measures against Bergerac wines and others from the Haut Pays or interior. Not only were the wines from the interior subject to taxes from which Bordeaux wines were exempt, but interior wines were not permitted to enter Bordeaux before November 11—a restriction changed in 1373 to December 25 (Pijassou 1980:300). Consequently, these interior wines, some of which were already noted for their quality, suffered at the hands of a Bordeaux privilege bestowed on city elites by the English crown and thus were less favored than those of Bordeaux on a growing international market. Though the defeat of the English by the French king, Charles VII, at the battle of Castillon in 1453 ousted the English from the Aquitaine and thus dealt a blow to the privileges of Bordeaux, Bordeaux wines had gained sufficient renown in northern Europe to endure the hardest of times. As Enjalbert maintains: "The importance of Bordeaux wine is not based on climate but on their better organization of marketing to northern Europe" (1953:317). Thus the superior reputation of Bordeaux wines owes, at least initially, more to English hegemony and the city's economic history than to any special claim for climate and soil.

While the English occupation and the right of taxation did much to privilege Bordeaux wines, the differentiation of these wines themselves did not come until much later. Enjalbert has argued that competition from Spain and Portugal during the seventeenth and eighteenth centuries precipitated an economic crisis among French growers as foreign wines were being sold on European markets at a lower price (1953). Rather than seeking to compete directly with Spain and Portugal by increasing quantity of production and lowering price, Enjalbert maintains that French growers opted to improve quality by the creation of the *grands crus*.

The *grands crus,* or elite Bordeaux wines, were produced, in contrast to the mass or common wines that saturated European markets, from older vine stocks that often reached fifty years in age and on rare occasions one hundred years. The older stocks produce significantly smaller yields of grapes at harvest time, which most wine experts agree directly improves the quality of the final product. Moreover, after vinification, *grands crus* are aged for several years before being released for sale, a process that exceeded the resources and potential of all but the wealthiest growers.

The development of the *grands crus* had lasting social consequences as they ushered in a more intensive division of labor that undermined the paternalistic relation between large proprietors and their workers. Prior to the development of the *grands crus,* the proprietors of large estates provided housing for their workers and even met their health and other personal needs. Labor on the large estates was also less specialized as workers were trained to carry out a wide range of skilled tasks from pruning the vineyards to supervising the fermentation of pressed grapes in the making of wine. However, the specialization of labor that materialized with the arrival of the *grands crus* led to a differentiation and hence hierarchy among the work force and growers in general. This differentiation placed those with limited resources in a subordinate position to elites and thus marginalized their voices in the construction and reproduction of winegrowing discourse and knowledge. Moreover, the proprietors of *grands crus* moved politically to assure a special commercial and symbolic status for their wine through the creation of the 1855 classification.

The 1855 classification was established in response to a request by the organizers of the Universal Exposition that was to be held in Paris in the spring of 1855. The Universal Exposition was not only conceived to be a showcase for elite French culture and, as Rabinow notes, the imperial pretensions of the French state, but it was also an occasion for a highly selective representation and thus invention of national culture (1989:93). The 1855 classification succeeded where earlier ones had failed in establishing for the Bordeaux region a widely accepted hierarchy of growths or *crus* that has changed little to the present day. The conservatism of the 1855 classification is exemplified by the fact that only four châteaus were included as first growths with a fifth château being added in 1973. In short, the 1855 classification established five different growths of château wines with the *Premiers Crus* (first growths) as the most esteemed and the *Cinquièmes Crus* (fifth growths) as the least. However, even a classification as a fifth growth gave immeasurable status or cultural capital to the proprietor of such an estate over wines that were not classified. Classification was thus important to the marketability of the wines.

Although the 1855 classification gave considerable commercial advantages to elite growers, it did not prevent some merchants and growers from substituting "fraudulent" wines for those which were renowned. To the contrary, it can be argued that the 1855 classification opened the door to fraud in that the establishment of a hierarchy of wines provided an opportunity for "unscrupulous" growers and merchants to exploit the commercial success and potential associated with elite wines. For example, by the middle of the nineteenth century, and most likely a good deal earlier, consumers came to identify their favorite wines with particular regions, if not certain producers. Some merchants sought to commercialize their wine as the product of a particular region to customers who were unaware that it had been blended with less distinguished wines originating from any number of different places. This was a common practice with wines imported from Algeria. Algerian wines were known for their robustness and high alcohol content and therefore they were frequently used to fortify weaker French wines.

Apart from misleading customers by the blending of wines from different regions, merchants and growers were also known to practice chaptalization. Chaptalization involves the adding of sugar during the fermentation process generally to fortify wines that have an especially low alcohol content. While the amount of sugar that could be added during fermentation would eventually come to be strictly regulated, some merchants and growers routinely exceeded the currently accepted standards. Most consumers presumed that the wines they purchased were fermented "naturally" or like the purist, Constantin Bourquin, looked upon chaptalization as deforming a natural product (Loubère 1990:105).

There is some irony in the fact that the very system of classification that was designed to reinforce the privilege of elite growers actually contributed to the resistance to privilege. That is, without the establishment of a winegrowing hierarchy and clearly defined standards of purity, it would be impossible to conceive of the very existence of fraudulent wines. Even if those who produced fraudulent wines were more motivated by greed and self-interest than resistance, the production of fraudulent wines was nonetheless a challenge to elite hegemony. Moreover, as we shall see shortly, the assumption of elite production to the general standard of French winegrowing was internalized and reproduced mimetically by the very class of growers that these standards were designed to exclude.

NATURE AND AUTHENTICITY

While these examples are illustrative, they by no means exhaust the history and significance of the production and commercialization of fraudulent wines in France. In the nineteenth and early twentieth centuries, fraud also consisted in large measure of wines that were made from dried fruit and sugar which was then fermented. These wines were important not only because of their threat to individual and regional reputations but because they initiated a controversy concerning the criteria of "authenticity." If wine could be made from the fermentation of any number of dried fruits as well as pressed grapes, then the question arises as to what precisely constitutes "real" wine. This may appear as a peculiar question to pose in light of the generally held presumption that wine is a natural product. Would it not simply make sense to turn to nature itself to resolve the issue of the authenticity of wine?

This question is tied to a more general cultural and historical theme of Western society that affirms a dichotomy between nature and culture and thus supports distinct epistemologies for the human and natural sciences. However, the idea that culture is a social construction and that nature exists independent of the concepts through which it is grasped has moved well beyond our intellectual history to occupy a significant place in our practical consciousness and language. Consequently, it has become for many persons merely common sense to speak of social constructions such as human nature, gender, and national traditions as if they were natural.

There is much at stake in maintaining that nature exists independently of the concepts through which it is socially constructed particularly when our culturally specific or metaphorical views of nature become applied literally to the realm of human affairs. Nature has been invoked, for example, to support and maintain racial and sexual inequality and, as we have seen from the past and even more recently, to uphold nationalist claims to ethnic purity and cultural authenticity. Such a view of nature is clearly part of what Gramsci (1971) referred to as the practical consciousness of hegemony or what Foucault (1979) has described as the panopticism of power. According to Gramsci and Foucault, the particular effectiveness of hegemonic power to shape human affairs come from its embodiment in an unquestioned daily consciousness. While the hegemonic uses of the "natural" and the panopticism of power may appear quite distant from the seemingly less political and mundane question of whether or not wine is a "natural" product, I believe, nonetheless, that the theoretical connections are far-reaching. This is so because regarding wine as a natural product rather than a social invention has contributed significantly to creating and maintaining social inequality between winegrowers themselves.

The question of the "authenticity" of wine was eventually resolved in a manner consistent with the interests of elite growers or owners of the château estates.[7] Beginning with the Loi Griffe in 1889 and continuing through a series of national legislative reforms over a period of generations, wine came to be defined legally as a naturally fermented beverage made from pressed grapes (Loubère 1978:297). However, by defining wine in "natural" terms, French legislators inadvertently naturalized the criteria of "authenticity" and thus concealed the fact that wine is a social invention. Moreover, the naturalizing of authenticity, like the appeal to climate and soil, strengthened the power of elites by limiting alternatives to a system that they had influenced and largely shaped.

The invention and representation of wine as a "natural" product is consistent with the general tendency of the invention of tradition—and commodification—to naturalize what is social, cultural, and historical. This limits, in turn, the options as to what one can imagine contesting by making the "invented" appear as common sense or even continuous with a distant and unchanging past. However, even if we do recognize that wine is, like most agricultural products, a domesticated entity, the exclusion of all but grapes from its defining characteristics tends to gloss over, if not veil, the social grounds of its authenticity. There are no reasons apart from established customs and the threat of competition—social rather than natural reasons—that other domesticated fruits could not be fermented and then classified as a wine. However, the fact that we rarely think about wine as a social construction or invention and thus take its legal definition as self-evident or natural is precisely what contributes to its symbolic and social force.

The establishment of the authenticity of wine on reputedly natural grounds was furthermore coincident with the formulation of taste and quality in progressively uniform and thus natural terms. While the science of oenology did not become widely accepted until after the Second World War (Peynaud 1988), elite growers had associated quality, at least since the end of the eighteenth century, with both diminished yields harvested from older plants and wine that had been aged before being consumed. It is widely believed today, even if it is not possible for all growers, that reducing yield and aging wine produces a product that is more refined and subtle. However, as with the legal definition of wine, the social standards of quality, and by extension taste, are often veiled by the universalization of criteria that are particular to place and time.

The 1855 classification of Bordeaux wines initiated, therefore, a series of legislative reforms that would eventually culminate in the national *appellation contrôlée* legislation of the late 1920s and 1930s. The general intent of the *appellation contrôlée* legislation was to regulate both the cultivation of vineyards and the production of wine itself and to reinforce institutionally the authenticity and quality of wine. Although protection of producers and consumers has always been given as the justification for France's strict regulations, the winegrowing legislation aided the efforts of elite growers to distinguish their wines while marginalizing those who had insufficient resources to meet its many mandates.

Winegrowing legislation was not the only means by which elite growers engaged in the construction of a winegrowing hierarchy and the invention of the winegrowing tradition. Most important, elite growers sought to establish a cultural continuity between their wines and an aristocratic past. The cultural association of elite wines with the aristocracy influenced, in turn, the very system of legislation and classification from which elite growers benefited most. Nowhere is this more apparent than in the representation of French château wines.

THE CHÂTEAU AS INVENTION

While the development of French wines owes much to the early monasteries and estates of the Middle Ages, many aristocratic families lost their estates as a consequence of the French Revolution. Aristocratic and church lands were seized by the new national government and then divided and put up for sale. Although some of these aristocratic families managed to repurchase their estates through the use of an intermediary, as Albert Sobul has argued, they remained largely peripheral to the continued development of French winegrowing (Sobul 1977; Dion 1977; Lachiver 1988). This did not in turn lead, as one might suspect, to a vast acquisition of property on the part of peasants as peasants only benefited from the seizure of lands in areas that were most marginal to elite winegrowing and agriculture in general.

The powerful symbolic association of wine with the church and aristocracy nonetheless endured, as the production and consumption of wine in southwest France was taken up initially by the nascent bourgeoisie, many of whom were members of the Bordeaux Parliament and nobility of the robe, and then later on by wealthy merchant families.[8] Remarkably, many of these elite growers built châteaus during the late eighteenth and nineteenth centuries that were small-scale replicas of those constructed during the Middle Ages. The château was chosen as the architectural model because elite proprietors wished, as Roudié has noted, to distinguish themselves culturally from the masses by insisting on the ancient roots and quality of their wines (1988). While the actual ties to aristocratic wines are dubious, given that the oldest plants rarely exceed fifty years, the nostalgia for an aristocratic past succeeded in carving out a symbolic place for the elite wines at the center of French civilization. This invented connection supplied elite growers with sufficient cultural capital to insure their commercial success and to establish their role as leaders in local winegrowing associations central to the construction of French winegrowing discourse and knowledge.

The connection between elite wines and the culture of the French nation-state is supported by Loubère who argues that "all the regional wine economies were strongly influenced by geographic, economic and cultural ties to the nation" (1978:255). Moreover, Bourdieu maintains (1984), while commenting on an essay by Eveline Schlumberger (1973) on Château Margaux, that the relation between elite wines and French high culture is presented as so intertwined symbolically that it is impossible to invoke one without also eliciting the other. Bourdieu sees Schlumberger's essay as representative of the general self-referentiality of aristocratic culture that employs a circularity of language that in the end explains nothing.

Analogy, functioning as a circular mode of thought, makes it possible to tour the whole area of art and luxury *without ever leaving it* [emphasis his]. Thus Château Margaux wine can be described with the same words as are used to describe the château, just as others will evoke Proust apropos of Monet or

César Franck, which is a good way of talking about neither: "The house is in the image of the vintage. Noble, austere, even a little solemn . . . . Château Margaux has the air of an ancient temple devoted to the cult of wine. . . . Vineyard or dwelling, Margaux disdains all embellishments. But just as wine has to be served before it unfolds all its charms, so the residence waits for the visitor to enter before it reveals its own. In each case the same words spring to one's lips: elegance, distinction, delicacy and that subtle satisfaction given by something which has received the most attentive and indeed loving care for generations. A wine long matured, a house long inhabited: Margaux the vintage and Margaux the château are the products of two equally rare things: *rigour and time"* [emphasis in original]. (Bourdieu 1984:53)

While Bourdieu is no doubt right in arguing that Schlumberger's description is circular, that is, she uses the images of aristocratic culture to explain itself, I believe that he overlooks the poetics of her description and hence its power. Schlumberger's description is not simply circular but also metonymic in that references to the part—the wine or the château—are capable of eliciting the whole, aristocratic culture. This is precisely what the elite winegrowers of the Médoc hoped to accomplish in building their homes as replicas of the celebrated châteaus of the Middle Ages. That there were also commercial benefits to be reaped from this should be self-evident. However, by embodying the commercial benefits in a less strategic symbolic or cultural form, the message is much more subliminal and hence a good deal more seductive.

The association of elite wines with an aristocratic past builds upon and extends rhetorically, not to mention hegemonically, the discourse of wine as natural. That is, the value attributed to aged wines, older vine stocks, and aristocratic roots (metaphorically both age and depth) is represented in terms of a time that ostensibly passes naturally and therefore can be accounted for and measured objectively. Consequently, the positive value that is attributable to age is supported rhetorically through associating the superiority of age with nature or natural time. As is the case with unquestioned customs or habits, naturalized time as part of winegrowing discourse reinforces the privilege of elite wines and winegrowers through eclipsing the cultural mediation of time and hence the social construction of the natural.

THE PROLIFERATION OF THE CHÂTEAU LABEL

While the position of elites in the winegrowing hierarchy remains essentially unchallenged, entrepreneurial merchants and growers have sought to profit from the cultural capital of château wines by increasing the amount of wine commercialized under the château label. Apart from legislation that specifies maximum yield per hectare, percentage of alcohol, grape variety, and the delimitation of region, the laws restricting the château label mandate only that the harvested grapes come from a single property, no matter how parceled. This has worked against the interests of wine cooperatives and other producers who, for the most part, vinify their wines collectively. Consider, for example, the following comment by Marie Lescot of the Pauillac cooperative in response to my question about social class and marketing.

That is to say, for the cooperative the clientele is a little less classy than for the châteaus where you have the notion that the château always equals high quality; for certain clients, that's it. If there is not a château label on their wine, it won't be good. Therefore, there is a certain class that will only buy château wine. On the other hand, true connoisseurs, the truly initiated know that they can have a very good cooperative wine that will cost a minimum.

Moreover, the association of quality wine with an individual property or place has favored the elite wines in that the proprietors of these estates have been largely successful in consolidating their properties into a single domain against a long background of partible inheritance in France.

Small growers have been, to the contrary, far less successful in consolidating their properties in that it is not unusual for them to have as many as twenty different plots spread out over a delimited or classified area. Some of these plots may contain as few as six or seven rows of vines. In cases where the plots are in more than one delimited area, the wines must be bottled under separate classifications as it is not permitted in France to commercialize wines under an appellation that blends wines from two or more regions. Those who do so are committing fraud. Technically speaking, the small growers with fragmented properties have the right to bottle and commercialize their wines under a château label provided they do not combine their grapes during vinification with those of other growers. However, not only do these growers have a greater problem with efficiency of labor and time, as one would expect, but they must counter the general impression of both experts and consumers that grapes coming from a multiplicity of properties will not produce a high-quality wine.

While it is true that elite estates invest more time and capital in the aging of wines, the association of quality with single domains or place is vastly overemphasized and serves principally to support the distinctiveness of elite wines and by extension elite French culture. This is especially apparent in elite regions such as the Médoc where it is not uncommon for small and medium growers, including those who are members of cooperatives, to have vineyards that border directly—row to row—on those of the *grands crus*. This was confirmed by Nicole Ducros of the Pauillac cooperative in response to my question about the commercialization of wine and social class. Ducros explains why she would not sell her wine to the nearby renowned Château Latour and expresses outrage over the difference in price between her wine and that of the château.

> **Ulin:** Do you think that relations between social classes are important for the marketing of wine?
> **Ducros:** Yes, because you need all social classes, whether that be a worker or a doctor or no matter whom . . . . Why couldn't there be a good relation just because one type drinks a Lafite or a Latour, why? That's something I can't understand, because what I can't understand, namely, is that there are two hectares of my property that come within 80 centimeters of Château Latour. Château Latour has requested many times to buy this property. I've always said no. If some day I sell my property to Château Latour, they will then sell my wine. I sell my wine under Haut Pauillac. And overnight it will be sold under the label of Château Latour, but not at the same price. When you see that it sells at 800 to 900 francs per bottle, then that my wine sells at an average of 35 francs, that's a big difference. Yes, the difference is the transformation of genre. I don't understand how you can just pay for a label.

However, while cooperative members are well aware of the stigma and disadvantage associated with wines produced from numerous properties, some are quick to turn this to their advantage by asserting that cooperative wines best represent the region as a totality. Consider, for example, the following exchange with two other members of the Pauillac cooperative, Albert Bourgode and Marie Lescot. The Pauillac cooperative is located in one of the two most esteemed winegrowing communes of the Médoc.

> **Ulin:** Is this the mode of inheritance that you find often in France? Small parcels here and there?
>
> **Bourgode:** I think so.
>
> **Lescot:** Yes, that's customary. It used to be very parceled. Now we are trying, little by little, to regroup, but it was very parceled. And the large properties, the *grands crus* also, are the same. There are three rows that belong to Mouton-Rothschild, three rows of mine from the cooperative, then four rows from Lynch-Bages, etc. It is very divided.
>
> **Bourgode:** So let's finish. The old-timers said that they were doing it [parceling] in order to preserve quality, since the soil is not the same even 800 meters away. So it brought taste, the bouquet, etc.
>
> **Lescot:** It balanced things out.
>
> **Bourgode:** It balanced things out. Whereas at the cooperative, we have all the wine from Pauillac which is brought to the cooperative.
>
> **Lescot:** Therefore it is truly the wine of Pauillac.
>
> **Bourgode:** That's true, the ensemble of wine from Pauillac.
>
> **Ulin:** I've read books about co-op members who said they left the co-op because the co-op vinifies the grapes of all the members collectively and, in addition, they prefer to make the wine themselves.
>
> **Lescot:** You know, proprietors who make their own wine are also rather dispersed. Take Monsieur Perronet of Château Pombadé, who I know very well. His property is overall more than three times as dispersed as that of the cooperative. Yet, he vinifies Château Pombadé which is very renowned. So that's a bad argument, a very bad argument.

Although the proprietors of elite estates have sought to limit the proliferation of the château label through the judicial process, they have been largely unsuccessful with those producers who carefully follow the mandates of the law. Today, there are numerous smaller growers, merchants, and even cooperative members who have been able to claim as their own a small part of the cultural capital associated with château wines. What this means, apart from the commercial interest, is that growers of all sorts have accepted the standards of quality and taste associated with the château wines. In elite winegrowing regions such as the Médoc, virtually all the largest growers who are members of cooperatives commercialize their wines through the cooperatives but under château labels. This is accomplished legally by segregating their harvested grapes from the general lot of the cooperative and then pressing and vinifying the grapes separately. Moreover, cooperatives as a whole, even though they cannot commercialize the majority of their wines under the château label, have sought to emulate the standards of the elite wines by producing a greater volume of *appellation contrôlée* wine. The efforts from independents and cooperatives alike to emulate and thus reproduce the standards of the elite wines, combined with the not-to-be underestimated influence of advertising and popular wine guides, have done much to shape the consumption patterns of the general public.[9]

Emulating the standards of the elite wines does not however mean that social class has not had a marked influence on French consumption. Bourdieu has made this perfectly clear through evaluating consumption patterns of different French social classes over a range of cultural products from art to cinema to food. For example, Bourdieu has noted that skilled manual workers spend 555 francs per year on wine while industrial and commercial workers spend 1,881 francs (1984:182, 188–89). There is little doubt that the industrial and commercial workers are purchasing more expensive wine. However, the shelves of French supermarkets today are stocked with an increasingly diversified selection of château wines and other classified wines that cost a fraction of the elite wines. Consequently, it appears that the proliferation of the château image has done ostensibly for the "aesthetics and desire" of wine what Walter Benjamin claimed was true for art in the age of mechanical reproduction (1969). That is, the image or aura associated with great wines and the château label has generally become accessible to everyone, as great art has through mass reproductions. Nonetheless, since few people would actually confuse the lower-cost château wines with the *grands crus,* price alone being a significant factor, it can be asserted that the proliferation of the château label and its associated imagery have not, as Bourdieu's survey indicates, undermined the social distinctions of taste.

I have argued that the current status of southwest French wines follows conjointly from their political and economic history and a process of invention that links place and individual property with the authenticity and quality of wine. Moreover, I maintained that the invention of the winegrowing past contributed to the naturalization of conditions and criteria that are fundamentally social and historical. This, in turn, has reinforced social distinctions between growers and provided elites with cultural capital that is widely regarded as authoritative.

While I believe that there is much to be gained from viewing the winegrowing past, if not history in general, as invented, I have been careful to point out that the process of inventing is not autonomous. Unlike Handler and Linnekin, I argued that tradition itself, even when rightly regarded as pluralistic and contested, nonetheless serves practically and critically as the inextricable context, or better yet shifting terrain, from which our collective existence in the present is problematized and rendered potentially transparent. That is, the very idea that we can invent a multiplicity of pasts, or for that matter our daily sense of self and world, emerges dialectically from shared assumptions and unresolved questions and issues of our historical life-world. Furthermore, the historicity of tradition as it is engaged and then mediated contains both a sense of our limits and possibilities as social and temporal beings.

I maintain, moreover, that the invention of the past, as well as what counts as the limits and possibilities of social being, is positional, or in Raymond Williams's sense, selective. Consequently, not all discourses of an imagined and relativized past have an equal chance of being advanced and recognized as authoritative. This seems, for example, to have been the fate of women's history until relatively recently. While women have always been part of the making of history, their accounts have all too often been marginal to the "official" or hegemonic versions of the past as constructed largely but not exclusively by men. In like manner, the working class, among other subaltern populations, has been represented, with few exceptions, as marginal to the narratives of modern history in spite of their principal contribution to the making of capitalist industry. Their marginality, like that of the peasantry, is a consequence of being linked exploitively to the world system of political economy. The historical and sociocultural differentials of power thus occupy a central place in establishing which of a multiplicity of positioned actors will be able to advance their versions of the past as authoritative. The effort to gain recognition for an interpretation of the past involves a political struggle for self-identity and mutual recognition that should not be trivialized by a postmodern equivalence of discourses or, as pointed out by Jonathan Friedman (1991:105), a museum concept of culture.

There is some risk, however, that my qualifying of the invention of tradition as applied to the case of French winegrowers will be misunderstood as "history from above," particularly since I have argued that the elite growers or producers of *grands crus* have established the authoritative criteria of authenticity, quality, and taste. This is not to say that small growers, or for that matter recently proletarianized peasant-workers, did not in some significant way contribute to the invention of the winegrowing tradition. Nor is it my intention to argue that a univocal winegrowing tradition was constructed without points of resistance. The famous winegrowers' revolt of 1907 that erupted in the Midi stands as a case in point although it can be argued that the revolt challenged the French government's responsibility for a weak economy of wine and not the standards of wine excellence promoted by elites. Likewise, the creation of wine cooperatives in southwest France was predominantly a response to an economic crisis that was especially severe for small and medium-size growers. While members of cooperatives may have at the point of their regrouping expressed some political discontent at their subordinate position within a class-stratified wine hierarchy, in the long run, like the Midi growers, they embraced and reproduced the very standards established by the elite growers.

While the history of the political economy of wine in southwest France established, as noted above, the limits and possibilities by which growers advanced their versions of the winegrowing past and present as authoritative, surely it is the symbolic representation of wine that has distinguished this commodity culturally from the vast majority of other agricultural products in France. The building in the Médoc of small-scale replicas of medieval châteaus during the late eighteenth and nineteenth centuries to distinguish elite wines from those of the masses is a salient example of the exceptional symbolism associated with French winegrowing. However, it is important to understand that the advancement of the elite wines as the universal standard of quality is not simply strategic nor a conspiracy of elite growers and their supporters among the upper classes. Rather, as the 1855 Universal Exposition illustrates, the ascendancy of the elite wines went hand-in-hand with the struggles that ensued in general over the construction or invention of a French national culture modeled in many respects on the aristocracy and *haute bourgeoisie*. Just as invented French national culture would come to be experienced by the majority of the citizenry as essentially natural, for Eugen Weber (1976) the period following the First World War, so the cultural construction of the elite wines would eventually be taken as natural. Cultural associations and representations have the most power and persuasiveness, as the literature on nationalism and the invention of tradition has shown, when they are taken to be natural or, at the very least, subliminal.

The conjuncture of the political economy of winegrowing and the cultural representation of elite wines as authoritative have enabled elite growers to use the cultural capital associated with their wines to tremendous commercial advantage. While the invention of tradition has played a leading part in this success and the establishment of the French winegrowing hierarchy, it is clear that the small growers who were marginalized by the capitalist transformation of the French countryside have not had an equal claim to that of elites in the social construction or invention of winegrowing discourse and knowledge. To the contrary, it has been elites, now and then supported by the French government, that have shaped the discourse and knowledge of wine. The invention of tradition must, therefore, be regarded in terms of mediation so as not to overlook the power differentials that co-determine the invention of the past.

CAPITAL ACCUMULATION AND THE SOCIAL TRANSFORMATION OF WINEGROWING IN SOUTHWEST FRANCE

3

Although Marx wrote copiously and with acknowledged insight on the history and logic of the capitalist social formation, there continues to be significant theoretical disagreement among scholars as to what are the salient features of capitalism. Apart from the theoretical tensions between political economists and cultural theorists discussed previously (see Chapter 1), the issue of what constitutes the social dynamics and identity of capitalism remains unresolved. The famous debates between Maurice Dobb and Paul Sweezy over the transition from feudalism to capitalism, and subsequent critiques and points of departure from both sides, are a case in point (see Hilton 1978). These debates focused essentially on the analysis of modes of production and whether or not the demise of feudalism was due to internal contradictions or external factors such as expanding markets. In like manner, an Althusserian structural marxism precipitated considerable debate throughout the 1970s on the issue of social change by raising the question as to whether or not the economy was determinant in the "last instance."[1] While these debates are no doubt important to understanding the capitalist transformation of the European countryside and social change in general, their somewhat mechanistic or formulaic approach to economic and social history has tended to essentialize the mode of production and thereby diminish the significance of a historically constitutive human agency.[2]

The Dobb and Sweezy debates, however, as well as those precipitated by structural versions of marxism, by no means exhaust the controversy over what constitutes the essential features of the capitalist mode of production. The introduction of global political economy or the world-systems approach on the parts of Andre Gunder Frank and Immanuel Wallerstein has done much, for example, to redefine the theoretical terrain of economic and social history while stimulating considerable discussion concerning the identity and origin of the capitalist system. Both Frank and Wallerstein have shown convincingly, and in a manner that has been highly influential in the social sciences, that local economies and social systems are parts of larger national and international hegemonic systems. A critical understanding of a region must therefore proceed from an analysis of its articulation with the larger system. We have seen, however, that in spite of its merits, the world-systems approach tends to reduce local systems and their human agents to a reflex of the international order. From this perspective, as with economistic and structural paradigms, it becomes impossible to understand the dialectics of local resistance, especially its cultural manifestations, and the potential influence of regional systems or peripheries on what Frank and Wallerstein identify as the core areas (Wolf 1982; Ulin 1991a; Comaroff and Comaroff 1992).

Wallerstein has argued, moreover, that the world system of political economy, and therefore capitalism, can be traced to the incipient political and economic structures of the fifteenth century (1974). While there is little disagreement that capitalism has agrarian roots and that international commerce is significant to the process of primitive accumulation or capitalist development, Eric Wolf maintains that the mercantile capitalism of the fifteenth century, or long-distance trade, should not be taken as the central or defining characteristic of the capitalist system (1982). Mercantile capitalism, although important to European empire building, coexisted with numerous noncapitalist systems of labor. Furthermore, capitalist markets have existed throughout history under different social circumstances and in widely differing civilizations and states without capitalism being dominant. For Wolf, unlike Wallerstein, the salient feature of capitalism is not the circulation of commodities but the creation of a market in labor. That is, capitalism is essentially defined by the separation of workers from their means of production, a historical process that is focused more on the productive relations between classes than on the circulation of commodities. Moreover, Wolf believes, following Marx, that the circulation of commodities is in fact largely determined by the social relations of production.

The theoretical difference between Wallerstein and Wolf as described above is not only germane to understanding the emergence of wine cooperatives in the early twentieth century, as we shall see, but it is also important to the social history of southwest French wine in that the circulation of French wine as a capitalist commodity can be traced to the Middle Ages or perhaps even earlier. However, I will argue, following Wolf, that the capitalist circulation of wine essentially coexisted with noncapitalist systems of labor right up to the middle of the nineteenth century. While wage labor became more prevalent as a consequence of expanded long-distance trade and the consolidation of properties that ensued from the Religious Wars of the sixteenth and seventeenth centuries, it was only with the development of the *grands crus* in the late eighteenth and early nineteenth centuries that a market in labor in the wine-producing agricultural sector began to predominate. Moreover, I maintain that there was no uniformity to the development of capitalist agriculture in southwest France, as some sectors of agriculture developed a market in labor before others. Consequently, the development of capitalist agriculture in France was uneven, often marked by different social consequences. This goes against the general impression, often supported by a world-systems approach, that capitalism is a homogeneous, totalizing system producing similar effects in all places and at all times.[3]

It will not, however, be my objective to trace the whole history of capitalist agriculture in France nor to discuss the fine points and ensuing debates concerning capitalist transformation in general. Such a task would be monumental, and would take us far from the theme of the historical development and analysis of the multiple social purposes fulfilled by wine cooperatives. Moreover, the history of capitalist agriculture in France has been well documented on both the local and national levels by numerous scholars, and most especially in France by those associated with Braudel and the Annales school. Rather, I seek in the following to sketch the historical background that would give rise in the early twentieth century to the wine-cooperative movement. While such an account could conceivably commence with the early twentieth century or even later with the economic crisis of the 1930s, I will begin somewhat unconventionally with the twelfth century since this period was a watershed in the production and circulation of southwest French wines. Moreover, the twelfth century saw a realignment of the significance and power of wine-producing regions that has continued to the present and which has important consequences for cooperatives located elsewhere. However, my account of southwest French winegrowing will not be strictly linear or chronological, tracing the history of wine decade by decade or century by century, nor will it be historically exhaustive. I am primarily interested in elaborating significant historical junctures, such as the Religious Wars, the development of the *grands crus* and the phylloxera blight, and social processes that matured or changed the direction of wine production. An elaboration of wine production along these lines will, in turn, help us to appreciate the particular social circumstances and alignment of social classes that were in place at the dawn of the wine-cooperative movement in the early twentieth century.

THE ENGLISH OCCUPATION AND ITS CONSEQUENCES

The social landscape of winegrowing in southwest France at the beginning of the twelfth century is practically the inverse of the interregional alignment of power and social significance that one conventionally attributes to wine production and commerce today. Although the quality wines of Bordeaux have often been romanticized in the oenological literature as timeless, prior to the twelfth and thirteenth centuries Bordeaux wines had a secondary status to those of La Rochelle, those of the interior or Bergerac, and those of the Haut Pays of Quercy, Agen, Toulouse, and the Dordogne or the Périgord. Moreover, Bordeaux's wine production was meager compared to the standard of La Rochelle, where an important culture and commerce of wine had developed. Bordeaux wines were, furthermore, indistinct and often did not compare favorably to those originating from the interior (Enjalbert and Enjalbert 1987:21–22; Roudié 1988:14).

Pijassou points out, furthermore, in an important work on Médoc winegrowing, that there was no intrinsic uniformity or common significance that one could attribute to the early history of Bordeaux's several winegrowing regions (1980). This was true, moreover, not only for Bordeaux but for France as a whole. Prior to the sixteenth century French wines lacked a common identity—"French" wines referred only to the wines produced in the vicinity of Paris (Lachiver 1988). According to Pijassou, at the dawn of the English occupation, the Médoc, located directly to the north of Bordeaux, was a relatively minor winegrowing area compared to the other Bordeaux regions of Graves, Entre-Deux-Mers, and the Côte de la rive droite de la Garonne—these regions themselves being secondary to the interior and Haut Pays.[4]

The system of labor in the Médoc, like much of southwest France, consisted of a widespread seignorial system whereby serfs fulfilled their obligations to lords through payment of agricultural products, including grapes and cereals, and labor services. According to Pijassou, some of these serfs were housed directly on the lord's estate as tenants while others simply were required to turn over a portion of the produce from their own meager holdings. In addition, Médoc serfs bore an extra burden of having to pay the lord an estate tax.

Land ownership, as Pijassou notes, was highly parceled in the Médoc's four principal seigniories, several religious communities, and the holdings of a number of privileged bourgeois from Bordeaux. Wine production was rivaled, moreover, by the production of cereals. Unlike today, significant parts of the Médoc were covered by forests. Pijassou maintains that in spite of differences between regions, the wine production of Bordeaux as a whole was not substantial in that it rarely surpassed 120,000 hectoliters, much of it being consumed locally. However, this would gradually change as a consequence of the commerce and realignment of winegrowing regions precipitated by the English occupation of the twelfth to fifteenth centuries.

It is widely acknowledged by scholars who write on French wine that the English occupation of southwest France or the Aquitaine opened up an important period of growth for Bordeaux wine (Roudié 1988). The marriage of Eleanor in 1152, heiress to the Aquitaine, to Henry Plantagenêt, duke of Normandy, set the stage for the English occupation as

Henry would succeed to the English throne. Although the English were present in southwest France since the latter part of the twelfth century, the occupation did not truly realize its historical importance until La Rochelle fell to the French king, Louis VIII, in 1224.

La Rochelle had been under the English the preeminent southern French port, enjoying a more favorable location than Bordeaux—directly on the Atlantic Ocean—as well as a greater proximity to England. In addition, much of the wine produced in southwest France as a whole prior to the twelfth century passed through the port of La Rochelle rather than Bordeaux. However, the defeat of the English at La Rochelle established Bordeaux as the exclusive supplier of wine to England, as Louis VIII prohibited La Rochelle merchants from engaging in trade with England (Dion 1977:372).

The trade in wine originating from Bordeaux became, as noted previously, so important that English warships marked their size by the *tonneaux* of wine that they could carry. The average annual wine consumption in northern European cities at the time was forty liters per capita, while inhabitants of Bruge were known to consume as much as one hundred liters. Although some beer was consumed, wine predominated as tea, coffee, and Eau de Vie (brandy) did not become important until the sixteenth and seventeenth centuries (Lachiver 1988:108). Roudié argues, furthermore, that after the fall of La Rochelle, forests were cleared in the Bordeaux region to make way for vineyards to meet rising northern European demand for wine, and that Gascon merchants, due to the political unification of Gascony with the Aquitaine, became formidable competitors to English merchants (1988:14–16).

While the English occupation did much to advance the commercial success of Bordeaux wine, it also had an opposite effect on wines coming from the interior. Henry III made a trip to Bergerac in 1254 to put both diplomatic and military pressure on the inhabitants of the town, including an embargo on wine, to submit to his rule. The inhabitants of Bergerac agreed to submit to English authority in 1255 and, in turn, adopted a new system of government similar to that of Bordeaux. The new government included the administrative division of the commune with a mayor and *jurats* or council. The new government gave special authority to the bourgeois in preference to nobility traditionally loyal to the French king and opened, moreover, new opportunities for commerce with England on the part of Bergerac wine merchants. However, the inhabitants of Bergerac continued to owe the English king one *tonneau* or cask on each boat that carried at least twenty (Lachiver 1988).

Beauroy notes that prior to the twelfth century, vineyards in the Dordogne Valley and the Périgord were maintained and developed by powerful nobles and church elites who had control of the best land (1976). The nobles would let some of their land for winegrowing for which they would receive a tax. These nobles were also attached to particular abbeys, which they supported through the collection of tithes. The nobles also controlled the circulation of commodities by controlling transport along the Dordogne River. The nobles would cast a net across the river and demand a toll before a boat or barge could pass. Although nobles and church elites played a central role in the expansion of vineyards in the Dordogne Valley, the vineyards were widely scattered and few properties were devoted to winegrowing alone. However, as with Bordeaux, England was the principal market for wines of the Dordogne Valley and high country of the Périgord.

Beauroy maintains that between the twelfth and fifteenth centuries the control of wine production shifted from the nobility and church elites to bourgeois from Bergerac.[5] This was especially the case with vineyards south of Bergerac that were seized from the nobility by the bourgeois, who invoked their municipal authority. It was not, however, the bourgeoisie in general who gained control of wine production but those, such as traders, who had occupied important positions in the commerce of the town, and others, such as doctors, who were important professionally. While the nobility was not eliminated from wine production and commerce, their role became secondary to that of the bourgeoisie.

While the English occupation alone does not account for the changing social composition of wine production in the Bergerac region, the occupation did result in an important transformation between Bordeaux and interior wines that has endured to the present. The wines of the interior were of sufficient quality with respect to price that they competed well with those produced in the vicinity of Bordeaux. However, in order to reach distant markets, especially the lucrative ones of northern Europe, interior wines, including those of Bergerac, had to pass by Libourne where the Dordogne joins the Gironde. The principal means of transport and access to coastal ports and thus distant markets in this period was the system of southwest French rivers. The main river coming from the interior is the Dordogne, which joins the Gironde River just above the city of Bordeaux. Prior to the English occupation, interior wines, like those of Bergerac, and even those of Bordeaux, would be shipped to distant markets by way of La Rochelle. However, with the fall of La Rochelle, Bordeaux became the principal port for the interior—thus leaving these wines subject to the control of Bordeaux merchants and elites.[6]

The Bordeaux elites and city officials approached the English crown through the duke of the Aquitaine in order to request protective measures against wines coming from the interior or Bergerac and the Haut Pays such as the Périgord (Pijassou 1980:299). Lachiver notes, moreover, that from the thirteenth century on, wines coming from Castile and Andalusia also competed with those from southwest France (1988). It is important to recognize that although inhabitants of the southwest did not in this early period have a social or cultural identity linked to the French state, they were, nonetheless, capable of mobilizing a local or regional identity to resist their English occupiers.[7] One way that the English crown thwarted the potential of resistance was to grant concessions to local officials. As Roudié remarks, the English crown granted the inhabitants of Bordeaux an exemption from taxes and duties on wine which, in turn, gave them a considerable commercial advantage (1988:15–16). Local inhabitants were also given permission to sell their wines in other than local taverns. On the other hand, wines coming from the interior and the Haut Pays, as well as Castile and Andalusia, were subject to taxation and duties, which made them more expensive and less competitive on local and long-distance markets. In addition, the *jurats* or magistrates of Bordeaux were given the right to limit the periods in which wines from the interior could enter the city—which also had a negative impact on their commercial competitiveness and viability.

The English occupation, in short, by shifting the flow of commerce away from La Rochelle to the port of Bordeaux, contributed significantly to a redefinition of the commercial importance and reputations of winegrowing regions and the power of winegrowers that persists today. Bordeaux elites made use of their ties to the English crown to gain special privileges that would make their wines favored over those of the interior on an expanding market system. This is of no little significance in that the privileged position of Bordeaux wines is often explained, as we saw in Chapter 2, in terms of its favorable climate and superior soil.[8] Moreover, English clients showed a preference for clarets, or red wines, and so proprietors in the Bordeaux region as well as the interior planted their vineyards to meet consumer demands. The Médoc, for example, to this day is a region that produces almost exclusively red wines.

It is important to recognize, nonetheless, that although the English occupation contributed significantly to the transformation of southwest French winegrowing, it did not substantially alter a mode of production that was essentially feudal. To the contrary, the new capitalist markets opened up through Bordeaux coexisted with the seignorial system even in cases where the bourgeoisie and merchants gained control of winegrowing estates. However, the realignment of winegrowing regions that ensued from the English occupation was not static, but a process that would continue. Although the reconquest of the Aquitaine by Charles VII in 1453 was disastrous for Bordeaux's commercial ties to England in that Charles VII severely limited the accessibility to Bordeaux of English ships and merchants for nearly a decade, southwest winegrowers proved to be, with the help of Charles's successor, Louis XI, sufficiently resilient to generate a recovery. In 1461 Louis restored and expanded Bordeaux's commercial privileges granted by the English crown. Unlike his predecessor who was resolved to punish Bordeaux's citizens politically and economically, Louis was determined to win their loyalty by recognizing the importance of the English wine trade to the Bordeaux economy (Penning-Rowsell 1969:61–62).

THE RELIGIOUS WARS OF THE SIXTEENTH AND SEVENTEENTH CENTURIES AND THE POSTOCCUPATION RECOVERY

While the retaking of the Aquitaine by the French in 1453 imperiled the southwest French wine trade, the social consequences of the Religious

Wars of the sixteenth and seventeenth centuries and the postoccupation recovery contributed, albeit sometimes indirectly, to the growth and expansion of capitalist markets. Prior to the sixteenth century, the circulation of commodities between French regions was often hindered by strong local restrictions as France lacked an integrated national market. However, the postoccupation period saw a liberalizing of local restrictions on trade that facilitated the circulation of commodities nationally. Moreover, the period of the Religious Wars witnessed an opening up of new markets with northern Europe, the growth of monocropping and specialized labor, and the securing of a prominent place for the bourgeoisie, particularly those who were Protestant, in the social hierarchy of the southwest interior, especially the Bergerac region. The importance of these changes is evident in that vineyard hectarage in the vicinity of Bergerac grew faster than in any other region from the 1720s on.

The Religious Wars were not only reflective of ecclesiastical or doctrinal differences between French Huguenots (or Protestants) and Catholics but they also exhibited, at least in southwest France, tensions which can be understood in terms of economic privilege. This is not to diminish the significance of religious prejudice. Protestants were not permitted to be buried in Catholic cemeteries. Protestant churches, such as at St.-Émillion, were fortified against Catholic assaults. Nonetheless, Beauroy asserts that it was Protestant families, such as the Eymas and Poumeaus, who played a leading role in the development of the wine trade in Bergerac right through the eighteenth century. For example, the Eymeric de Meredieu, seigneur of Ambois, Boir-Bru, Boulagac, and Naillac, managed his property as an absentee landlord preferring to live in nearby Bergerac. The ownership of vineyards on the part of Protestant families reinforced, furthermore, their dominant position in the political life of the town, as it was not uncommon for these same families to occupy positions on the town council. The urban community would determine, in turn, when the harvest would begin—thus exhibiting their power over the countryside. It is likely that the preeminent position enjoyed by Protestant families was resented by Catholics who were either competitors or subaltern dependents.

The consequences and outcome of the Religious Wars has been, of course, well documented. Many Huguenot families were forced to flee from Catholic France. Due to the reputation of the Dutch for religious tolerance, Huguenots settled permanently in Holland. This was fortuitous for the Bergerac wine trade and that of the interior of southwest France in general in that families newly settled in Holland maintained strong ties with Huguenots who elected to remain in the Bergerac region. Many of the Huguenots who remained in the Bergerac region had already made, as noted, considerable reputations for themselves as merchants or winegrowers. The personal ties between the Bergerac region and Holland precipitated a trade in wine of such magnitude that it nearly rivaled that which had developed at Bordeaux.

The Dutch had a maritime monopoly and thus set up a system of transport and distribution that was commercially significant for the whole Dordogne Valley. Moreover, the trade with Holland was so important that it also stimulated copper production of which Bergerac was a center. The Dutch had a proclivity, furthermore, for sweet white wines and so the increase in wine trade led to an extensive plantation in the muscadelle vine stock from which sweet white wines could be made.[9] Beauroy sees the introduction of muscadelle between 1600 and 1640 as the first phase in the transformation of wine production in the Bergerac region. As Médoc specializes in reds today, certain areas of the Bergerac region, such as Monbazillac, continue to favor the production of sweet white wines to satisfy the preferences of their northern European market.

Although the period of the Religious Wars was marked by renewed prosperity, winegrowers of the Bergerac region or interior had to contend with the interruptions precipitated by hostilities. This took the largest toll on the harvest, which as a labor-intensive activity could ill afford to lose workers to the interruptions precipitated by military conflict. Beauroy relates, moreover, that taxes were imposed on wines particularly during periods of hostilities. However, in spite of these problems, the Religious Wars ushered in an important change in the organization of the system of production as sharecropping became widespread in the interior during the sixteenth century.

Sharecropping not only became common to winegrowing but also to the cultivation of cereals. The owners of large estates leased portions of their vineyards to peasants for which they would receive at least 50 percent of the yield in return. A portion of the sharecropper's yield would be retained for personal consumption while the rest would be sold at the market or to a middleman. As Sobul has noted, the relation of the sharecropper to the proprietor was more than economic as the sharecropper would look to the proprietor for advice, medical assistance, and other social needs that deepened their interdependence (1977). According to Beauroy, the winegrowing sharecropper in particular was both an entrepreneur and a partner to the proprietor. Sharecroppers often acted as managers and marketing agents for absentee proprietors—a mutual dependency that was distinctive to winegrowing up to this period.

The opening up of new markets with Holland, combined with the already established ones of England and Flanders, thus contributed to changes in Bergerac's system of production and to advancing its importance among the winegrowing sectors of southwest France.

While the Religious Wars were widely important and influential throughout France, they made less of an impact on wine commerce in Bordeaux than was the case in Bergerac. This was due, in part, to the greater involvement of Protestants in Bergerac winegrowing than in Bordeaux. In terms of the postoccupation recovery, Pijassou adds that the involvement of merchants and parliamentarians in wine cultivation and commerce did much to improve the situation in Bordeaux's major winegrowing regions (1980:317). According to Pijassou, the nobility had become indebted and was therefore unable to invest needed capital in winegrowing. This capital came, rather, from the merchants and parliamentarians. As in Bergerac, Bordeaux merchants and parliamentarians pursued a system of sharecropping whereby the lessor became more involved in the property's management. There was also an attempt to regroup the parceled land of the peasants—the result of a long tradition of partible inheritance—although this transformation would prove to be slow and incomplete.

The merchants and parliamentarians who became involved in Bordeaux winegrowing and commerce purchased their properties from the traditional nobility. These individuals assumed, furthermore, a new social status through the purchase of offices, a practice that was common in sixteenth-century France. The extent of the purchase of properties on the part of merchants and bourgeois of Bordeaux is reflected in the fact that 40 percent of the properties in the Médoc changed hands between 1595 and 1603 (Pijassou 1980:323). Although the example of Haut-Brion predates this specific period, it is typical of the change of ownership that would take place at the end of the sixteenth century. Haut-Brion was bought in 1533 for 1,800 *livres* by a merchant of Basque origin, Jean Duhalde. This same individual, known as Jean de Pontac, was not only interested in purchasing the best sites of Graves in Pessac, just outside of Bordeaux, but he was also interested in investing money in the Haut-Médoc (Pijassou 1980:323).

The sale of so many properties led, furthermore, to a concentration of holdings on the part of the new owners. For example, in the sixteenth century, the bourgeois and merchants of Bordeaux, consisting of only 9.7 percent of the proprietors, controlled 40.7 percent of the surface area in vineyards. Furthermore, the nobility who had purchased titles, in this case 9 percent of the property owners, controlled 34.2 percent of the vineyards (Pijassou 1980:323). On the other hand, Pijassou maintains that the winegrowers and workers who constitute the majority of the "agricultural crowd" controlled only 12.9 percent of the land (1980:336). Moreover, the large elite landowners resided in Bordeaux and had their properties managed or sharecropped by others. The sale of land and its consequent concentration in the hands of fewer owners proved to be disastrous for the peasantry. Many small peasant proprietors found themselves evicted, with few options other than to become agricultural workers or to leave the parish altogether.

The postoccupation period for the Bordeaux region led to the concentration of land in progressively fewer hands as properties changed ownership at a remarkable and unprecedented pace. This, in turn, led to a disenfranchisement of the peasantry forcing them to seek work on the large estates or to leave the countryside in search of a livelihood elsewhere. While this form of primitive accumulation or capitalist development no doubt led to the introduction of wage labor, it was on a limited basis as sharecropping and paternalistic social relations continued to be the predominant means through which absentee estates were managed in the Bordeaux region.

The sixteenth and seventeenth centuries continued to present high and low points for Bordeaux winegrowers—which seems to be typical of the history of French winegrowing in general. For example, the Dutch, beginning in 1672, demanded less French wine and more from Spain—which precipitated a crisis in Bordeaux. This was combined with an embargo on the part of England against French wines because Colbert, the finance minister under Louis XIV, had refused to sign a commerce treaty with England in 1679. However, in 1685 the embargo was lifted and Bordeaux wines reasserted their supremacy on the English market (Pijassou 1980:365). The vicissitudes of the wine trade in Bordeaux thus followed the course of periodic European conflicts and the international character of ascendant European empires, thus making local history, as Wallerstein has argued, part of a larger global narrative (1974). This can be seen not only through commerce in wine but also through the Caribbean connection, as Bordeaux also became a major center for the processing of sugar.[10]

THE GRANDS CRUS AND THE SOCIAL TRANSFORMATION OF SOUTHWEST WINEGROWING

The appearance of wine cooperatives in the early part of the twentieth century owes much to transformations in the capitalist production and marketing of wine that occurred concurrently with and, in part, as the consequence of the development of the *grands crus* during the eighteenth and nineteenth centuries.[11] This is not to deny the importance of the English occupation and the Religious Wars to the formation of the historical context from which cooperatives would emerge insofar as these two seminal periods contributed to the rapid expansion of capitalist markets and the ascendancy of Bordeaux as the principal center of wine production in southwest France. This continues, furthermore, to have enormous significance for the subordinate or secondary status of growers in the interior compared to those in the immediate vicinity of Bordeaux and has, in addition, established a link between particular vine stocks and grapes and delimited winegrowing regions.[12] However, as I argued at the outset of this chapter, it was in the context of the domination of the capitalist mode of production and not simply through capitalist circulation that the social basis of wine cooperatives was forged. The English occupation and Religious Wars, although furthering the ends of capitalist exchange, did not create a market in labor and hence did not elevate the capitalist mode of production to a position of dominance in the French countryside. Rather, between the twelfth and seventeenth centuries, capitalist markets and social relations coexisted, as we have seen, with feudal relations and their remnants, as well as small dispersed family plots worked by peasant households.

Although the Republican reforms that followed from the French Revolution, including a more direct role played by the state in the economy, set the eighteenth and nineteenth centuries apart from the preceding periods of expanding capitalist markets, the assertion of the capitalist mode of production as dominant was slow to mature. Theda Skocpol has argued that competing interests of the upper classes and monarchy, as well as local restrictions on trade, were an obstacle to capitalist development (1977). She maintains, furthermore, that throughout much of the eighteenth century, the upper classes did not pursue entrepreneurial interests—they used their wealth to purchase state titles. Although the French Revolution served to consolidate bourgeois property by challenging communal holdings and control over production, the encumbrances of complex proprietary rights and the predominance of the small dispersed family holding prevented a rapid transition to the capitalist mode of production.

Skocpol's notion that the transition to the capitalist mode of production was gradual is further supported by Albert Sobul, who argues that the French Revolution in general did little to alter feudal relations in areas of France where sharecropping was dominant (1977). According to Sobul, the traditional tithe so hated by peasants throughout feudalism was merely absorbed into the rent structure of land leased to peasants.

Even though feudalism was abolished once and for all by the decrees of the convention of 17 July 1793, certain aspects of feudalism persisted throughout the first half of the nineteenth century and sometimes until the very dawn of the twentieth. Essentially, these aspects affected the regions where small scale farming and sharecropping were prevalent, that is, western and southwestern France, where the "agricultural revolution" had scarcely penetrated. (Sobul 1977:50)

Although Sobul's comments on the prevalence of sharecropping and persistence of certain aspects of feudalism in southwest France are well taken,[13] winegrowing was considerably more advanced along capitalist lines than other sectors of agriculture. This was attributable, in part, to the enormous northern European demand for the wines of the southwest and the capitalist markets that this demand had created since the twelfth century. In addition, vineyards suffered somewhat less from the extreme parceling of agricultural lands, and were not subject to traditional rights of common use.

Even through the currents identified by Skocpol and Sobul did slow the development of the capitalist mode of production, the eighteenth-century reforms that followed from the Republican government created new economic and social potentials. At the very least, the Republican constitution fortified, in a formal sense, private property and the rights of citizens to pursue their individual interests unfettered. Charles Tilly has argued that the Republican reforms, by establishing a uniform system of taxation and by reducing use rights, traditional controls, and fiscal hindrances on trade and industry, contributed to the process of capital accumulation or development—in part by consolidating property rights for individual parcels (1975). A uniform taxation system and the reduction of local restrictions on trade made it easier for merchants to circulate commodities throughout France, thus curtailing, but not eliminating, the commercial privileges of certain areas. The reduction of use rights in land affected most severely those peasants with little or no land—forcing them in many cases to sell their labor power to the large estates, thus advancing the creation of a rural proletariat. In short, the commercial potentials generated from the Republican reforms stimulated not only wine commerce and consequently the area devoted to vineyard cultivation and monocropping but it also redefined property rights.

The development of the *grands crus* during the eighteenth and nineteenth centuries, combined with the Republican reforms that ensued from the French Revolution, greatly transformed the social relations of winegrowers and the symbolism associated with French wine. Enjalbert has noted that although French wine generally fared well on the international market, especially in northern Europe, French growers began to face significant competition from wines produced in Spain and Portugal (1953). Spanish and Portuguese growers emphasized high yields. The abundant production of Spanish and Portuguese wines permitted merchants from these countries to sell their wines at a lower price than French wines on local and international markets, thus precipitating a crisis.

French growers had essentially two options to meet the challenge from Spain and Portugal. They could either increase the yield from their own harvests and thus lower the price, or they could seek to develop a wine that was altogether distinct. French growers, especially the owners of large estates in regions like the Médoc, opted to develop a distinct wine by decreasing the yields from the harvest and thus, they believed, improving quality. It was decreased yields coming from older plants, combined with the aging of wine, often in oak barrels for the reds, that would come to characterize the *grands crus* of southwest France. It is important to note, however, that the development of the *grands crus* was gradual and went hand in hand with wines, such as Haut-Brion, that already had been associated for some time with particular estates by consumers in European and American markets.[14]

The development of the *grands crus* in the course of the eighteenth century initiated a change in both the social and technical character of wine production. Pijassou argues that it was the *grands crus* or château wines that assumed a predominant role in "colonizing" vineyards and promoting monocropping (1980:466). The proprietors of the château vineyards managed to consolidate parceled properties and thus promote the association, as exemplified by Haut-Brion, between quality and place. Pijassou maintains that while the consolidation of properties, monocropping, and the association of quality with place did not eliminate peasant growers, it resulted in their being at the bottom of a wine hierarchy not subject to change. Moreover, as argued by Loubère, "In the area of fine wines, peasants were nearly but not entirely excluded from purchasing land during the revolutionary era and also during most of the 19th century" (1978:217). According to Loubère, these lands were purchased by middle-class urbanites, rural bourgeois, and nobles—thus reinforcing the class distinctions cultivated by the *grands crus*.

The impact of the *grands crus* on the social relations of production was also noteworthy and, as we will see later, would in the long run influence the social organization of wine cooperatives. Sharecropping continued to be, as noted, one of the most prevalent forms of production in southwest France. In addition to sharecropping, production on the large estates was typified by a combination of a yearly pension, known as *prix-fait,* and piecework. Wine workers were paid an annual pension based upon their carrying out a range of activities that included planting of vine stocks and pruning. Pensions were not usually sufficient to guarantee the reproduction of the wine worker's household so that supplemental income acquired through piecework was necessary. In addition to work in the vineyards, wine workers also tended sheep and raised pigs for the proprietors. In the case of pigs, the wine worker would split the profit with the proprietor at the time of sale.

Housing was provided, furthermore, directly in the vineyards by the proprietors of the large estates for their pension wine workers or *prix-faiteurs.* Houses were equipped with pigsties, stables, furnaces, and winepresses. Since the fundamental part of the wine worker's diet was composed of cereals such as wheat and rye, payments made to the wine worker tended to be in one or both of these staples. The price of grain greatly influenced the quality of life for wine workers. At the end of the eighteenth century, for example, there was widespread discontent among the wine workers and winegrowers because of the high price of grain. Consequently, uprisings such as *la révolte frumentaire* at Bergerac in 1773 were not uncommon. While women had limited roles in the cultivation of vineyards and the processing of grapes into wine, the wives of wine workers and winegrowers were among the leadership of these revolts at the end of the eighteenth century. According to Beauroy, the winegrowers employed by the large estates had a social standing above the peasantry at large but beneath that of sharecroppers (1976).

It was those peasants who acquired some land who were able to obtain a partial subsistence by working household vineyards and by selling their labor to nearby estates. This group, although less numerous than sharecroppers and pension workers, was often sympathetic to the vine workers of the large estates and supported them in their periodic revolts for higher wages and improved working conditions. Revolts among the wine workers and growers were, however, sporadic and for the most part were tied to local issues. Periodic gluts on the market resulted in a drop in wine prices, a situation that was most directly felt by small proprietors and wage laborers.

The development of the *grands crus* in the eighteenth century changed the social contour of an already stratified group of winegrowers and small proprietors. This was the case because the production of *grands crus* involved the application of new technology and hence more specialized labor. For example, the pruning of grape vines is an activity that requires considerable judgment and which, according to oenologists, is crucial to the cultivation of quality grapes. On the large estates, pruning became a specialized task requiring knowledge and skill and thus pruners occupied a social status considerably above that of other wine workers. On some estates, it was the pruners who supervised other vineyard workers, particularly in the case of an absentee proprietor. Otherwise, estates such as Château Lafite and Château Latour hired a *regisseur* to oversee or manage the estate in the proprietor's absence. The *regisseur* at Château Lafite at the end of the eighteenth century was a Bordeaux merchant who himself owned a small vineyard in Talence near Haut-Brion. It was common for such *regisseurs* to receive 2 to 4 percent of the total sales as commission.

The case of vine trimmers exhibits the potential relation between specialization and social control, a point that has been argued theoretically by scholars sympathetic to the marxist tradition and which has been well documented in general through the history of the capitalist division of labor (Marx 1967; Braverman 1974). However, specialization and social control developed gradually from the rupture of the formerly unified processes of viniculture and viticulture that resulted from the development of the *grands crus*. Viniculture is the process through which harvested grapes are pressed and the resulting juice or must is fermented and then aged to produce wine. Viticulture refers to all the activities, from planting to chemical treatments to prevent disease, that are involved in the cultivation of vineyards. Throughout much of the eighteenth century and earlier, as indicated above, proprietors provided for the personal and social needs of their winegrowers. The same workers, furthermore, both cultivated the vineyards and processed harvested grapes into wine. Although the development of the *grands crus* eventually came to serve the rationalization of production, the assault on the older or traditional methods of winemaking did not come to fruition until the nineteenth century. The point here is to recognize that capitalism and its modes of social control had an uneven development in the southwest of France, making a profound impact on certain geographical areas and winegrowing regions before others. Furthermore, specialization, as we shall see later, did not make much of an impact on small proprietors who continued to produce wines for daily consumption. At the dawn of the nineteenth century, it was the incipient urban working class that served as the primary market for small proprietors.

The specialization of wine production that ensued from the *grands crus* doomed many of the sharecroppers and those who were housed as workers on the large estates. Proprietors of these estates relied on a more rationalized organization of production whereby productive tasks were allocated according to the particular expertise of the labor force. This, in turn, undermined the older organization of labor in which wine production was a unified process. The employment of specialized workers attacked the mutual bonds that had marked the relations between proprietors and their wine workers since the early Middle Ages.

Such specialization is not incommensurable with the process that typified the division of labor in capitalist industry. It was more profitable for the capitalist proprietor to utilize capital-intensive labor when needed, such as during the harvest, rather than be responsible for the support of winegrowers and their families on a continuous or yearly basis. The movement toward specialized seasonal labor and away from wine workers housed on large estates was accompanied by a deepened social and political assault on community ties, symbolized by the enclosure of common lands. From here on, the transformation in the organization of production on the large estates was reinforced at the political and legislative levels by guarantees given to the free acquisition and disposal of private property. The consequences of the enclosures in France, although not as extensive or severe as in England, contributed to the creation of a wage labor force available to the proprietors of the large winegrowing estates.

The development of the capitalist mode of production, however, typified by the domination of a market in labor, was not uniform throughout the southwest of France. The winegrowers in the Bergerac region, for example, both large and small, produced wines that for the most part were best consumed young. Sharecropping and the housing of nonspecialized winegrowers persisted well into the nineteenth century with remnants of the former still visible as late as the 1940s. It was in the Bordeaux region that the consequences of the development of the *grands crus* were most manifest. Bordeaux merchants had played a lead-ing role in marketing wine throughout the southwest as a whole since the late twelfth and thirteenth centuries. Moreover, as we have seen, Bordeaux asserted its supremacy by controlling the circulation of wine and the price that it would obtain at market. This was the case even though the 1776 Edict of Turgot guaranteed the free circulation of commodities throughout France, thus ostensibly challenging the control by certain commercial centers of goods that passed through their mar-kets. While the capitalist mode of production among Bordeaux wine-growers was articulated in advance of that at Bergerac or elsewhere in the interior of the southwest, it was not long afterwards that the com-mercial dominance of Bordeaux drew Bergerac into its fold.

The *grands crus* precipitated changes not only in the organization of production and the political economy of southwest French winegrowing in general, but they also facilitated changes of a more cultural nature that served to reinforce and reproduce the social bases of the winegrow-ing hierarchy and thus the inequality between classes of growers. The large growers in the Bordeaux region not only sought to distinguish their wines from mass-produced Spanish and Portuguese wines but they also desired to set their wines apart from those produced by the vast majority of French small and medium proprietors, not to mention peas-ant growers.

The proprietors of the large estates thus sought to associate their wines with a long history of aristocratic production in France. These proprietors set out to emulate what appeared to them to be the most ostensible cultural characteristics of the "traditional" aristocracy. For example, as I mentioned in Chapter 2, proprietors of *grands crus* estates built small-scale replicas of medieval châteaus as a means of representing their direct historical ties to a glorious but invented French past. In fact, as Roudié has pointed out, the houses of the traditional aristocracy were not châteaus but were merely known as a noble house or *un maison noble* (1988:1444).

Moreover, these self-same proprietors assumed a leading role in es-tablishing in 1855 a widely accepted hierarchical classification of Bor-deaux wines that has changed little up to the present day. The 1855

classification was established in response to a request from the organizers of the Universal Exposition in Paris—itself an event that was
important to the invention of French nationhood and the advancement
of an elitist and hegemonic national culture (Clifford 1988). The 1855
classification, like the invention of tradition or culture in general, naturalized the social conditions of wine production by making it appear
that the preeminent wines enjoyed their elevated status as a consequence
of a favorable climate and soil, rather than, as argued by Enjalbert, a
superior organization of marketing to northern Europe (1953). The
appeal to nature enabled elite growers of the Bordeaux region to deny
a Bordeaux classification to wines of the interior, such as those from
Bergerac, which, in turn, gave them a measurable commercial advantage. The representation of elite wines on the part of Bordeaux growers
and merchants thus illustrates the profound interrelation between political economy and an incipient hegemonic national culture.

THE PHYLLOXERA BLIGHT

By the time the phylloxera blight struck the southwest of France in the
1870s, capitalist social relations had asserted their dominance in both
the Bordeaux and Bergerac regions.[15] Capital accumulation was aided
throughout the eighteenth and nineteenth centuries not only by the
Republican reforms and the hegemony of Bordeaux merchants and
grands crus proprietors but by the ruination of many small independent
winegrowers as a consequence of crises ensuing from overproduction
and the decline in the price of wine at market. When the phylloxera
blight commenced, a frail accommodation had been achieved between
the proprietors of the large estates and those with small holdings. The
proprietors of the large estates, especially in areas of Bordeaux such as
the Médoc and Sauterne, concentrated for the most part on quality
wines while the vast majority of small proprietors produced table wines
for the incipient urban working class. The phylloxera blight shattered
this accommodation.

Phylloxera is a louse that attacks and destroys the roots of some grape
stocks. It is suspected that the parasite that caused phylloxera was

brought into France during the early 1830s by elite growers who imported grape plants from America (Dion 1977). In the area between Bergerac and the departmental capital to the north, Périgueux, 75 percent of the vineyard area was destroyed. The phylloxera epidemic was, however, less severe in the immediate vicinity of Bordeaux. According to Roudié, of 170,000 hectares in the Gironde, less than 70,000 were infected with phylloxera (1988:156–58). Initially, growers attempted to address the phylloxera blight through sulfur treatments of the vineyards or through flooding the fields to drown the parasites. These techniques did not prove to be especially effective. Roudié remarks, however, that after 1884 producers did not hesitate to uproot dead and sick plants and to replace them with phylloxera-resistant American stocks such as Reparia and York's Maderia (1988:172). Unlike previous efforts, the grafting of American vines onto the French stocks proved to be effective.[16] In spite of the success of grafting, numerous winegrowers whose vineyards were destroyed by phylloxera, especially from the area between Bergerac and Périgueux, decided to leave the countryside to seek employment in urban areas while others turned to agricultural pursuits such as the growing of tobacco or the search for valuable truffles.

A sizable number of the large growers elected to replant their vineyards with lower-quality high-yielding grapes. These vine stocks produced a beverage that was best consumed young, therefore avoiding the need for expensive long-term storage facilities. The shift to high-yielding stocks on the part of the large growers had consequences that were devastating for the small proprietors of ordinary or table wines. The capital resources of large growers enabled them to seek markets not accessible to the small growers and to invest in promoting their wines on national markets. However, the group that profited most from phylloxera was not the large growers but merchants with sufficient capital to invest in viticultural research. Research in viticulture proved to be necessary not only to prevent a reappearance of phylloxera but to prevent the destruction ravaged on vineyards by fungal infestations such as mildew and odium. Furthermore, these merchants also had the capital to invest in new vinicultural technology and so they managed to gain control of the winemaking process from proprietors whose resources were diverted away from viniculture and to protective viticultural measures.

Although the response of the small proprietors to the wine crisis that ensued from phylloxera was not uniform, Loubère maintains that the "blight was largely responsible for modifying the ferocious individualism of most vignerons and at least indirectly stimulated their willingness to modernize" (1978:173). Moreover, syndicates, which had played an important role in the lives of small growers since the beginning of the eighteenth century, took on renewed importance in assisting the peasant proprietor in avoiding disaster. Syndicates made agricultural resources such as fertilizer and pesticides available to the peasantry at a lower cost. However, because the leadership of the syndicates was drawn from the large proprietors, the *grands crus* proprietors from the Médoc being a prime example, they served more as a means to reinforce the traditional hierarchy of the countryside rather than as a viable means of political resistance against the excesses of capitalist development. [17]

Some small proprietors made an appeal to the central government to rectify the growing problem with fraudulent wines, yet another problem resulting from phylloxera and the ensuing mass-produced wines (see Chapter 2). It was not uncommon for both growers and merchants, due to the wine shortage precipitated by phylloxera, to pass off *piquettes,* or second wines, as firsts or to illegally fortify weaker wines by blending wines from different delimited regions. [18] After much debate in the French legislative body, the Loi Griffe was passed in 1889. This law defined wine as the product of naturally fermented grapes (Warner 1960). All other beverages which did not meet this specification, including wines made from dried fruits, had to be labeled accordingly. The Loi Griffe had the consequence, unforeseen by small growers, of upholding the wine hierarchy rather than giving those who were most marginal to winegrowing greater access to local and foreign markets.

Although the national government was at times responsive to the hardships precipitated by phylloxera and the pleas for social justice on the part of the small proprietors, it was equally the intention of French officials to establish a means by which they could control the production of wine. The first step was the recognition of syndicates in the middle of the nineteenth century—which up to this point had been illegal. However, syndicates merely reinforced the traditional hierarchy of the countryside, and thus did not provide an effective means to unify the resources of independent peasant proprietors. Wine cooperatives would provide, on the other hand, the very institutional medium through which limitations could be levied on the quantity of production through the cooperative's centralized administration. Control over production was, moreover, strategic to curtailing the periodic economic crises that had challenged the viability of capitalist viticulture and viniculture since the sixteenth century. Even conservative members of the French legislature who were uneasy with the idea of cooperative efforts in the countryside or city voted in favor of the creation of wine cooperatives because their potential contribution to state control was recognized.

The government, in short, authorized the state bank, Crédit Agricole, to make loans available, beginning in the early twentieth century, for the establishment of wine cooperatives. Crédit Agricole was specifically instructed to make financial assistance available only to those groups or individuals who were motivated to modernize their means of production. The most destitute of small wine producers, including those who clung tenaciously to the older methods, were not part of the national government's plan for agricultural development. The phylloxera blight and its social consequences thus reinforced the inequalities in both the Bordeaux and interior winegrowing regions.

Southwest French wine cooperatives are, as I will elaborate further in the next chapter, a historical product of and dialectical response to the development of capitalist viticulture and viniculture—a development that is both local and international in scope. Moreover, wine cooperatives enabled small and medium growers to adjust to ongoing changes in capitalist winegrowing and marketing while, as noted, providing a means for the French government to monitor or control the quantity and quality of production. However, while wine cooperatives definitely emerged from a condition where capitalist social relations were dominant, I have argued that the historical context that enables us to grasp the development of the wine-cooperative movement and its current articulation, particularly the relation between winegrowing regions, is broad and long.

The importance of the English occupation of the twelfth to fifteenth centuries cannot be overemphasized insofar as it radically transformed the relations between the interior of southwest France and the Bordeaux winegrowing region. Not only did the English occupation dramatically expand the wine trade with northern Europe and elevate Bordeaux over La Rochelle as the principal coastal port, but it established commercial privileges for Bordeaux that have endured to the present day. For example, wine cooperatives located today in the immediate vicinity of Bordeaux and extending as far as St.-Émillion to the east enjoy a reputation that is unequaled by those of the interior. In winegrowing, reputation generally translates into commercial advantages, which means that Bordeaux wines obtain a higher market price for their producers than wines produced elsewhere in the southwest of France. Moreover, Bordeaux is the center for virtually all the major wine merchants and exporters as well as the numerous associations and syndicates of winegrowers.

While the English occupation contributed to the commercial ascent of Bordeaux, the postoccupation recovery and the period of the Religious Wars advanced the interests of new technology, marketing, and capitalist social relations in the winegrowing sector. Even with the protectionism that existed for Bordeaux wines throughout the English occupation and the advantages of lucrative English markets, local restrictions on wine continued to be an obstacle to the development of a national market and thus hindered trade. This would change during the sixteenth and seventeenth centuries as the gradual elimination of local restrictions permitted a free circulation of commodities throughout France and hence a better articulation between local, national, and international markets.

Moreover, the period of the Religious Wars brought a change in the ownership of large vineyards as numerous estates in the southwest were acquired by the bourgeoisie, especially merchants who had amassed considerable fortunes from the wine trade. Although these new owners purchased aristocratic titles, they departed from the managerial objectives of their predecessors by reinvesting profits in their winegrowing estates. In a manner reminiscent of the English occupation, proprietors in the interior planted their vineyards with vine stocks designed to meet the demands of Dutch clients. Unlike English consumers who preferred red wines, the Dutch liked sweet white wines. Even today, vineyards in the vicinity of Bergerac, such as Monbazillac, are still noted for the production of quality sweet white wines.

While we have seen that the English occupation and Religious Wars did much to further the development and maturation of capitalist markets, they did not, as I have argued, create a market in labor and thus did not establish capitalism as dominant in the French countryside. To the contrary, a paternalistic relation between large proprietors and their winegrowing workers, including those who were sharecroppers, appears to have endured. This is not to say that wages played no part at all in the social relations between proprietors and growers as clearly this was part of the structure of the *prix-fait* or pension arrangement. However, the ethos that predominated in the winegrowing sector throughout the sixteenth and seventeenth centuries, with the provision of a house and other means of assistance, was one that promoted an interdependency that was much more than a simple monetary exchange.

The development of the *grands crus,* beginning in the late seventeenth century, and continuing throughout the eighteenth and nineteenth centuries, marks the greatest period of change in southwest French winegrowing history. Not only did the *grands crus* undermine the special paternalistic relations between large proprietors and their winegrowers but they also articulated well with the reforms that followed from the French Revolution. The development of the *grands crus* introduced specialized labor that divided the formerly unified processes of viticulture and viniculture. This, in turn, would produce a hierarchy of workers and in the long run would lead to a situation whereby hired seasonal labor would largely replace, but not entirely eliminate, yearly workers housed on the winegrowing estate. In addition, while specialized labor no doubt increased the responsibilities for some workers, it simplified and degraded the work of others; a process that is coincident with the capitalist division of labor (Braverman 1974).

The development of the *grands crus,* like earlier acquisition of properties on the part of the bourgeoisie, led to a consolidation of properties in the most favored winegrowing regions. This process, combined with the proprietary rights gained through the Republican government following the French Revolution, especially those rights, as Tilly has argued, that undermined communal lands and reinforced private property, began to disenfranchise peasant proprietors who owned land in or in proximity to the region of the celebrated château vineyards. Disenfranchised peasants had few options other than to sell their labor to the proprietors of large estates or to leave the region altogether to look for work in the towns and cities of southwest France.

The economic consequences of the *grands crus* combined with the legal reforms of the Republican government were by no means the only channels, as we have seen, through which capitalism was elevated to a position of dominance in the southwest French countryside. To the contrary, the cultural construction of elite wines was an equal if not at times more significant counterpart to the economic and political hegemony of Bordeaux merchants and proprietors of château estates. While it is often difficult to establish the intentions of historical actors, it appears that the construction of small-scale replicas of medieval châteaus on the part of *grands crus* proprietors was an attempt to establish an "imagined" relation to an aristocratic past that would make their wines undeniably distinct. Moreover, as I argued in Chapter 2, the cultural capital accrued through the links to an aristocratic past enabled the proprietors of the elite estates to assume a leading role in the establishment of a winegrowing classification and hierarchy that concealed the social and historical foundations of winegrowing privilege in a discourse that appeared to be natural. The economic and political advantages that ensued from the naturalization of what is social and historical have produced enormous commercial returns for the proprietors of elite estates while marginalizing the vast majority of small-scale producers culturally, politically, and economically.

The development of capitalism in the winegrowing sector of southwest France was not due to mutually exclusive internal or external factors, as the Dobb and Sweezy debates would suggest, nor was it a product of the economy taken, in the sense of Althusser, as dominant in the "last instance." Moreover, although capitalist exchange, or mercantile capitalism, did much to stimulate and develop capitalist social relations, in a manner consistent with the world-systems theory of Wallerstein, it did not by itself challenge or undermine the ethos of paternalism that predominated in the French countryside well into the nineteenth century. Rather, as I have shown, the domination of capitalism followed from the conjuncture or articulation of local and international exchange, political reforms that guaranteed individual proprietary rights, and the cultural construction of the winegrowing hierarchy. I believe, furthermore, that what is particular to the southwest of France, while perhaps suggestive for capitalist development in general, should not be taken as universally prescriptive or formulaic. This has certainly been the shortcoming of those such as Althusser, or even Wallerstein, who have applied social theory in a mechanical fashion to concrete historical and ethnographic materials.

The phylloxera blight of the late nineteenth century had social consequences that were far-reaching for the wine-cooperative movement of the early twentieth century. The phylloxera blight shattered the frail accommodation that had been reached, albeit unintentionally, between large growers producing quality or classified wines and small peasant producers oriented toward the production of wines for daily consumption. Once the phylloxera blight ravaged vineyards in the southwest, the interior more than those of Bordeaux, large growers electing to produce mass-consumption wines imperiled the small producers. This was especially the case given that the French government opted to control the quantity of production to provide loans that would push growers, large and small, toward modernization. It was the effort to keep pace with rapidly changing circumstances of production and marketing, as we shall see shortly, that made wine cooperatives at the dawn of the twentieth century an inviting option for small and medium-sized winegrowers.

THE "MAKING" OF SOUTHWEST FRENCH WINE COOPERATIVES | 4 |

There is little doubt that wine cooperatives advanced the extent and import of capitalist social relations among small producers as well as the rationalization and control of the productive process. However, I remain convinced that a history of rural radicalism, class divisions between growers, the power of merchants, and a commitment to small-scale family farming made the formation of wine cooperatives, if not their current articulation, as much politically motivated as pragmatically informed. I hold this view in spite of the fact that the majority of my informants deny it and most scholars who have devoted some attention to the wine-cooperative movement think it implausible.[1]

That there are some points of difference on the part of informants and between scholars concerning the assessment of motives involved in the founding of wine cooperatives should not come as a surprise as the "truth" of the past is neither singular nor transparent. This has been well understood by historians such as E. P. Thompson (1966) and, more recently, by anthropologists such as Renato Rosaldo (1990), and John and Jean Comaroff (1992) who, among a growing number of scholars, regard ethnographic and historical narratives as polyphonic and shifting and thus as much culturally and historically mediated as mediating.[2] These scholars, especially Thompson, view the social world as equally a product of an agency engaged in its own making as well as of an agency that is shaped or even overdetermined by external social forces and social processes.[3]

I argue that the wine-cooperative movement arose from a number of imperatives some of which were politically motivated while others were more clearly pragmatic in nature. This middle course between political and pragmatic motives is not a retreat from the controversy over how we should interpret the founding of wine cooperatives. Rather, I maintain that both past and recent transformations in the world system of political economy, combined with the practical exigencies of running a modern cooperative, have eclipsed the somewhat radical nature and political character of the wine-cooperative movement's early history. This has foregrounded retrospectively its essential pragmatic characteristics.

My discussion of the "making" of wine cooperatives begins with a review of the social consequences of the phylloxera blight before addressing how these consequences were deepened, if not surpassed in some winegrowing areas, by the appearance of mildew. The transformed social relations that ensued from these vineyard maladies, combined with economic crisis and the French state's effort to manage the continual problem of overproduction and fraud, take us to the dawn of the wine-cooperative movement in the early twentieth century. I proceed by exploring the social and political conditions of subsequent decades including the activism of winegrowers in southern France. Finally, I turn to the Popular Front and the economic crisis of the 1930s to explain the possible motives of growers who were the founding members of cooperatives in the Médoc and the Dordogne, the two winegrowing regions of my research.

FROM CRISIS TO COOPERATION

The phylloxera blight of the last quarter of the nineteenth century ravaged the vineyards of the southwest. Significant numbers of growers uprooted or even abandoned their vineyards altogether. Some of the most imperiled growers sought work in urban areas or when possible turned to the large winegrowing estates for employment. Others struggled, as in the Dordogne, to retain possession of family farms by replanting fields with tobacco, or they gave up winegrowing for livestock or dairying. Pijassou remarks that phylloxera was so widespread, especially among small producers, that table wines became scarce, leading the French government to ease restrictions on the import of inexpensive Spanish and Italian wines (1980:817).

Most significant, however, was the pattern of replanting that was undertaken by some medium and large proprietors, including Bordeaux merchants who owned winegrowing estates. These growers sought to recover their losses as quickly as possible and so departed from the production of quality wines by replanting with high-yielding vine stocks conventionally used in the production of mass wines. This placed them in direct competition with small peasant producers (Ulin 1986, 1988). The shift to high-yielding stocks on the part of some large growers precipitated a crisis for the small producers who lacked the financial and technical resources necessary to compete. Moreover, the shift to high-yielding vine stocks, combined with increasing imports and the continuing problem of fraudulent wines, augmented the supply of wine overall and thus led to declining prices, a situation that was most difficult for small producers to endure.

Although the social consequences that ensued from the phylloxera blight were noteworthy and contributed significantly to the social context from which wine cooperatives would emerge—in that phylloxera heightened divisions between classes of southwest French winegrowers—this process of social differentiation was exacerbated, as Pijassou maintains, by the outbreak of mildew in the Bordeaux region between 1882 and 1892 (1980:763). Mildew is one of several cryptogamic maladies that had especially severe social consequences for winegrowers in the late nineteenth and early twentieth centuries. Mildew is a fungus that grows on the leaves and grapes of the wine-producing plants and which prevents the grapes from maturing. Pijassou argues that the consequences of mildew, especially for the *grands crus,* were even more serious than those of phylloxera in that mildew reduced the production of the *grands crus* by 44 percent (1980:763). Treatment of the leaves and grapes with copper sulfate eventually proved effective against mildew. However, copper sulfate was expensive and treatments were labor-intensive. Consequently, as with the phylloxera blight, the burden of treatments was most heavily felt by the small growers, a point that is emphasized by Pijassou. "It is no exaggeration to conclude that for nearly forty years, from 1882 to 1920, cryptogamic diseases put the small growers at a disadvantage whenever the year was damp, thus accentuating the gap between them and the large domains" (1980:772).

Perhaps the most salient consequence of mildew was that it challenged the individualism for which southwest French winegrowers were known (Pijassou 1980:772). As with phylloxera, mildew forced many growers to share resources and information through collective organizations such as syndicates. These syndicates, as noted in Chapter 3, were not radical in that their leadership came from among the largest and most established growers. Syndicates purchased winegrowing supplies such as copper sulfate in bulk. They passed the savings on to small growers.

Although French winegrowing had always experienced crises throughout its long history, whether from war, vineyard maladies, or overproduction, the combination of the phylloxera blight and the outbreak of mildew in the last quarter of the nineteenth century changed the social composition of winegrowing. This can be explained from the relatively early maturity and advanced stage of capitalist social relations in viticulture compared to other agricultural sectors in France. Class distinctions between growers were rendered more severe with large-scale replanting and production of mass wines on the part of some large growers. Fraud precipitated a crisis of "authenticity" that both threatened the marketability of regionally classified wines and contributed to the general problem of overproduction. Bartoli and his coauthors assert that the postphylloxera period witnessed an increase in social stratification, an intensification of specialized regions dependent on the market, an augmentation in the costs and quantity of production, and finally, increased competition from cheap imports and artificially produced wines (1987:9). It is important to note that although the postphylloxera period was one of general crisis among winegrowers, that is, all growers experienced some difficulty and hardship, the effects were not uniformly distributed among social classes of winegrowers or among regions.

Although the French state was periodically responsive to pleas for assistance from winegrowers, government officials were primarily resolved to establish a means to monitor and control both the quantity and quality of production. The first step was taken early on through the official recognition of syndicates in the middle of the nineteenth century. However, while providing some relief to small growers, syndicates did not unify their productive and marketing resources and in actuality tended to duplicate the winegrowing hierarchy in that elites were generally the founders and leaders of syndicates. Wine cooperatives would come, on the other hand, to provide the very institutional medium through which limitations could be levied on the quantity of production and quality monitored through the centralized administration offered by the cooperative's organization.

Control over production, in particular, was strategic to curtailing the periodic crises that had threatened capitalist viticulture since the sixteenth century. Even the conservative members of the French legislature who were largely suspicious of cooperative efforts in agriculture came to support the wine-cooperative legislation of 1908–10 because they clearly recognized the potential for state control. Moreover, the cooperative legislation authorized the state bank, Crédit Agricole, to make loans available to cooperatives at low interest rates. Crédit Agricole was specifically instructed to make financial assistance available only to those groups and individuals who were motivated to modernize their means of production. The most destitute of small winegrowers, especially those who clung tenaciously to the old methods of cultivation and vinification, were not part of the state's plan for agricultural development. The majority of these growers thus passed into the margins or silences of French winegrowing history.

THE DAWN OF THE WINE-COOPERATIVE MOVEMENT

The first French agricultural cooperative, founded in 1888 in Charente-Inférieure, was a dairy cooperative that produced milk and butter (Lachiver 1988:482). According to Lachiver, cooperation in agriculture, including wine production, was not a new European idea as cooperatives had existed in Germany, Catalonia, Portugal, Hungary, and Italy from as early as 1868. Lachiver maintains that the dairy cooperative was infused with political motives as it was under the influence of both socialists and communists. From the socialist side, argues Lachiver, came the principle of self-management while the communists advanced the collectivization of individually owned property.

Unlike Pijassou, Lachiver conceives of the early cooperatives as building upon the collective potentials and organization of the mid-nineteenth-century syndicates, although he recognizes that the leadership of syndicates essentially came from the larger proprietors. Lachiver is not, however, alone in his assertions concerning radical politics as Bartoli and his coauthors also maintain that the winegrowers who created cooperatives were pulled by the forces of the Left (1987:3). Lachiver believes, furthermore, that cooperatives, like syndicates, eased the pressure experienced by small growers from both merchants and large proprietors.

The first French wine cooperatives were founded in Languedoc and Var. This should not come as a surprise as Languedoc, especially following the phylloxera blight, became most noted for the production of mass or table wines. It was growers in this region who were most imperiled by the replantation on the part of large growers in vine stocks that produced mass wines and by cheap imports coming not only from other European countries but from French colonies such as Algeria. According to Lachiver, the wine cooperative not only provided small and medium growers some freedom from the domination of merchants but they also solved the problem of wine storage and new technology not available to small-scale individual growers.

The first wine cooperative was founded at Mudaison in the Hérault in October of 1901 followed by the founding of Maraussan in December of the same year. The political self-consciousness of the cooperative movement in this early stage was evidenced by the fact that the members of the Maraussan cooperative referred to themselves as *les vignerons libres*, "free winegrowers" (Bartoli et al. 1987:3). Maraussan is unusual in the history of the wine-cooperative movement in that the vineyards of its members were collectivized. The uniqueness of this feature cannot be overemphasized as all of my informants insisted that they would have nothing to do with a wine cooperative if in fact they had to relinquish ownership and control of their individual- or family-owned vineyards. However, the experiment of collectivizing vineyards at Maraussan only endured for less than a year before returning to individual proprietorship. French peasants and farmers account for this reluctance to collectivize vineyards and lands with a long-standing ethos of individualism.[4]

CRISIS AND GROWTH

Although the earliest French wine cooperatives, and cooperatives in general, exhibited some advantages to the small and medium proprietors, they were slow to take root in the southwest of France. Most growers in the two southwest regions where I conducted my field research did not join wine cooperatives until the middle to late 1930s. In order to understand this reluctance and the desire to collectivize that would eventually prevail, it is necessary to have some grasp of the conjuncture of crises and economic circumstances that unfolded during the first third of the twentieth century, as well as the consequences of new legislation.

While overproduction and the decline in prices that ensued from a large surplus of wine on the market were by no means a new problem, the growing division between classes of winegrowers that followed the phylloxera blight and the outbreak of mildew imperiled those growers with the fewest and weakest productive and marketing resources. These problems, along with the French state, pushed elite proprietors toward the modernization of the viticultural sector. The widespread use of treatments such as copper sulfate and the introduction of new techniques of winemaking, including the broader use of bottling, are representative of this development. Most important, winegrowers of all classes and regions had incentives to change their techniques as loans and direct grants were made available from the French state contingent upon their willingness to modernize.

While the small proprietors in southwest France largely followed, with few exceptions, the discipline and logic of capitalist winegrowing established by the elite growers and merchants, the winegrowers and workers of the Midi challenged the changing conditions of capitalist winegrowing of which they felt themselves to be the primary victims. Midi winegrowers participated in strikes in 1903 and 1904 that raised the wages of salaried workers and thus helped to reduce the gap between large proprietors and worker-growers. Moreover, these workers organized themselves as the Fédération des travailleurs agricoles du Midi which later became affiliated with the larger and more influential Confédération Générale des Travailleurs. Lachiver remarks that it was over-abundant production, fraud, and imports from Algeria that led the winegrowers of the Midi to revolt in 1907 (1988:463).

Marcelin Albert, a Midi grower, emerged as a primary leader in the 1907 revolt. According to Lachiver, Albert came to symbolize the revolt by supporting a campaign in favor of defining wine as a "natural beverage" (1988:467).[5] While Albert attacked government officials for their seeming indifference to the production of fraudulent wines, he had little to say about wine imported from Algeria because these wines were often used to fortify those produced in Languedoc. The 1907 revolt was one of the most violent in French winegrowing history. However, in spite of the attention that it drew to the plight of the small producer of ordinary wines, its organizers and participants failed to recognize overproduction as a cause of the crisis. Their primary objective was to strike against taxes.

Lachiver argues, furthermore, that the rapid replanting following the phylloxera blight not only sharpened class divisions and contributed to overproduction but it also furthered monocropping in the Midi and throughout the southwest of France in general (1988:473). This had important repercussions for both small proprietors and those who gained their livelihood as wage workers on the large estates. According to Lachiver, monocropping in the viticultural sector reinforced and furthered a system of absentee landlordship whereby proprietors of large estates lived in the cities and had their vineyards worked by day workers. Lachiver maintains that after 1900, the salaries of these day workers declined. Moreover, with the replacement of workers housed on the large estates by day laborers, the periods of unemployment increased between the periods of principal work required in the vineyards, thus exacerbating the austerity with which small growers and wage workers were faced.

Lachiver concludes that although the organizing around the activism of the 1907 revolt and the formation of growers' associations was a professional success, it did not resolve the social problem between large growers and their workers. On the other hand, legislation passed in 1907 did begin to address the problem of fraud but without seriously addressing the problem of overproduction. With the legislation of 1907, winegrowers had to declare the size of their harvest as well as the size of their stocks. Records were maintained, furthermore, on the quantity of production by department, the principal French administrative division. The law of 1907 also sought to improve the overall quality of wine produced by limiting the amount of sugar used in the fermentation of wine and regulating the products that were conventionally added to improve defective wines.

While the complex of social circumstances that followed from phylloxera and mildew produced especially harsh conditions for Languedoc growers, elite regions such as the Médoc were not spared hardships. According to Pijassou, twenty-four *crus classés* were sold between 1889 and 1901, which amounted to 40 percent of *crus classés* in the Médoc (1980:815). The sale of these properties was precipitated by rapidly declining prices for wine. In some cases prices fell to 20 percent of what they were previously. Many of these proprietors, if not forced to sell their properties, were compelled to sell their wines as a bulk commodity in barrels, a type of marketing normally only associated with table wines.

However, the period between 1900 and 1910, while also witnessing the sale of numerous large domains, saw for the first time the presence of finance capital of foreign origins, thus reinforcing my earlier assertion that the local conditions of winegrowing have been and continue to be mediated by a world system of political economy. Pijassou remarks that while the "changing of hands" of the large properties had been common since the introduction of the *grands crus* (as illustrated by wealthy Bordeaux merchants that purchased vineyards), the purchase of elite vineyards by investment groups from countries such as Germany and England was wholly new (1980:817).[6] The main consequences of this intrusion of foreign capital were to inflate the price of vineyards and to increase an absentee landlordship that was increasingly indifferent to the plight of estate employees and small growers in general.

Although small winegrowers and wage workers in the elite regions of the southwest were not nearly as militant as their counterparts in Languedoc, they were capable of organizing and periodically taking actions of a more political nature. In February of 1913, the growers of Pauillac and St.-Julien-Beychevelle in the Médoc formed a syndicate largely for the purposes of addressing the grievances of the salaried workers. While Pijassou believes that it is difficult to attribute the formation of this syndicate to the Left, he acknowledges that this syndicate and others like it established an agenda for change that markedly improved the working condition of the average worker. For example, the St.-Estèphe syndicate of winegrowers redefined the length of the working day to seven and three-quarters hours for men and six and three-quarters hours for women. In addition, they managed to win higher remunerations for the most difficult labor, payment for supplementary hours or overtime, and better meals and lodging for harvest workers (Pijassou 1980:848). Moreover, in a manner that was unprecedented in the Médoc, some salaried workers managed to advance their interests by striking. While this was effective on some elite estates, there were proprietors who responded by dismissing the striking workers. Some proprietors, who were not sympathetic to the syndicates, saw the firing of striking workers as a way to weaken or at least slow down their activities.

Although the organizing that the syndicates offered did improve the working and living condition of small growers and salaried workers, the First World War brought some unexpected advantages to these individuals that actually reduced the division between elite and peasant wines in southwest France. While many peasants found themselves drafted to military service, those who were left behind benefited from a shortage of labor that pushed wages higher. This was only partially offset by an increase in the cost of living. However, the most noteworthy impact of the war on the winegrowing sector was that it pushed the prices up for peasant wines while decreasing the price paid for elite wines. For example, a cask of Lafite or Margaux, as a consequence of being purchased under contract,[7] sold for 1,650 francs while peasant wines sold for as much as 1,000. Merchants were hesitant, adds Pijassou, to invest in fine wines as they could not sell their reserves and so consequently they invested in what Pijassou refers to as the "small wines" of the Médoc (1980:854).

The war also generated problems with the international marketing of wine. Not only was transport more difficult and dangerous but economic resources in those countries at war were diverted away from the purchase of imported wines. Political turmoil also produced serious problems in areas of the world that were primary clients for southwest French wine. Czarist Russia, for example, had long been a good market for Bordeaux wine, importing sizable quantities especially from the celebrated French vineyards. The fall of Czarist Russia in 1917 and the ensuing economic problems of the new Bolshevik government nearly put an end to those imports and thus contributed to a growing range of hardships. Moreover, although not a consequence of war, the ratification of Prohibition in the United States in 1919 intensified the crisis experienced by all French winegrowers as America had long been one of the largest importers of southwest French wines.

The legislation of the 1920s enacted by the French government was designed to ameliorate years of crisis and a growing sense of malaise among all classes of French winegrowers. This legislation, proposed largely through coalitions of elite growers and merchants, principally affected the processes of vinification and marketing as much else apart from the treatment for maladies was slow to change. "In fact, up until the appearance of the tractor, the manner of cultivation and the methods of caring for the vineyards changed but little" (Pijassou 1980:785).

The legislation of the 1920s, especially the *appellation contrôlée* laws, while designating a wine by geographical origin and grape variety, also established regional standards for vinification. These laws, combined with the fact that the elite Médoc châteaus forced the merchants to accept estate bottling in 1925, went a long way toward addressing the problem of fraud while ostensibly seeking to augment the overall quality of wine production. However, as I argued previously, these laws did not solve all problems nor did they solve the problems of all growers in a uniform manner. To the contrary, numerous small growers found it beyond their capacity to meet the mandates for vinification advanced by the *appellation contrôlée* legislation.

While the inability to meet the mandates of the legislation did not in itself put small growers out of business, it did mean that they were not able to enjoy the economic advantages of new regional classifications of wine that resulted from this legislation. This factor combined with pressures toward modernization and problems of marketing both local and international in scale made the worldwide economic crisis of the

1930s especially daunting for individual small growers with limited resources.

THE CRISIS OF THE 1930S

The economic crisis of 1929, represented by the unprecedented and dramatic plummet of the American stock market, was not actually experienced in the French economy and French viticulture prior to 1931 (Pijassou 1980:899). Once the economic crisis did touch French viticulture the consequences were severe. Winegrowers had a difficult time selling their accumulated supplies as clients were unable to pay their bills. This was combined with consecutive harvests of low quality in 1930, 1931, and 1932 due to heavy rains and problems with mildew. Some growers responded to the difficult times by electing to pull up a portion of their vineyards to reduce the costs of cultivation. Eight thousand hectares of vineyards were pulled up in 1936 alone in the Gironde as a whole. Pijassou remarks that before the crisis of the early 1930s, the area of vineyards cultivated was 17,100.56 hectares while after the crisis only 13,286 hectares remained—amounting to a reduction of 22.3 percent (1980:931). On the vineyards that had been uprooted, some winegrowers elected to raise cows and pigs.

Another indicator of the severity of the crisis is the impact that it had on merchants who had long been influential in the commerce of southwest France. "The Bordeaux merchants, who controlled the markets, took advantage of difficult times for the proprietors to impose prices by a politics of subscriptions (d'abonnements). But in 1930–32, the agricultural world and the merchants were equally stricken" (Pijassou 1980:915).

Commerce was, in part, made more difficult for merchants in that the countries that normally imported wines from the Bordeaux region, especially England and those of northern Europe, increased their customs barriers (Pijassou 1980:916). Moreover, the gold standard was abandoned in the early 1930s which led to instability in the currency markets. While the ending of American Prohibition in 1933 was a relief of sorts to French merchants and growers, the dollar had lost approximately 40 percent of its former value and this clearly hurt French imports to America.

According to Pijassou, the 1930s challenged the traditional hierarchy that existed in the Médoc, one of France's most elite winegrowing regions. The St.-Estèphe cooperative sold 450 casks of wine at 2,000 francs per cask, a price that rivaled that of the elite châteaus. However, the crisis of the 1930s brought higher debt to both large and small growers. Small growers had difficulty obtaining loans and therefore had to wait until they sold their harvests before they could pay off debts. Pijassou remarks that for the small growers some of these debts were paid off in *piquette,* or wine made from multiple pressings of already pressed grape skins to which was added water and sugar. The *piquette* was then transported to the butcher in the middle of the night to whom the grower owed money (1980:931). This would appear to undermine Pijassou's earlier statement that the 1930s crisis challenged the traditional hierarchy of growers as proprietors of large estates never had to resort to such surreptitious activities. With respect to the plight of the small growers Pijassou adds:

They live frugally. They work their vineyards and try to work a few days at the neighboring châteaus. They have two or three cows, a pig; they cultivate potatoes; they log the trees when they have some; they sell wood for heating when they have cut vines; they fish in the river; they gather mushrooms; they live as best they can, waiting for times to change. (1980:931–32)

It would appear that rather than having climbed the hierarchy, the small grower was making do on a day-to-day basis.

The 1930s was also a period of great political change in France as the Popular Front, France's first socialist government, came to office in May 1936. The Popular Front was led by the reformer Leon Blum who had a principal interest in improving the working conditions for the French labor force. Under the Popular Front, salaries for all workers in France rose approximately 10 to 15 percent while the length of the work week was reduced from forty-eight to forty hours as early as June 1936. It is generally believed, however, that the Popular Front primarily had an impact on the industrial work force, leaving the working conditions in the countryside relatively untouched. I was certainly given this impression when inquiring about the possible political motives of wine cooperatives founded during and just after the Popular Front. Consider, for example, the following from my interview with Pierre Chauvet and his assistant, Robert Cardon. Chauvet is president of an organization of southwest French cooperatives concerned exclusively with the marketing of cooperative wines.

> **Ulin:** Were there political objectives among the winegrowers who founded the cooperatives?
> **Chauvet:** No, I think that during—well, if I'm saying it, that's what I think—at first the wine cooperatives, you should know, were suspected of being vehicles for ideas that today one would call rather leftist or collectivist. In fact, the reality is totally different, because often, not to say always, the elite of the villages founded the wine cooperatives. Because they were intellectually best suited to consider the situation dispassionately and to undertake or to put in place the most appropriate solutions.
> **Ulin:** Yes, I understand. But those were also the years of the Popular Front.
> **Chauvet:** Yes, yes indeed.
> **Cardon:** However if there was a political relationship, it was between a cooperative movement born in a rural milieu which had economic and sociological needs and another political movement, the Popular Front, which essentially developed in the Parisian milieu.

There is little doubt that Chauvet is correct in arguing that the wine-cooperative movement was led by village elites, a point that I shall take up shortly. While Cardon believes that the wine-cooperative movement was distinct in origin from the urban, Parisian social climate of the Popular Front, he is less certain about their political relationship. However, as noted, the years from the phylloxera blight up to the Popular Front were austere for small and large growers alike, and so in some areas such as the Dordogne there was not only an uprooting of vineyards but an exodus to urban areas sometimes amounting to 25 percent of the population. Individuals who left rural areas for the cities often returned to visit relatives and friends in their natal villages, especially during summer festivals. Although it is difficult to prove, it is likely that these visits also produced a lively exchange of political ideas that found some fertile grounds in both rural and urban areas.[8]

While the ties of the Popular Front to rural areas may be difficult to pin down in terms of specific persons and rural organizations, some historians and geographers such as Pijassou have argued for its manifest influence on rural winegrowers (1980:928). That the Popular Front was a real presence in the southwest French countryside is exemplified by the anxiety experienced by merchants and large growers over changes initiated by the socialists at the national level and by the decline in the stock market and devaluing of the franc that ensued. Pijassou remarks that workers in the vineyards demanded, in a manner consistent with urban workers, an adjustment to their salaries. These demands led to strikes in elite winegrowing regions such as the one that occurred at Pauillac in the Médoc in June 1936. The pressure brought by the strikers at Pauillac forced Rothschild to raise the salaries of his workers by 10 percent. Moreover, the strikes led to the creation of a society consisting of both workers and owners to study the working conditions and salaries of the winegrowing labor force (Pijassou 1980:928).

As noted previously, it is widely recognized that village elites played the leading role in the creation of the southwest French wine-cooperative movement and therefore it is often concluded that political motives were clearly secondary to economic exigencies. This was the explanation put forward by the majority of my informants and a view that was expressed widely by cooperative directors and presidents that I interviewed. Michel Lebrun, for example, who is a winegrower and president of the Pauillac cooperative, argued that political objectives were not in the least involved with those who founded the Pauillac cooperative in 1934. Though Lebrun himself was not involved in the founding of the Pauillac cooperative, his father was among several who were.[9]

Ulin: Why was the cooperative founded in the 1930s?
Lebrun: It was founded for a very simple reason. It was because individually the small proprietor could no longer make it. He could no longer make it because of the level of competition occurring on the markets. Because some wine merchants knew how to use the situation to their maximum advantage and managed to negotiate their business with small

proprietors at such a low level that finally the proprietors could no longer survive. So then my father and several others decided to look around and get some information. They made several trips to cooperatives that were a little older than those of this region to see how things worked. So in '33 and especially '34, when things really started, the cooperative was then founded. It's a question of large-scale revenues (*C'est un problème de revenues sur un grand compte*).
Ulin: Yes. Were there political objectives?
Lebrun: No.
Ulin: No? Not at all?
Lebrun: No, not at all political. No politics.

Lebrun's comments on the founding of the Pauillac cooperative are, however, particular to Pauillac and cannot be generalized to all of southwest France and not even to the Médoc as a whole. What is not stated by Lebrun is that Pauillac is a specific area of the Médoc that had long been noted for elite château wines and that those who became involved in the cooperative movement were more politically centrist than in other winegrowing regions. This is apparent when the same question was put to Gilles Blanchard who is also a winegrower and president of the Listrac cooperative. While Listrac is well known today for producing very good wines and even some thought to be excellent, its overall reputation falls short of that of Pauillac. Moreover, it is a particular part of the Médoc that is less dominated by the presence of elite château wines.

Ulin: Why was the cooperative founded during the 1930s?
Blanchard: So yes, the cooperative was founded in 1935. All the wine cooperatives of the Médoc and the Gironde in general were founded in '34, '35, and '36 following the wine crisis. So what they call the wine crisis was a period when wine sold badly and the revenues did not permit the winegrower to subsist. The wine crisis began in the years 1930, '31, '32, '33, and the winegrowers who had wanted to try and survive this crisis felt a need to unite. And it was the ideal solution; you had to unite or abandon winegrowing (*Et c'était la solution idéale: il fallait se regrouper ou abandonner la viticulture*). So here at Listrac twenty-five winegrowers, mostly small growers, got together. They created the Listrac wine cooperative and that produced good results; the cooperative has grown and

evolved. They achieved what they hoped to, and since the cooperative still exists, I believe that it will exist for a long time to come.

Ulin: But how did they find the resources? It's expensive.

Blanchard: Yes, they constructed a small building with some backing, personal savings they had, and which made possible other forms of financing. And then loans, they borrowed a lot from the Crédit Agricole at the then-current rate of 3 percent. And they dared to borrow and let's say they succeeded, because they reduced costs and had a more important economic clout in terms of commerce. . . . And they had a power of spending by virtue of the volumes they harvested.

Ulin: But at the beginning of the cooperative, were there political objectives among the winegrowers?

Blanchard: Yes, yes there were. There were, because the wine cooperative was somewhat socialist. All winegrowers, especially those from the Médoc, are individualists who like to manage what they do themselves. In the wine cooperative, it was necessary to accept certain constraints and to have a single director. That went somewhat against the grain, but despite that some winegrowers managed to get along, and on the other hand some were critical of it. They succeeded in creating some benefits and through the years it turned out that what they put into place was beneficial for all on a very important scale, since cooperatives have taken their rightful place in the Médoc. But, initially, to belong to the wine cooperative was to go toward a planned economy, seizures, socialism and even beyond.

Blanchard's comments about the individualism of Médoc winegrowers is consistent with attitudes throughout southwest France and was in fact, according to all of my informants, a primary obstacle to the formation of cooperatives. Consider, for example, Jean and Anne Bosquet's response to my question concerning the cooperative spirit at the Sigoulès wine cooperative where they are members:

> **Ulin:** Do you often discuss the wine cooperative with the other cooperative members?
>
> **Anne Bosquet:** The French do not have a cooperative spirit. They are very individualist and it is for that reason that they are . . .
>
> **Jean Bosquet:** Independent.

The individualism to which my informants refer is not, however, rooted in cultural origins although culture is central to its reproduction.

Rather, it is more likely that the individualism is attributable to a household or family organization of production and, as Harriet Rosenberg suggests, the agricultural policies of the French state. Rosenberg argues that throughout the nineteenth century French agricultural officials "supported individual initiative, the breakup of the commons, and the dismantling of collective labor systems" (1988:182). By discouraging collective undertakings, especially those involving labor, the French state indirectly promoted and reinforced an individualism that was intrinsic to household production.

When I asked informants if they had ever considered relinquishing ownership of their vineyards for the potential benefits of the increased scale of common holdings, their responses were uniform. They maintained adamantly that they would never have joined a cooperative if collectivizing private property had been an imperative. Even those informants who identified their politics as socialist or communist concurred on this point with their more conservative colleagues at the wine cooperatives. As Blanchard has indicated, even giving up managerial autonomy over certain activities concerned with the care of their privately owned vineyards was perceived by many to be threatening. This hardly seems like a fruitful social environment for politically motivated activity. Nonetheless, I believe that many winegrowers were acutely aware of the nature of the economic crisis with which they were faced and that this crisis was especially hard for them to endure because of the subaltern position that they occupied in the winegrowing hierarchy. Though the political activity of Dordogne and Médoc winegrowers in the first third of the twentieth century may not be comparable to that of Languedoc, the periodic strikes by winegrowing workers, the joining of syndicates, even if these syndicates were founded by village notables, and the widespread influence of the Popular Front that linked village to city should not be overlooked or ignored as part of the social fabric from which the wine-cooperative movement in the southwest arose. I emphasize the probable influence of the Popular Front in particular as there has been a long-standing tendency in anthropology, and perhaps in Western scholarship in general, to regard European villages as if they were isolated entities. This model of scholarship in anthropology was taken over from the wholly inadequate model of research in the European colonies of the Third World. However, if we can argue that the southwest of France had ties to significant other European regions since the twelfth century, or even earlier, then it is hardly a large step to assert that a socialist government at the national level, even if responding to urban working-class demands, would also have a measurable and important influence on the countryside.

Although the founders of southwest French wine cooperatives were mostly village notables and that the Popular Front was principally an urban working-class movement, the founding of wine cooperatives emerged from a social and historical context that combined economic crisis with a range of individual or collective political motives that in some cases were pronounced, such as at Listrac, while in other cases more subtle. The degree to which these political motives were manifest was in large part a reflection of existing hierarchical social relations among winegrowers. The workers who struck the Rothschild estate in Pauillac were not all proprietors and therefore not suitable candidates to join wine cooperatives. However, as noted, Pauillac, in comparison to Listrac, or for that matter the cooperatives that I studied in the Dordogne, was a region dominated by famous châteaus and thus it was often pragmatic motives that dominated over those that could be characterized as more political.

There were other reasons, apart from the predominance of château vineyards, that account for why political motives were not more pronounced, or at least secondary if not deemphasized, in the founding of some cooperatives. Apart from the Languedoc in the south which was well known for its radical winegrowers, southwest France was composed of winegrowing regions that with few exceptions were more renowned and thus more dominated by elite growers. This simply means that there was a greater emphasis on producing aged classified wines rather than wines for daily consumption and consequently the social structure in the southwest was more internally stratified than in the Languedoc. However, in spite of the internal stratification of southwest wine-producing regions, there was considerable political diversity among the small and medium growers who were potential adherents to the wine-cooperative movement. In order to draw these individuals of virtually all political persuasions into the cooperative, it was necessary to promote the economic advantages that regrouping or collectivizing offered and to deemphasize political motives. Moreover, as Lenin noted in regard to the peasantry—though the social and historical context is quite different—it was no surprise that village notables should assume the leadership in the formation of cooperatives.[10] Small growers supplemented their livelihoods through working on the large estates and thus were most dependent on maintaining strong ties to the proprietors of these estates. The medium-size growers, on the other hand, had the most potential, especially given the benefits of collective vinification and marketing that the cooperatives would bring, to obtain their livelihoods solely from winegrowing. While many of these growers wished to maintain amicable relations with proprietors of elite estates, they were also far less dependent on the château vineyards and thus more able to assume the risks associated with the new cooperative venture.

It is important to recognize, however, that even in cases where the leadership of newly formed cooperatives was socialist and where political motives were involved in the founding of wine cooperatives, this leadership wished to draw a diversity of growers into its fold. It was thus not uncommon to find among the earliest cooperative members, communists, socialists, centrists, and those of the far Right working side by side to ensure the success of the cooperative venture. What made this possible was the incorporation into the founding charter of wine cooperatives of a statement that specifically forbids the discussion of politics at the cooperative. The importance of this censuring of political discussion is emphasized by Raymond Frossard, an informant from the St.-Estèphe cooperative:

> **Ulin:** Were there political motives or objectives at the cooperative during the 1930s and 1940s?
> **Frossard:** There were none in 1930. That took place only in 1934. I don't think there were political things. The cooperative was a daughter of poverty (*une fille de la misére*).
> **Ulin:** Because at the Listrac cooperative, Monsieur Blanchard told me that the socialists had been very strong at the cooperative during the 1930s and that afterwards there were others that followed their political lead.

Frossard: Yes. Here I think not. There were some socialists who took part, but in that period they were real socialists. Me, I had a teacher who was a Radical Socialist. Well, that man was as upright, perhaps more upright, than the priest. Whereas now, the socialists—I don't like the pretenders at all, eh (*je n'aime pas de tout les rateliers*). That I am sure of. They have become a club.
Ulin: Yes, I have a sense that the people at the cooperative try to avoid politics.
Frossard: Yes, otherwise it's a catastrophe.

While Frossard quite obviously feels that present-day socialists lack the integrity of those involved in the early cooperative movement, it is thus clear from his final comment that the potential divisiveness of political discussion and argumentation was realized by all.[11]

The primary objection to overcome in recruiting new members to the cooperatives was the ethos of individualism that southwest French winegrowers associate with their own sociocultural identity and that informs their desire to preserve the self-management of their vineyards. The French state helped by making the cooperative appear as an attractive option to small growers through subsidized loans.

Apart from loans made available through the French national bank, the French government, according to Leo Loubère, was reluctant before 1939 to get involved with the problems of viticulture. Loubère argues that the state was a reluctant partner to the winegrowers and had to be "dragged in by growers who were already organized politically and professionally" (1990:261). However, private companies were quick to exploit an opportunity. For example, la Compagnie ferroraire d'Orleans (the Orleans railroad company) saw in the organization of cooperatives an opportunity to transport large volumes of wine from the southwest of France. They organized trips for southwest French winegrowers to the wine cooperatives of the Midi and Burgundy that provided an opportunity for the curious, skeptical, but not close-minded to witness actual cooperatives in action (Guichard and Roudié 1985:61). By talking to cooperative members the most recalcitrant were able to discover that much of their autonomy would be preserved and that the cooperatives offered a competitive edge through collective marketing and a greater degree of leverage with the large merchants who were the conventional buyers of peasant wines. There is little doubt, therefore, that these organized trips did much to alleviate the concerns of southwest growers over collectivization and thus contributed in a period of economic crisis to the growing impression among small proprietors that the wine cooperative was a tenable solution to their economic woes.

The question still looms as to why many larger growers, or in Yoon's terms "gentleman farmers," did not perceive wine cooperatives as a threat and why in some cases it was local notables, such as Pierre Martin in Entre-Deux-Mers and Robert Villepigue of St.-Émillion, who took the first step in the formation of wine cooperatives (Guichard and Roudié 1985:61). Moreover, as we shall see later, Pierre Martin not only used his charismatic personality to found a wine cooperative but he also showed leadership through establishing marketing relations that were international in scope between cooperatives. Perhaps the answer to the question of elite participation in cooperatives can be found in the following observation of Soon Young Song Yoon.

The cooperative, in fact, operates in order to cushion the shocks of capitalism as it reaches the small landowners . . . . Why cooperation should take such a strong anti-capitalist stand is, no doubt, an outcome of the liberal, socialist-like origins of the cooperative movement . . . . It is also a response to local tendencies toward agrarian individualism and competition with large land-owners. The cooperative brings, then, the small landowning peasants and gentlemen together by opposing them to stronger capitalist classes. (1973:36–37)

While Yoon's comments are specific to the wine cooperatives of Provence where she carried out her field research, I also believe that they are relevant to the wine cooperatives of southwest France. Small and medium growers of southwest France formed an alliance out of practical necessity ensuing from capitalist economic crisis and their subaltern position within the French winegrowing hierarchy. Because wine cooperatives initially produced wines of lesser distinction, the movement was not perceived as a threat by the elite growers as their wines were destined for different clients and hence different markets.

Yoon also attributes the initial appeal and success of the wine cooperatives to their maintenance of the household unit of production, something which, as I indicated earlier, winegrowers were unwilling to abandon. The family or household was the unit of production for both small and medium growers in the southwest, although medium growers supplemented household labor with wage labor. For the most part, though, Yoon argues that the cooperative enabled the precapitalist family structure to persist under capitalist modernization, a point with which I concur and which is likewise supported by Susan Rogers's important work on modernization in rural France (1991).[12] Yoon adds that under this family unit the incentive to work "was not just profit but also obligations which were familial" (1973:52). However, the formation of cooperatives intensified the ties of independent small producers to capitalist social relations and made them more successful capitalists and more able to compete on both national and international markets (1973:40).

By the time that the Médoc and Dordogne cooperatives that I researched appeared, most between 1934 and 1940, the wine-cooperative movement in France was already in full swing. There was a large expansion of cooperatives between 1919 and 1939 when 750 new cooperatives were founded, 340 of these in Languedoc-Roussillon alone. By the end of 1939, the numbers of cooperatives had grown to 827, a mark of their appeal and success (Lachiver 1988:498). There is little doubt that the success of cooperatives in the Languedoc-Roussillon, Provence, Champagne, and Burgundy regions did much to increase their appeal in the self-proclaimed individualist southwest.

Pijassou notes that the first wine cooperative created in the elite winegrowing region of the Médoc was at Pauillac in April 1933 (1980:933). At its founding the Pauillac cooperative had fifty-three members and in its first year produced an impressive 1,764 hectoliters of wine. Five other cooperatives quickly followed in the Médoc in 1934—Bégadan, St.-Estèphe, St.-Sauveur, St. Seurin de Codourne, and St. Yzans de Médoc. Cessac, Listrac, and Vertheuil appeared in 1935. Ordonnac in the lower Médoc was founded in 1936, making ten cooperatives total founded within a period of four years of crisis. By 1939, Acrins, 1937, and Queyrac, 1939, were established thus making twelve cooperatives in all with a total membership of 948. Pijassou adds that between 1936 and 1939, Médoc cooperatives augmented their total production from 18,303 hectoliters to 63,507 hectoliters, a remarkable achievement in a period marked by economic duress (1980:933).

The evolution of Dordogne wine cooperatives, although similar, was a little slower with Sigoulès being founded in 1939 and Monbazillac in 1941. There are nine cooperatives in the Dordogne with Sigoulès being the largest and Monbazillac the only one producing wines that are widely acknowledged for their quality.[13] However, although the wines produced in the Dordogne are not as celebrated as those of the Médoc, the wine cooperatives of the interior parts of the southwest were equally successful in augmenting both the quantity and quality of production while keeping within the guidelines for production that had been set by the French state. Apart from these evident commercial advantages, some of these cooperatives also became centers for village life and thus facilitated a greater exchange among growers concerning their political and economic plight.

The period leading up to the founding of wine cooperatives in the early twentieth century was, as I have shown, marked by duress especially for medium and small winegrowing proprietors. Although the phylloxera blight was a natural disaster, destroying as much as 70 percent of the vineyards in areas such as the northern Dordogne, its true import was experienced at the level of the winegrowing hierarchy. Some large growers who normally oriented their production toward quality wines sought to quickly recoup by replanting with high-yielding vine stocks. This shattered the frail accommodation between smaller and larger winegrowers in that the large growers placed themselves in direct competition with small growers who had long been known for the production of mass table wines. Small and even medium growers lacked the resources to compete with the large growers and moreover did not have the leverage to demand higher prices from the merchants to whom the majority, especially the smallest growers, sold their harvests.

The problems that followed from the phylloxera blight were exacerbated by the outbreak of mildew at the end of the nineteenth century. While mildew did not lead to replanting, it did require expensive treatments of copper sulfate that were often beyond the means of the least secure growers. Syndicates proved to be a partial relief from perilous consequences of both the phylloxera blights and mildew in that these organizations made products used to treat the vines, from fertilizer to copper sulfate, available to all members at greatly reduced prices. However, it is important to note that these syndicates were not radical in that they were largely founded and controlled by the elite growers. Even with the assistance of the syndicates, some growers, especially those who were most marginal, gave up winegrowing and left the countryside for the cities. This was more the case in regions such as the Dordogne where the production of ordinary wines was predominant. Other growers contended with the problems resulting from these natural blights by uprooting portions of their vineyards and turning to the raising of cows and pigs. Once again, this was more likely to be the response in regions where the production of elite wines was not the primary objective.

It would be wrong to conclude, however, that natural blights alone precipitated the miserable economic and social conditions of the early twentieth century that would lead to the wine-cooperative movement. Overproduction, which had long been a problem for French growers, combined with fraud to make the winegrowing sector one that was especially precarious. The legislation of the early twentieth century, whereby wine was defined as a product made from pressed grapes that were then naturally fermented, helped to alleviate the problem of fraud but did not and to this day does not provide an ultimate solution.[14] On the other hand, the wine-cooperative legislation of the early twentieth century did much to address the problems of overproduction. At the very least, a wine cooperative centralizes the vinification and marketing processes. When a regional limit is placed on the quantity of production in a particular period, this can be administered more directly through the centralization that the cooperative offers.

However, the majority of cooperatives in the regions of my research were founded in the 1930s. These were horrible years for southwest French winegrowers. Not only had these winegrowers experienced a deepening of class divisions in the winegrowing hierarchy but the 1930s combined a series of poor harvests with the consequences of the worldwide economic crisis. Even though American prohibition had ended, the unfavorable exchange rate of the dollar hurt French exports to North America. Unlike the earlier phylloxera and mildew blights, the problems of the 1930s were somewhat of an equalizer. These were years in which the price of all wines plummeted, especially the price for elite wines, which approached the price of those produced by peasant winegrowers. The wine cooperatives, especially in elite regions like the Médoc, offered some stability to both small and medium growers. However, the large elite growers preferred to sell their vineyards to merchants or investors rather than mix their wines with those regarded to be common at the cooperatives.

I have argued, moreover, that political motives were equally intertwined with practical considerations in the founding of the earliest Médoc and Dordogne cooperatives and those of southwest France in general. This is not to say that there was a uniformity of political motives and political action manifested across winegrowing regions. To the contrary, the potential of winegrowing proprietors and workers to identify and to act on common political objectives was markedly variable. I have attributed these differences to the specific context of social relations that can be found from commune to commune in both the southwest and south of France. Languedoc has never been dominated by large elite growers of *grands crus* and thus as a region it has been able to respond politically to the changing historical conditions and increasing concentration of capital in the hands of elite growers and merchants. The Médoc, by contrast, has some communes like Pauillac which are dominated by châteaus while in others such as Listrac this is far less the case. It is therefore not surprising that the respective presidents of the Pauillac and Listrac cooperatives have seen the importance of political motives in the founding of the cooperatives with which they are associated in quite different terms.

I have asserted, moreover, that there is a connection between the founding of southwest French cooperatives in the 1930s and the Popular Front and that the self-identified individualism of French winegrowers has more to do with the history of peasant household production on family farms than it does with an abstract cultural ethos, even though this ethos does contribute strongly to supporting the persistence of small family farms in France. The connections, however, to the Popular

Front, acknowledged by some informants, are not direct. Rather, it is likely that urban visitors to their natal villages, especially in summer, were a rich source for political discourse and exchange and are likely to have had a mutual influence on both the countryside and urban working-class movement. This is not to eclipse a radical socialist movement indigenous to the countryside as both Frossard of the St.-Estèphe cooperative and Blanchard of the Listrac cooperative testify to the importance of the socialists in the founding of Médoc cooperatives.

There is little doubt that the cooperatives, although often founded by village elites, did much to alleviate the most serious consequences among small and medium owners of winegrowing properties of the development of capitalist viticulture and its periodic crises. We will see, furthermore, in the following chapter the tremendous economic and commercial advantages that came with the collectivization of vinification and marketing. However, I will argue that with the abandoning of vinification on the part of individual winegrowers came consequences that did not always work to their advantage and interests. Consequently, wine cooperatives are not simply pragmatic mediums of accommodation to the emergence and proliferation of capitalist production, but they also furthered its division of labor and hence its potential for social control.

CYCLES OF LABOR 5

The annual cycle of labor in winegrowing is profoundly shaped by both the seasons and by the historically developed division between viticulture or the cultivation of vineyards, and viniculture or the processing of harvested grapes into wine. As we have seen previously, this division of labor initially appeared with the introduction of the *grands crus* and then matured and proliferated as the *grands crus* ascended culturally and economically to their paramount position in the southwest French winegrowing hierarchy and thus became the standard of winegrowing excellence. Moreover, the division between viticulture and viniculture assumed in the early twentieth century an institutional form for small and medium cooperative growers through the structure and organization of wine cooperatives. Any discussion of the labor of wine-cooperative members must take this socially constructed division into account, for it has gradually eroded the knowledge of winegrowing and winemaking as a unified process. As a consequence of this erosion of knowledge, cooperative members have become less skillful, thereby increasing their dependency and subordination to cooperative administrators—a point that will be more fully addressed in subsequent chapters.

In spite of the consequence that has followed from diminished knowledge and skill, cooperative winegrowers have not experienced the profound degradation of labor described by Braverman in the industrial working class (1974) nor have they suffered a commensurate decline in their knowledge of viticulture.[1] This is primarily the case because cooperative members have maintained private ownership of their vine-yards and have largely depended on household labor, sometimes supplemented by wage labor and apprenticeship, to work their family holdings.[2] The ties to labor in their own vineyards have thus remained direct and immediate, without necessarily implying, as we shall see shortly, that they are unmediated. The relative autonomy that follows from private ownership of vineyards and household production would seem to make the conditions under which cooperative members labor analogous to the autonomy of labor of fisher families that are described by Gerald Sider in his highly acclaimed ethnography on Newfoundland fishing (1986). Moreover, this analogy is significant for what it suggests about the social location of appropriation in general—more specifically Sider's view of merchant capital—and by comparison serves to highlight the limits to the autonomy of cooperative winegrowers.

Sider's account of Newfoundland fishing, which integrates cultural analysis with that of political economy or class, takes a somewhat unconventional theoretical position on the development of capitalism among Newfoundland fishing families, although he concedes that Newfoundland may be a special case of a more general process of capital formation. Sider argues that because the fisher families were able to maintain control over their own equipment and allocation of labor, the process of appropriation of their product, and thus domination, took place at the point of transfer—the transfer of fish to merchants—rather than at the point of production. According to Sider, fisher families were especially vulnerable because they produced a single product which they were then compelled to exchange with merchants for the provision of essential subsistence resources.[3] This is not to say, however, that control over the allocation of labor made the fisher families immune from the influence of merchants in the sphere of production. To the contrary, Sider challenges the conventional marxist position that merchant capital only operates in the sphere of circulation. He argues that in spite of the apparent autonomy of fisher families at the level of production, merchant capital penetrates the process of production by drawing producers into an interregional economy, with numerous consequences. Sider maintains that not only does the penetration of merchant capital drive down the unit costs of production and increase the division of labor, but it also undermines family and village customs and ceremonies in the long run (1986:42–44).

The situation for southwest French winegrowers at the dawn of the twentieth century was not all that different from what Sider describes in Newfoundland prior to the introduction of an industrial model of fishing. Small and medium proprietors of vineyards, especially in regions like the Médoc where monocropping predominated, found themselves dependent upon and thus dominated by Bordeaux's numerous and powerful merchant houses—a condition that would be partially alleviated by the founding of wine cooperatives.[4] Moreover, Bordeaux merchants played an important role in expanding and thus disseminating winegrowing along capitalist lines, even if it cannot be maintained, as I argued earlier, that merchant capital alone was responsible for capital accumulation and transformation in the French countryside.

While winegrowing families to this day maintain a large degree of control over the allocation of household labor, they are engaged in the cultivation of an agricultural product that is one of the most regulated in the world. The types of vine stocks that can be planted in a specific region, the quantity of yield, and even when the harvest can commence are all strictly regulated. Consequently, the view of wine cooperatives as a medium of state control that I presented in earlier chapters is not limited to the vinification process but can and was necessarily designed to be extended to the vineyards as well, thus having a significant influence on labor in the vineyards.

THE CYCLE OF VINEYARD LABOR AND THE SOCIAL CONSTRUCTION OF WORK

There are, as Penning-Rowsell (1969:17–21) and Peynaud (1988:160–72) have argued, some noteworthy differences in vineyard labor among growers, based upon distinct regional traditions and mandates that are reinforced legally. For example, some winegrowers will plow their vineyards four times per year, as in Margaux, while others will only plow two or three times per year. Moreover, there are strict regulations concerning permissible yields that will affect both the planting and the harvest. In St.-Émillion to the east of Bordeaux the permissible yields are forty-five hectoliters per hectare while in the Haut-Médoc they are forty-eight. Although wine connoisseurs and experts maintain that these differences are important to quality and taste, most of these fine distinctions relate more to the production of elite wines than they do to the production of cooperative wines. With a few exceptions related to class and gender, it will be possible to discuss the labor of cooperative members in common terms so that we can appreciate more precisely as a group what it is that cooperative winegrowers do and, moreover, gain some understanding of how they view or constitute their own labor and *métier* as winegrowers.

Once the grapes have been harvested and turned over to the cooperative for processing into wine, usually during the month of September, cooperative winegrowers uniformly regard this as the culmination and highlight of a process that varies little from year to year. The harvest is viewed as an important juncture practically and symbolically in that it means the growers have made it through another year without serious maladies in the vineyards and have been spared from natural catastrophes such as extreme cold in winter or hail in summer that can cause immeasurable damage to the fragile grape plants, thus affecting the yield and quality of the harvest. Apart from the sense of pleasure and relief that comes from a successful harvest, some cooperative winegrowers look forward to the period immediately following the harvest in that it affords an opportunity for a brief vacation before the agricultural cycle recommences in early October. The younger winegrowers, most particularly the full-time growers, will use this time to visit siblings or friends who have moved elsewhere while others will frequent resorts in France or travel to vacation spots in France's former colonies. However, the older generation of winegrowers, generally those in their fifties or older, and growers who have agricultural pursuits that are polycultural, as in the Dordogne, are likely to take much more circumscribed trips to nearby cities or to devote the time to catching up with projects on the family farm.

One of my informants from Sigoulès, Gilles Darnaud, used this particular time to visit his married daughter and grandchildren in Bordeaux but remarked that it had been years since he had traveled to more distant places such as Paris. Not traveling to more distant places for the older generation of winegrowers is common as they pride themselves on never taking vacations and remark that they have no desire, as others do, to visit the French capital—a point of view that is indicative of the continued tension between the French center and its peripheries.[5] Although not opposed in principle to a vacation, especially to visit her daughter who lives in the French Pyrenees, Nicole Ducros of the Pauillac cooperative explains why she often does not have the time to take a vacation. Her case may be somewhat special in that her husband is deceased and so she must manage her estate alone.

No, I don't go on vacation, well, because being alone doesn't always make it possible. This year it may yet happen, because the season will be finished early. Let's hope that by the 15th of August we'll have finished the treatments [of the vines with chemicals]. Because after all you have to stop the treatments at least a month before the harvest. Because it certainly wouldn't help the vinification if you did treatments too close to the harvest. So it may be that on the one hand I can't easily leave and that I feel at home here because I have large lawns, flowers, gardens that I have to care for, because if I let them go for fifteen days then it will hardly be worth the work any longer.

Ducros has conveyed to me on numerous occasions that being a winegrower is a demanding and time-consuming occupation that provides her with few opportunities to take a vacation—a situation in which she, like others, takes pride.

Those however who are part-time winegrowers and thus work in nearby factories tend to take their vacations during the month of August when the majority of factory workers take their annual vacation of four weeks. At a cooperative like Sigoulès, the part-timers are in the majority as only fifteen of its over three hundred members pursue winegrowing on a full-time basis.[6] These part-time winegrowers in general do not enjoy the leisure and control over the rhythm of work that is enjoyed by full-time growers, a difference that is marked by social class. Part-time growers are thus back at work during the period immediately after the harvest and consequently this was not a time of leisure for them.

The agricultural cycle for winegrowers recommences in October after a brief interlude with the cleaning of the vineyards of debris that is generated by the harvest and from the leaves as they begin to fall from the vines. This is also a period in which the first plowing will occur. Soil is taken from between the rows of plants and placed at the base of the vine stocks to protect them against winter frosts. Winter frosts are much more feared than snow, as snow will provide a layer of protective insulation against the freezing of the ground.

Following the cleaning of the vineyards and the first plowing is perhaps the most important phase of work, pruning. Pruning generally begins sometime in November when all the leaves have fallen from the vines. Ducros describes this work, which she carries out with her two wage workers, one of whom is Portuguese and the other French.

So in mid-November we begin to prune. We begin to prune and it takes four months. As for the men's work [her employees], it takes organization for them to work. After pruning the vines, they change the wires that are broken. They change all that, and then following from behind I begin to attach the vines [to the wires]. And it's the same for me. It takes two months at least. In the meantime, I help the men. That's our winter's work.

Pruning is arduous work. It requires a fair amount of hand strength to cut the vines, it continues throughout the winter in the worst weather, but it is a labor that requires judgment and a significant amount of skill. While I often volunteered to assist my informants in the carrying out of their multiple winegrowing tasks, pruning was the one task in which my role was restricted to that of observer.[7]

That pruning is among the most important work performed in the vineyards is also confirmed historically. During the eighteenth and nineteenth centuries when winegrowing labor became more specialized, it was the pruners who were given the responsibility of supervising the other vineyard workers and often the estate as a whole, especially in the cases of absentee landlords. Moreover, pruning was an activity that was strictly orchestrated and carried out by men. While women worked in the vineyards during the time of pruning, they would follow behind the male pruners and collect the cut vines from the ground. Once the vines were collected and bound they were then sold to the local baker to fire the ovens. However, today all the ovens are gas-fired and so the vines or *sarments* are burned or used to sear the beef for a regional culinary specialty. Consequently women's labor in the vineyards suffered a partial decline with the introduction of gas-fired ovens.

Proper pruning is believed to directly affect the yield of the plant and thus is thought to be important by all winegrowers and oenologists to the quality of the wine. The plants themselves are aligned in rows of one plant per meter. The distance between rows is approximately two and a half meters, wide enough to permit a tractor to pass. In the Médoc and the Dordogne, the vines or branches are attached to three wires that run parallel to the rows of plants. Prior to the pruning, each plant has numerous vines that grow densely upward and outward from the vine stocks, nearly concealing the wires to which the pruned vines will be attached. The skilled pruner has to decide which vines to cut and which will remain to produce the grapes in the following season. While the style of pruning varies widely by region, the Médoc and the Dordogne generally allow, for vine stocks that produce red wines, two widely spaced vines, each of which keeps two to three buds, which are then attached by twine to the wires (Penning-Rowsell 169:18). The sémillon vine stock, for whose sweet white wines the Monbazillac cooperative has become renowned, are much closer to the ground and when pruned only have one vine remaining which is attached with twine to parallel wires. For most of the small growers who are members of cooperatives, the pruning goes on throughout the winter and may even extend into the earliest days of spring, depending upon the severity of the winter. The larger proprietors at the cooperatives sometimes have to make use of hired workers in order to complete the pruning in a timely fashion.

Winegrowing as a whole was generally thought to be man's work. It is now common to find men and women working side by side in the vineyards. This was also confirmed by Nicole Ducros in describing her work with her husband before his untimely death. However, she and her husband did maintain a clearly defined division of labor.

So the division of labor was mainly in summer. My husband would take care of plowing, cutting, and sulfuring the vineyards. I was never involved in that; that was his domain, his domain. Pruning. But nevertheless I still pruned with him. I learned everything, all the tasks, everything you can do to a vine, as well as fertilizing. . . . My husband taught me everything. So the difference between him and me was that he took care of the plowing and the sulfuring, and I had nothing to do with that, he took care of that.

On the other hand, Jean Bosquet of Sigoulès shares ownership of his vineyards with his two brothers. The brothers prefer to work collectively rather than divide their family inheritance into three independent parts. Bosquet and his wife both expressed the pleasure that they take in working together in the vineyards. However, Bosquet's two brothers do not work with their wives reputedly because their wives do not enjoy the work in the vineyards. Gilles Darnaud, also of Sigoulès, did not discriminate against women in the hiring of his three employees. Nonetheless, Bosquet, who was most reflective on this issue, did remark that there were tensions between men and women regarding the gender identity of work. While most men welcomed the labor of their wives and daughters in the vineyards, there was some anxiety. New technology introduced in the vineyards, such as pneumatically powered pruners, were in fact labor-saving devices. Bosquet remarked that as the men had more spare time, increased demands were likely to be made on them by their wives to assume some responsibility for housework. It was Bosquet's opinion that many men were reluctant to use such labor-saving technology because they wished to avoid the possibility of doing work that was traditionally defined as female.

The tensions between men and women concerning work in the vineyards are also intensified by the fact that it is not uncommon for the women to own the vineyards. When I first began my field research in Sigoulès I was confused by the list of cooperative members in that it was periodically the case that the wife of a winegrowing informant was listed as a member of the cooperative even though I had no experience of her working in the vineyards. I came to understand, and Gilles Darnaud is a case in point, that it was not uncommon for daughters to inherit property from their fathers. When these women married, it would almost always be their husbands who would work the vineyards and would be regarded as the "true" members of the cooperative by their largely male colleagues—although the formal or legal evidence was to the contrary. One way of reinforcing the legitimacy of a male wine-grower whose wife was the actual proprietor, once again especially among the older growers, was to institute a strict division of labor between household and vineyard. Gilles Darnaud managed all the affairs related to the family farm while his wife, Mireille, was responsible for managing the household and a small grocery store, or *alimentaire,* in the village of Sigoulès.

This goes to show, as Susan Rogers (1985) has demonstrated in France and likewise Jill Dubisch (1993) in Greece, that women are not subordinate to men in spite of a persistent gendered division of labor that is commensurate with a division of social space in rural areas between a male public and a female private sphere.[8]

While the pruning is continuous for most cooperative members throughout the winter, there are other tasks that also have some degree of importance. Penning-Rowsell remarks that the vineyards are generally treated in January with manure so as to fertilize the soil (1969). However, fertilizer is not used in the vineyards more than once every five years otherwise the yield from the harvest will exceed the communal limit, and quality, as experts maintain, is likely to suffer. However, in the ten years that I have been conducting field research in the southwest of France, and I have been there throughout the growing cycle on more than one occasion, I have yet to witness my informants treating their vineyards with manure. I suspect that this is a practice of the elite estates. Penning-Rowsell describes January as a period in which defective staves are replaced and some proprietors spray against diseases. The staves are important as they support the wires to which the pruned vines are attached. However, the increasing replacement of wooden staves with metal ones has decreased the necessity of this type of maintenance. I have, nonetheless, witnessed my informants spending considerable time ensuring that the wires are taut. Once again, winter spraying seems to be an activity more exclusive to the elite estates.

A second plowing takes place toward the end of February. This plowing is important in that it exposes or "opens up" the vines by removing the soil from the foot of the plant to the ground in between the plants. This work is generally completed by the end of March and is followed in April by the replacement of the plowed soil onto the feet of the vines.

Penning-Rowsell remarks that there are several other plowings, ending in May with soil being left on the feet of the vines to protect them from the summer's heat. I noted that my informants were not as consistently concerned with the numerous plowings as were the proprietors of the elite estates.

Planting is frequently undertaken in the spring but it is an activity that is strictly regulated. This is the case because winegrowing in the past was perennially plagued by overproduction and winegrowers seemed unwillingly to regulate both the quantity and quality of their production. While growers do not have to obtain permission from their cooperatives to expand the size of their vineyards, they must obtain permission from the Institut Nationale des Appellations Origines (INAO) on a communal basis for all wines that are classified. The INAO will then visit to make sure that there are no hybrids and to verify the location of the parcel within the appellation (Pijassou 1980:1004). It is argued that the strict regulation of plantings preserves the integrity of the communal appellation while also protecting its economic viability. Moreover, the growers are restricted to certain plant varieties such as cabernet sauvignon, petit verdot, and merlot in the Médoc. However, Michel Besson of St.-Estèphe conveyed that it is not that difficult to obtain permission to plant, particularly if one is pulling up old vines.

Over the years that I have worked with cooperative winegrowers, I have only infrequently witnessed expansions in the size of their vine-yards and then only among the largest growers. Albert Colineau, for example, who is the vice-president of the Listrac cooperative, has been slowly augmenting his holdings. Planting is time-consuming work and involves considerable financial investment and some financial risk. On the other hand, Pierre Besson, who is vice-president of the St.-Estèphe cooperative and son of the previously mentioned Michel, decided to purchase vineyards outside of the commune of St.-Estèphe rather than undertake new planting. Besson went outside the commune to purchase vineyards because he was interested in experimenting with vinification which is not otherwise possible in that the cooperative mandates that he bring the total yield from his St.-Estèphe vineyards to the coopera-tive at the time of the harvest.

With the arrival of warm weather in June, most of the winegrowers will commence spraying their vineyards with pesticides and other chemicals designed to protect the plants against maladies that in any given year could seriously damage the plants and thus the expected yields at the time of harvest. Spraying is also done to kill the weeds that appear in the soil around the base of the plants. The majority of growers use a backpack sprayer. However, some of the larger growers use a sprayer that is attached to a tractor and therefore is more time-efficient. The tractor sprayer also reduces the contact that the worker has with the chemicals and therefore is thought to be safer. However, while chemical spraying is used in virtually all types of agriculture, the cooperative growers of St.-Estèphe are reluctant to use chemicals and will manually remove weeds from the vineyards. This is so because the Dutch are among the best customers of St.-Estèphe wine and insist on purchasing wines that have not been treated chemically. Nonetheless, the majority of cooperative growers in other communes of the Médoc and Dordogne continue to spray their vineyards and do so throughout the summer months.

The month of August tends to be a fairly inactive time in the vineyards, except for those who are part-time winegrowers. The part-time winegrowers, especially if they are on vacation from factory jobs, will use this time to catch up with work in the vineyards. Some of the larger growers, especially those who are cooperative administrators, will spend more time at the cooperatives in August giving tours to the many summer tourists.

The harvest is generally in the month of September. However, depending upon the summer weather, the period of harvest has occurred as early as late August and as late as early October. Even though cooperative members own their vineyards, they have no control over when the harvest will commence. Rather, a group of administrators from the cooperative will travel to a select number of vineyards owned by cooperative members to test the grapes for sugar content. It is this group of cooperative members who will decide when to harvest, a time that varies from commune to commune depending upon the strict regulations of the communal appellation established by the INAO.

The harvest is not only labor intensive but it must be accomplished in a timely manner as the ripe grapes are in a fragile state and must be picked with expediency. For example, a thunderstorm with strong winds and hail can cause severe damage by easily puncturing the fragile skins and destroying an entire year's crop. The risk of severe summer storms is much greater in the Dordogne than the Médoc. The Médoc is located between two bodies of water which I am told has a moderating effect. Most of my informants from the cooperatives relied on the hiring of university students to work the harvest as classes at the French universities do not resume until the first week of October. The harvest thus provides an excellent opportunity for students to earn some money and perform work that is challenging but generally enjoyable. Growers also rely on family members and friends to assist with the harvest. This contrasts with the large estates which import foreign workers through the Office National de l'Immigration, predominantly from the Andalusian region in Spain and only for the purpose of working the harvest (Pijassou 1980:1020). However, wages for both foreign workers and French citizens are strictly regulated by the government, and the growers also provide them with room and board for the duration of the harvest.

The men and women who are hired for the harvest work as a team. It is not uncommon for the larger cooperative growers such as Ducros or the Bessons to hire as many as forty workers. This is in contrast to the part-time cooperative growers who rely principally on family labor and help from friends. Most of the workers hired by the larger growers are employed as *coupeurs* or grape pickers. The work is generally arduous as it is hot in the vineyards and the grape pickers must bend over moving from plant to plant as they detach the grapes with a small pruner-like device known as a *sécateur.* The harvested grapes are placed in a hand-held basket which when full is emptied into a large pack carried on the back of a worker. While both men and women worked as *coupeurs,* only men were employed to carry the large packs on their backs.[9] Given the difficulty of this work and its physical risks, these workers were paid a supplement above that of the grape pickers. Once the backpacks were full, they were then emptied into a large bin or wagon, a technique that requires some skill so as to avoid depositing oneself in the bin with the grapes. The bins full of grapes were then transported to the cooperative to be registered in the proprietor's name.

The work during the harvest is routine and thus does not vary from day to day. However, the boredom is broken by verbal banter and the teasing that seems to go hand in hand with the work in the vineyards. I was told that in former times song was part of the ritual of harvest work but this tradition has been all but lost or confined to evening meals. The most festive times are the noontime and evening meals, the noontime meal in the past being held in the vineyards but now in the home of the winegrower. Each day the work stops at noon and the harvest workers go to the home of the proprietor to be fed a meal that consists of meat or poultry, vegetables, potatoes, salad, cheese, and wine. Here again the division of labor is significant in that the immense amount of work that goes into the preparation of these meals is carried out by the females of the household, usually with the assistance of several generations. In the case of a female proprietor such as Ducros, she not only manages the harvest workers in the vineyards but also assumes primary responsibility for supervising and participating in the preparation of the meals. The meals are taken collectively at long tables and the conversation ranges from world politics to the work that will be carried out in the afternoon. An equally large meal is prepared and consumed in the evening. However, the evening meal is more relaxed and festive as it marks the end of a hard day's work. There is a constant flow of wine and the after-meal hours are punctuated by song and dance. It is the conviviality of the evening meals that had so often been communicated to me by my informants from the cooperatives and which highlighted the memories of the harvests that growers recall from year to year.

All the winegrowers, whether members of cooperatives or independents, throw large parties for their harvest workers on the last day of the harvest. My wife and I had the opportunity to attend the party given by Ducros of the Pauillac cooperative. These parties resemble the previously described evening meals with the difference that the proprietors bring out better wines and generally prepare one special dish of regional renown. The parties last throughout the night and are famous for their excess, the objective being to outdo the celebration from the year before. At the Ducros celebration, I was told that it was conventional to make toasts and so I like others was called upon to thank my gracious hostess and the acquaintances that I had made during the harvest. The harvest festival was also the time at which the workers were paid, thus contributing to the intensity of the celebration.

The gradual introduction of the mechanical harvester threatens to eliminate everything ritual, invented or otherwise, that is associated with the harvest. Given the expense of mechanical harvesters and the tenacity of tradition, especially on the elite estates, harvesting by hand still predominates among cooperative growers in both the Dordogne and the Médoc. Nonetheless, some cooperative growers, such as Albert Colineau of Listrac, have made use of a mechanical harvester in conjunction with his team of university students. Colineau is a not only a member of the Listrac cooperative but also of a machinery cooperative. That is, a group of growers from Listrac have pooled their resources to buy equipment that they could not afford alone. This works well as long as the members are careful to plan when the equipment will be used by whom.

The mechanical harvester works very quickly and does in one day what would normally take a small group of harvesters nearly a week. The mechanical harvester straddles the row of plants. It has mechanical arms that shake the plants as it travels along the row. The bunches of grapes fall onto a conveyor belt and are deposited in an enormous bin in the rear of the machine. Apart from speed, the advantage of the harvester is that it only requires two workers; one to drive the machine and another who guides the driver to make sure that he follows the alignment of the rows.[10] The use of a mechanical harvester avoids the necessity of hiring workers for the harvest thus reducing costs to the proprietor and the enormous amount of time and labor that goes into the housing and feeding of harvest workers. However, even Colineau admitted that his long-term plans to replace all his harvest workers with a machine would decrease some of the pleasures of the harvest time and thus would be experienced as a loss. He added though that his decision was driven by practicality and economic exigency.

There is presently a fair degree of controversy over the use of mechanical harvesters. Some growers believe the mechanical harvester collects rotten grapes along with those that are ripe and also gathers branches, leaves, and snails—making for a far less clean product com-

TOP: Woman pruning the vines in the vineyards of Gilles Darnaud of the Sigoulès cooperative.

BOTTOM: Michel Besson of the St.-Estèphe cooperative performing the second plowing to remove the soil from the feet of the plants.

TOP: Hand spraying in Listrac Médoc.

BOTTOM: Mechanical spraying in Albert Coliner's vineyards, Listrac Médoc.

TOP: Harvest workers in the Besson vineyards, St.-Estèphe.

BOTTOM: Transporting the grapes to the bin collected from the grape pickers or *coupeurs*.

TOP: Grape collection site in the vineyards.

BOTTOM: Author at work.

TOP: Harvest play.

BOTTOM: Tradition lives at the Pauillac cooperative—the harvest delivered in wooden barrels.

TOP: Aging of wine in oak barrels at the Pauillac cooperative.

BOTTOM: Bottling of wine at the Listrac cooperative.

TOP: A local Médoc summer festival that features cooperative wines.

BOTTOM: The judging of local wines at the Sigoulès wine festival.

TOP: Besson family vinification of their non-cooperative grapes.

BOTTOM: Three generations of the Besson family.

pared to hand picking. Ducros is fairly typical of those who oppose mechanical harvesters.

> **Ulin:** Do you use a harvesting machine here?
> **Ducros:** No. No. No. Manual harvesting.
> **Ulin:** Because the vine stocks are too low?
> **Ducros** : Yes, because the vine stocks are very low, but there are never-
> theless machines that can reach all the vine stocks. Because people who
> now have machines, obviously, adapt their machines to the level of the
> vines rather than the vines to the level of the machine. Now the people
> who plant, true, let their vines grow higher so that it's easier to work on
> them. That's true. But there are no machines in this shop.
> **Ulin:** Is it cleaner with the manual method?
> **Ducros:** Sure, you pick only grapes. You don't pick leaves. If you gather
> leaves, you need a person on the cart to remove the leaves. You don't get
> snails, you don't get weeds. So the manual method is cleaner. I can tell
> you that three years ago, someone, a colleague, telephoned me because he
> had bought a machine and said: "Come see, you'll see the work it does."
> I had no time because just then I had a lot to do and after all I had 40
> persons [harvest workers] from morning to evening the entire week. So I
> told him that I didn't have the time. So he said that he would hold onto
> the grapes (just harvested) until the following morning and that I should
> come whenever I wanted. So I was there at 7 a.m., the machine was in
> the garage, I went to see his beauty, and he didn't like my comments at
> all, but I am a blunt woman. I said that there were as many snails as
> grapes. It wasn't strictly true, but on top, it was full of snails. I said he
> was going to eat and drink at the same time, eh (*Je lui ai dit tu vas manger
> en même temps que tu vas boire, eh*).

The proprietors of the elite estates concur with her view of the harvest-ing machine but also invoke the mystique of tradition in arguing that hand picking is necessary to the production of a quality wine. They have no desire to break continuity with the past as it is this continuity, as we saw previously, that contributes to the successful marketing of the wine. It thus seems that it will yet be some time before the me-chanical harvesters totally replace the labor and ritual of the harvest teams, especially given the recalcitrance of the elite growers.

The principal technical change in viticulture that was most noted by cooperative growers was the gradual introduction of tractors beginning in the 1950s. This is confirmed by Bourgode, a retired member of the Pauillac cooperative. Bourgode is eighty-one years old and thus has experienced some of the most important changes in winegrowing and rural French society:

I'll tell you, what happened is simple. We had a government which completely changed workers' habits. They took all their money, not out of the banks, forget them, but out of their stockings to buy equipment, equipment we still have and use, tractors, cars, televisions, etc. Those were the important changes. Between 1945 and 1960, that's what happened between '45 and '60. So then things really changed because from '45 to '55 we needed agricultural tractors. From '55 to '65 they were everywhere. That's the difference. Those were very important steps. I'm not saying it's necessarily better. We've completely changed our way of life and mode of work.

While the technological changes are important, as Bourgode remarks, the most important transformations were initiated through the French government and, as Bourgode fails to acknowledge, the very banking system whose loans made wine cooperatives possible in the first place.[11] The question as to whether all these changes have been for the better has less to do with viticulture and more to do with Bourgode's own ambivalence for a transformed rural society and his nostalgia for a bucolic past.

It would be shortsighted to conclude a section on vineyard labor without remarking on the considerable exchanges of labor that I witnessed among cooperative growers. While most cooperative growers relied on household or hired labor, it was the case, especially in polycultural regions such as the Dordogne, that members of the cooperative would assist each other in carrying out a wide range of agricultural tasks from the caring of cows to tending the vineyards. More than once my appointments with cooperative growers were interrupted or simply canceled with the explanation that they must help an *agriculteur* who lives down the road. The general rule of thumb was that no immediate reciprocity was expected. However, it was widely recognized that favors would be returned when a particular need should arise. Hence, in spite of the avowed individualism promoted by a household mode of production, the connections between cooperative growers for the sharing of labor, information, and even tools were in fact significant.

THE CYCLE OF LABOR AT THE WINE COOPERATIVES

The vinification at the cooperatives, unlike work in the vineyards, is carried out by cooperative employees. The process as a whole is overseen by oenologists hired from nearby oenological centers and by the cooperative's *maître de chai,* "wine-cellar master."[12] Since cooperative members are occupied with their own harvests and know little about the process of vinification, it is these hired experts who are responsible for ensuring that the wine will be fermented properly and that the quality will be assured. Once the fermentation process is complete, it is then the skill of the cooperative's *maître de chai* that is counted on to monitor the process from aging to the bottling of the wine.

Most of the cooperative winegrowers transport their harvested grapes to the cooperatives in tractor-pulled metal bins that are either owned by the cooperatives and thus lent to the growers or are part of the growers' personal equipment. At some cooperatives such as Pauillac in the Médoc, there are older growers who take pleasure in maintaining tradition. These growers will transport their harvested grapes to the cooperative in wooden barrels rather than the more sterile metal bins, thus contributing to the sense of nostalgia that envelops much of wine-growing and contributes to its symbolic and commercial value.

All the cooperatives are now equipped with computerized control rooms that contribute to the efficiency with which the harvested grapes are processed. Throughout the harvest, cooperative members will bring their full bins to the cooperative where computerized machines will weigh the grapes and take their sugar content. Since it is sugar that will be converted into alcohol as the grapes ferment, the sugar content of grapes is strictly regulated, the limits being established by the communal appellations. For example, the classified red wines of the Sigoulès cooperative must not exceed 178 grams of sugar per liter—being after fermentation a minimum of 10 degrees alcohol. If the grapes should exceed the communal limit, the cooperative must obtain a variance from the INAO before the grapes can be pressed and processed. I have been told that this variance is generally given. If the variance should be denied, then the cooperative is unable to accept the member's grapes. I was, however, aware of no cases where members' grapes were rejected, as the cooperatives enforce strict standards of quality in the vineyards. The computer will assign a number to the cooperative member and keep track of his or her contributions as they are brought in throughout the harvest.

The process of vinification itself is essentially standard from cooperative to cooperative, as confirmed below by Ducros, and only differs with the type of wine, such as red or white, that is being produced.

The vinification remains the same whether you do it here or in the United States, it is always the same thing. There are not fifty ways to vinify. There is only one way, either at the Pauillac cooperative or at Lafite-Rothschild or Château Latour, the methods are the same. Now what's different is that at Château Latour you will still find wooden fermentation vats, at Château Latour you will find stainless steel vats, and here, admittedly, at Pauillac you will find stainless steel and cement vats. But the process of aging the wine happens in wooden barrels like at Lafite, like at Château Latour. What we don't do, because it is too expensive, is to put all of our wine in new barrels. Our wine isn't expensive enough, because one barrel costs 1,900 francs. So it's too costly. So we buy barrels from what the big châteaus call second wines (*deuxièmes vins*), and we put our wines in those barrels. But the process of vinification is exactly the same.

All the cooperatives in the Médoc produce red wine exclusively while Sigoulès in the Dordogne produces red, whites, and rosé. Monbazillac, also of the Dordogne, produces largely dry and sweet white wines. For the red wines, the production process begins with *égrappage,* or the removal of the stalks from the harvested black grapes. The black grapes are deposited into a cylindrical machine, called a *fouloir-égrappoir,* which removes the stalks and pierces the skins. The stalks are then filtered out or separated from the grapes and deposited by a conveyor belt in a bin located outside the cooperative building. Generally, the stalks are not removed from the white grapes in the making of white wine (Penning-Rowsell 1969:22).

Once the *égrappage* is completed, the grapes, skins, and juice are pumped into fermentation vats. In the past, these vats were made of concrete. However, concrete vats are difficult to clean and often collect gases that make them somewhat dangerous to cooperative employees. With few exceptions it is stainless steel fermentation vats that have replaced those of concrete. The stainless steel vats also have the added advantage of quality temperature control that is so central to the fermentation process. Some of the elite estates such as Margaux and Mouton Rothschild use, as Ducros has noted, oak fermentation vats. However, these vats are beyond the means of cooperatives.

Fermentation generally commences within twenty-four hours of the skins and juice being pumped into the fermentation vats. It is the fermentation that will transform the natural sugar of the grapes into alcohol by means of the yeasts found on the grape skins. Sometimes, yeast will be added to facilitate this process as well as sugar in amounts strictly regulated, especially if the alcohol content is not commensurate with the communally established limits. For example, the Sigoulès cooperative is permitted to add 25 to 30 grams of sugar per liter in order to raise the alcoholic content 1.4 to 1.6 degrees, the legal limit being 2 degrees. The process of adding sugar to fermenting wine is known as chaptalization. It is, however, illegal to add sugar to wine that has already been fermented. The fermentation process usually takes about five days but can last as long as two weeks. It is crucial that the temperature in the vats be kept between 30 and 34 degrees Celsius, otherwise the fermentation process will slow down to uneconomic levels. Once the fermentation is complete, there is no prescribed amount of time that the wine will be kept in the vats and thus it varies from cooperative to cooperative.

One way that the temperature of the fermenting wine is kept below the crucial limit is to pump the wine from the bottom of the vat to the top through water-cooled pipes. However, the skins will float to the top of the vat and form a hard crust, sometimes a foot thick, known as the *chapeau*. As Penning-Rowsell remarks, the *chapeau* "prevents essential air reaching the must as well as reducing the contact of juice with the skins" (1969:23). The *chapeau* thus must be broken up so that the juice from the bottom can reach the top, a process known as *remontage*. The fermented wine is generally left in the vats for a period of two weeks in order to enhance its color and tannin. During this period, the wine also undergoes a second or malolactic fermentation; that is, the transformation of malic acid into lactic acid. Penning-Rowsell (1969) and Emile Peynaud (1988) concur that this second fermentation is important for red wines and should not take place once the wine is in bottles.

The processing of white wines is distinct from that of reds in that the grapes are pressed three or four times and on the elite estates the fermentation will take place in casks. However, casks are expensive and so for the majority of cooperatives, fermentation vats are used. For rosé wine, the must is removed from the skins almost immediately. With the sweet white wines the process is distinct in that the grapes in the vineyard are not picked until they have been nearly shriveled by the *pourriture noble* or noble rot, thus accounting for the elevated price of these wines.

After the second fermentation is complete, the wine is drawn off into storage vats or tanks. Some cooperatives, such as Pauillac, will purchase used oak casks from the elite estates which will then be employed to store and age their wines. The used casks are far less expensive than new ones as casks are still produced by skilled artisans and thus are costly.[13] There appears to be no uniform amount of time that wine is stored in vats before being bottled. However, because the Médoc has an esteemed reputation, even the cooperatives will age their wines before releasing them for sale. This is a significant contrast to Sigoulès where the wines are not aged due to the fact that they are generally best consumed young. Moreover, all the storage vats used at Médoc cooperatives were located inside buildings so as to protect the wine from the summer's heat and the chill of winter. The storage vats at Sigoulès are located outside, a factor that more than once drew critical commentary from my Médoc informants.

Whether located inside or outside of the cooperative buildings, the storage vats are extremely important to the financial well-being of cooperative members. In the past, small growers did not have the ability to age wine or even to store it during periods of declining prices. They were, like the Newfoundland fishing families described by Sider, at the mercy of merchants and essentially had to sell their wines at whatever price the merchant was offering. Today a cooperative such as Sigoulès, which has a storage capacity of 80,000 hectoliters, is able to store wine for approximately two years given that their annual harvest averages just under 43,000 hectoliters. The cooperative thus has the potential to wait out a weak market before releasing the wine for sale.

Payments to members are generally made four times per year, in December, March, June, and September. The amount of the payment depends upon both the weight of the harvest delivered and the type of the appellation. At Sigoulès 80 percent of the wine produced is *appellation d'origine contrôlée* (AOC), with two different qualities of red noted as AOC1 and AOC2, while the rest is sold in bulk as *vin de table* (CC). Sigoulès members, who actually receive five payments per year, are paid the following per hectoliter at 10 degrees alcohol, one hectoliter being the equivalent of 150 kilograms of harvest: Rouges CC 100 francs; Rouges AOC1 167 francs; Rouges AOC2 125 francs; Blancs 108 francs; Sauvignon 160 francs; and Monbazillac 160 francs. For cooperatives in the Médoc, the primary difference in payments is between those members whose wines are sold under the cooperative label and the small number whose wines are sold under a château label. In both the Dordogne and the Médoc, however, approximately 10 percent of what a cooperative member delivers to the cooperative is held back to cover the overhead expenses of the cooperative. In all cases, members are allowed to collect wine for their personal consumption proportionate to the size of the harvest that they deliver to the cooperatives.

All cooperatives have a handful of employees. Usually, in the front office, one finds at the very minimum a secretary who takes care of the paperwork related to orders for wine and an accountant or bookkeeper who keeps track of cooperative finances. However, larger cooperatives like Bégadan may employ three secretaries and a bookkeeper to manage the sizable volume of business with merchants and independent clients. Several employees are also necessary to monitor the stored wine and to prepare orders for shipping. These employees work under the direction of the *maître de chai* who has a good deal of responsibility and autonomy. The *maître de chai* of the Bégadan cooperative told me that although he is paid less than he would be in a large winery he enjoys working at the cooperative because of the conviviality of the work environment and the freedom that he is given to make decisions, albeit related to his specific expertise.

The bottling is sometimes done by cooperative employees and sometimes by independent companies. These companies transport bottling equipment in a truck and travel from cooperative to cooperative contracting their services. Apart from the employees, the work at the cooperative is generally supported by elected members of the *conseil d'administration,* "Board of Directors" who donate their time as they are able. Their donated time is especially important in summer when most cooperatives welcome tourists anxious to sample the wines.

In summary, the process of vinification—like the cultivation of the vineyards—is strictly regulated. While the cooperatives, like the growers themselves, have a fair amount of autonomy, there are clearly limits when it comes to meeting mandates that are both communal and at the level of the nation-state. Although improving the quality of wine produced by small growers may be a principal objective of wine cooperatives, the necessity of meeting the defined objectives of communal appellations has also brought new responsibilities and demands to cooperatives that in the long run have curtailed their autonomy. It was after all the autonomy of small producers that the cooperative legislation was meant to challenge. Those who refused to comply, as I argued in earlier chapters, were relegated to the margins of winegrowing history and eventually were forced out of winegrowing altogether.

IDENTITY AND WORK: WINEGROWING AS ART OR SCIENCE?

Although the seasonal cycle of winegrowing labor described above appears largely constant in its formal properties from region to region, the relation of this labor to the self-identity of southwest French cooperative winegrowers is nevertheless contingent and variable. That is, the identity that winegrowers construct with respect to their work or labor, while not exhaustive or all-determining, is profoundly dependent upon the particular reputation of their winegrowing region and its articulation with the nation-state.[14] I argued therefore in Chapter 2 that by associating their wines with an "invented" aristocratic past and by building small-scale replicas of medieval châteaus (the invoking of mimesis) to distinguish themselves and their wines from the masses, elite Médoc proprietors sought during the nineteenth century to forge an identity that participated in the incipient symbolism of French national culture.

The 1855 Universal Exposition held in Paris is testimony to the close association between elite wines and the formation of an aristocratic national culture. Only the proprietors of elite Bordeaux estates were invited to exhibit their wines at this exposition which was also the occasion for the enduring 1855 classification of Bordeaux wines. Such universal expositions, like the world's fairs of the twentieth century, were central to the invention and representation of national cultures.

As their wines came to be viewed as part of the French national heritage, and thus recognized as a national treasure, elite growers, their wines, and their châteaus elicited the symbolism of the nation-state. Médoc growers are thus able to benefit from the cultural capital associated with their region in a manner that is not duplicated in the Dordogne or other areas where the production of mass wines predominate. This is not to say, however, that identity is simply univocal or uncontested. To the contrary, we should recall Lescot and Bourgode's contention that the wines of the Pauillac cooperative are, rather than those of elite estates such as Lafite, the "authentic" wines of Pauillac because cooperative wines are made from the grapes of all of the members and thus come from a large number of properties of the region. This does not prevent Médoc cooperatives such as Pauillac from using the reputation and identity of this esteemed region to their commercial advantage.

My informants from the Sigoulès cooperative invoked, in like fashion, the winegrowing hierarchy as a point of reference but, in contrast to Médoc growers, also as a source of self-effacement. For example, they questioned why I was interested in their wines, and by extension themselves, when the esteemed vineyards of Bordeaux were in such proximity to their own. Such a comment indicates that they understood their social position in the national winegrowing hierarchy and thus had a minimal claim on the esteem associated with French wines.[15] In fact, the distinction between regions, in my case the Dordogne and the

Médoc, was profoundly implicated in the winegrowers' distinct attitudes toward their work and their product which, in turn, contributed, as I have suggested above, to their sense of self-identity.

The vast majority of winegrowers from the Sigoulès cooperative understood their labor in essentially practical terms. This is perceptible through the comments of some informants, confirmed also by the director of the cooperative, that *"la rentabilité est la plus importante"* (profitability is most important) and in their general desire to produce a wine that was standardized or did not vary in taste from year to year.[16] Moreover, the fact that most of the large growers in the Dordogne cultivated a variety of crops contributed to their essentially pragmatic attitude about their viticultural pursuits, since wine was often ancillary to the raising of cows, the cultivation of tobacco, and cereals. Their identities were thus tied, in a manner commensurate with the overall reputation of the Dordogne region, more to the general categories of *agriculteur*, "agriculturist" and *paysan*, "farmer" than to the specific identity of *viticulteur*, "winegrower." Moreover, among the younger growers who attended the regional agricultural schools, it was common for them to refer to themselves as *agriculteur* rather than *paysan*, especially given the often negative connotations of the latter.[17] On the other hand, for the part-time growers of the Dordogne, winegrowing contributed to only a small part of their livelihood and thus most of these individuals saw their own labor, no matter how enjoyable, in likewise pragmatic terms. If they worked in a factory, as many did, it was more common to identify with the industrial working class than with those who gained their livelihood from working the land.

Médoc cooperative growers, in contrast to those of the Dordogne, spoke first about their concerns for producing and improving the quality of their wines and only secondarily about profitability. Moreover, the identity of most growers as *Médocain* was largely borrowed from the established reputation of the Médoc as an exclusive winegrowing region. This was even true for the vast majority of part-time growers who gained their livelihoods as wage workers on the elite estates and thus identified with the reputations of those estates. While many of the older growers still referred to themselves as *paysans*, it was more common than in the Dordogne for these growers to identify themselves as *viticulteurs*. With few exceptions, therefore, winegrowing and self-identity go hand-in-hand in the Médoc.[18] Moreover, in contrast to the pragmatism of the Dordogne, many of these self-same Médoc cooperative growers saw their work much more as an art or craft than as a science.[19]

The relation between art and science has several implications for how Médoc growers understood their own work and knowledge, not to mention the bearing that it has on their identities. This became evident to me in a discussion with two elderly members of the St.-Estèphe cooperative, Yvês Diouf and the aforementioned Michel Besson.

Ulin: You are an artisan?

Diouf: Yes, we are artisans. But you need learning, and more learning.

Besson: Yes, you need learning for everything.

Ulin: You prefer artistry to science?

Diouf: Yes, it is rather craft-like. It is more artisanship than science.

Besson: Vinification is evolving like a science, with oenology now.

Diouf: Yes, but it's still craft-like (*Mais, c'est artisinal quand-même*). There are methods of work that are still identified with the Médoc region. That's why it's called a craft, because there are methods of work different from those in other areas. That's why we say it's a craft. They're identified with this region.

Besson: It's a craft, yes, because people who go to school, who never come to this region and who go to learn in schools, they then come here. . . . They aren't the ones who do best. . . . To the extent that they adapt, what they have learned will help them all the more, but I think it is necessary to learn here at work, next to the vines (*il faut aussi avoir appris ici sur le tas, à côté des pieds*). You have to combine the two. And I think that with the vinification it is the same. It is necessary. . . . There's a skill on the large estates that must be joined with oenology. I think that the two must be paired to do what we do here, to do it well. In short, that's my point of view. It is nevertheless a craft, the two must be combined, but it is necessary that the fundamental artisan themes and methods endure. From my point of view.

It is clear that both Diouf and Besson believe that it is necessary to integrate scientific methods with those of the artisan, even though, as Peynaud argues, oenology has only relatively recently gained widespread acceptance (1988). However, by artisan, Diouf and Besson have in mind knowledge, techniques, and skills which are specific to the Médoc. This is obviously in marked contrast to Ducros who argued that vinification is everywhere the same. Nonetheless, it must be kept in mind that Ducros's comments were made about the technical process of vinification and not, like those of Diouf and Besson, in relation to regional identity. Moreover, Diouf and Besson exhibit some contempt for the agricultural schools where classroom learning is not linked to practical experience in the vineyards, a point of view, as we saw with Frossard, that is common among the older growers. Nonetheless, Diouf and Besson see themselves as caretakers of traditions that are particular to place and thus they regard their own labor in the vineyards as analogous to that of an artisan. It is the linking of labor to the particularity of place through the concept of the artisan that creates and reinforces the Médoc identity while distinguishing winegrowers of this region from those of the Dordogne. Winegrowing labor is thus not simply technical but it is also culturally framed and mediated in its association with both regional identity and national culture.

I have argued that cooperative winegrowers in both the Médoc and the Dordogne maintain, like the Newfoundland fisher families described by Sider, a large degree of autonomy over the work carried out in their own vineyards. The extraction of surplus and thus domination of small-scale southwest French winegrowers takes place predominantly at the point of exchange rather than simply at the point of production. However, the analogy between winegrowers and fisher families exhausts its potential once we recognize the special symbolic and commercial connection of wine as a product and thus the unique restrictions that are imposed on winegrowers from the cooperative, the region, and the nation-state. Cooperative growers must strictly comply with regional regulations regarding the planting of new vineyards, what vine stocks are permissible, the allowable yields per hectare, and the sugar content of the grapes at the time of harvest. Moreover, the cooperative growers must await permission of their cooperative before they can commence harvesting of their own grapes. Periodic checks of the vineyards of cooperative members by the cooperative administrators will insure that standards are being met and thus shows that cooperatives contribute significantly to the disciplining of their members, an objective that has long been consistent with the wine-cooperative legislation.

While there is much in common between the Médoc and the Dordogne in the formal properties of labor in both the vineyards and the cooperatives, we have also seen that winegrowing labor is mediated by gender, class, region, and the nation-state. In the distant past, although winegrowing labor was essentially characterized as male, men and women would work side by side during the pruning, the harvest, and the crushing of the grapes. However, with the introduction of new technology (some of which had little to do with winegrowing, like gas-fired ovens), the significant contributions made to winegrowing by women were diminished. More recently, much of this has begun to change as women have assumed positions of responsibility at the cooperatives and have thus, albeit with struggle, won the respect of their male colleagues.[20]

The winegrowing population in the cooperatives is also stratified according to class. This is most apparent between the full-time and part-time growers but also among the full-time growers themselves.[21] Consequently, not only is the seasonal rhythm of labor somewhat different for the part-time growers but they are also less likely to assume the identity of *viticulteur.* However, since the identity of winegrowers takes much from the reputation of the region, the difference between an elite region such as the Médoc and a region largely known for wines best consumed young, such as the Dordogne, is paramount.

While the winegrowing labor for cooperative growers in the Médoc and Dordogne is essentially the same, Médoc growers are far more likely to see their labor and knowledge as unique and thus akin to the work of an artisan. The analogy of artisan permits Médoc growers to perpetuate the mystique of tradition and the hermeticism of knowledge that can only be learned, as Diouf and Besson emphasize, *sur place* (on location). Most importantly, however, the profound interconnection between their identity as *Médocain,* their winegrowing work, and the esteemed regional reputation for winegrowing permits winegrowers of this region, cooperative and otherwise, to participate in and thus reproduce metonymically the symbolism of the nation-state. Consequently, they have benefited from the accumulation of significant cultural capital and consequent commercial advantages that perhaps are only equaled in France by the celebrated Burgundy winegrowing region. [22] However, in spite of these advantages, the domain of cooperative winegrowers from all regions remains profoundly conditioned by the structure and organization of the cooperative and thus it is to this arena that we presently turn our attention.

COOPERATIVE ORGANIZATION AND THE REPRODUCTION OF POWER | 6

I conducted fieldwork in both the Dordogne and the Médoc so as to compare the histories, winegrowing cultures, and institutional organization of wine cooperatives in areas known for the production of ordinary and elite wines respectively.[1] Moreover, I intended to determine whether the region's winegrowing reputation influenced a cooperative's identity and operational procedures and to evaluate conclusions reached earlier in the Dordogne against those to be formulated in the Médoc. Apart from a recognized emphasis on monocropping in the Médoc and polyculture in the Dordogne, I concluded that Médoc cooperatives are distinct by virtue of an invented tradition that emphasizes the natural superiority of the Médoc's climate and soil while promoting the historic and symbolic connection of its wines to an aristocratic past. This, in turn, has brought Médoc cooperatives, and the Médoc as a whole, considerable cultural capital and marketing advantages not accessible to the majority of Dordogne cooperatives.

In spite of the important practical advantages that follow from this symbolic or representational difference and the commensurate risks of monocropping versus polyculture, it nonetheless became apparent to me that the cooperatives from the two regions are remarkably similar in organization and government. This is evidently the case because wine cooperatives in France are exclusively vinification and marketing collectives. However, it is also true that southwest French wine cooperatives operate with a charter or statute that has been standardized since the early days of the wine-cooperative movement. A standardized charter appears to facilitate the establishment of a cooperative for those lacking legal acumen, as was the case with most winegrowers in the early twentieth century, and thus avoids costs of drawing up a new statute every time a cooperative is founded.[2] More important, the standardized charter was designed to articulate with the cooperative legislation at the national level and therefore has established, as Yoon has argued, an organizational framework that is thoroughly mediated by the French state.

> In each cooperative the president and administration were thus given powers to mediate between the coop and the state. The coop itself mediated between local producers and the state. But the penetration of the state was part of the original design of the whole coop structure. The state had written the by-laws and approved them. Perhaps even more significant, the coops had to rely upon the state and its laws in order to maintain order within the coop. Thus coops would have been inconceivable outside a state structure. There was a mutually interdependent relation between state and coop. (1983:174)

Therefore, the statute not only outlines the individual rights of cooperative members and mandates their responsibilities to the collective body but it also established a governmental and organizational structure of cooperatives that is consistent with the French state's policy of agricultural modernization. Although edited for illustrative purposes, the charter reproduced in Table 6.1 is exemplary of the principal points covered in the statutes of southwest French wine cooperatives. While many of these individual points may be elaborated or modified at the discretion of each cooperative, albeit within the constraints of the cooperative legislation, an effort is generally made to affirm and thus preserve their overall framework and intention.

A standardized charter may appear as nothing more than an organizational necessity—and this surely was the view of my informants, including the cooperative administrators. By establishing wine cooperatives as vinification and marketing organizations exclusively, the standardized charter unwittingly gave institutional form to and thus played a role in disseminating a capitalist division of labor between viticulture and viniculture. This division in the long run rendered cooperative winegrowers less skillful, and consequently sustained and re-

TABLE 6.1 COOPERATIVE CHARTER

1. The Board of Directors has fifteen members elected by the General Assembly (number may vary).[a]
2. All administrators must be of French nationality and must be from a member country of the European Economic Community.
3. The number of administrators over eighty years of age must not exceed one-third of the total.
4. The administrators are elected for three years and are renewable by one-third each year.
5. The candidates for election are made known to the General Assembly by the Board of Directors.
6. If someone leaves or dies, the Board of Directors proceeds to replace him/her subject to the ratification of the General Assembly at their next meeting.
7. All members of the Board of Directors can be recalled by the General Assembly.
8. The Board of Directors names a president. It also names one or more vice-presidents.
9. The Board of Directors must meet at least one time per trimester.
10. The president does not have to be paid.
11. The Board of Directors can name a director if he is a member of the cooperative. He should not then be a member of the Board of Directors.
    a. The director executes his function under the surveillance of the Board of Directors.
    b. He is not allocated any percentage of the profits realized by the cooperative.
    c. He cannot be charged with the direction of the cooperative.
    d. The Director hires and is responsible for all employees of the cooperative.
12. The General Assembly designates by secret ballot, one or more *commissaires aux comptes*.
    a. This person oversees and checks all financial affairs.
    b. He reports annually to the General Assembly.
    c. He cannot choose as *commissaire aux comptes* parents or relatives to the fourth degree.
    d. The person or persons holding this position receive some sort of salary for this work.
13. The General Assembly consists of all the regular *coopérateurs* inscribed on the register. Their decisions are binding for all those absent and dissident.
14. Meetings of the General Assembly are generally called by the Board of Directors.
15. Decisions are by a two-thirds majority of members of the General Assembly who are present at the meeting.
16. Dissolution: in the case of the loss of 75 percent of the cooperative's capital reserves, the General Assembly has the right to dissolve the cooperative.
17. The total harvest must be brought to the cooperative.
18. The cooperative will be responsible for the vinification and marketing of the membership's wine.
19. Payments will be made to cooperative members in December, March, June, and September.
    a. Payment is based on the weight of harvested grapes.
20. Political and religious discussions are forbidden at meetings of the General Assembly.

Source: This charter is from the Listrac cooperative. My informants at the Listrac cooperative told me that they simply adopted the standardized version and modified it to meet their individual circumstances.
[a]The number of members who serve on the Board of Directors varies from cooperative to cooperative and is largely dependent on the size of the cooperative's overall membership.

produced inequalities of some historical depth. While the diminishing of winegrowers' skill may have been an unintended consequence of the cooperative's organization and collective purpose, the dissemination of the capitalist division of labor was nonetheless consistent, as Yoon has reminded us above, with the French government's objective of viticultural modernization. The embodiment of this objective in the cooperative's organization, combined with the potential to monitor production through the centralization which cooperatives offered, ensured that the social organization and governance of virtually all French cooperatives would be hierarchical or stratified.[3]

In the following sections, I elaborate the social organization of southwest French wine cooperatives in relation to the capitalist division of labor and analyze its consequences for winegrowers who are members. Although the emphasis of this chapter, at least in terms of argument, will be on the cooperative's institutionalization and reproduction of power, it is also important to acknowledge the considerable advantages offered to members by cooperative organization and marketing compared to the uncertainties faced by independents. This is especially apparent once it is recognized, as we shall see in Chapter 7, that cooperatives offered some degree of independence from the direct domination of the large Bordeaux merchants.

VITICULTURE AND VINICULTURE: THE CAPITALIST DIVISION OF LABOR

I argued in Chapter 3, following Enjalbert (1953), that French winegrowers in the Bordeaux region elected to augment the quality of their wines in the development of the *grands crus* in order to combat stiff competition from Spain and Portugal at the end of the seventeenth and beginning of the eighteenth centuries. The introduction of the *grands crus* established a strategy of winegrowing that favored the harvesting of grapes from older plants that produced smaller yields, combined with the aging of the wine itself before being released for sale. The greatest transformation was marked, at least in social terms, by the undermining of the special paternalism that had long characterized the relation between proprietors of winegrowing estates and their workers. This relationship was more than economic in that winegrowing proprietors housed workers on their estates and assumed responsibility for the health and general welfare of their families. Moreover, the work on the estates itself was highly integrated and diverse in that the same set of laborers would both care for the vineyards and press the harvested grapes into wine. With the introduction of the *grands crus,* the labor tasks became divided between those who worked in the vineyards, a process known as viticulture, and those who assumed responsibility for the making and aging of wine, otherwise known as vinification. While the division between viticulture and vinification has been widely regarded as a mark of progress, if not a natural division, it simplified and thus devalued the labor for many who had a prior relationship to both winegrowing and winemaking. The split between viticulture and vinification also produced a hierarchy among the work force not previously present and led to proprietors preferring to hire workers seasonally rather than pay for their upkeep on a yearly basis. The special paternalistic relationship characteristic of winegrowing on the large estates was in the long run shattered by the development of the *grands crus* as the division between viticulture and viniculture became the standard for the production of quality wines on the large estates of southwest France and thus eventually a model for all French winegrowers.

The social consequences that followed from the introduction of the *grands crus,* especially the fragmentation and hierarchy of the work process and workers themselves, are reminiscent of what Harry Braverman has described as the degradation of work under the capitalist division of labor, although Braverman's principal concern is to critique Taylorism and industrial psychology (1974).[4] Nonetheless, Braverman shows that as work loses its unity, exhibited in factories by the separation of a concept of a labor task from its execution and thus the labor of planners from that of workers, the general character of labor as a fulfilling and nonalienated process—that is, the identification of workers with the product of their labor—is undermined.[5] This is not to suggest that the introduction of the *grands crus* directly paralleled the intentions, which they obviously predate, of industrial psychology to rationalize and control labor, or even approached the degree of alienation and fragmentation of labor experienced by assembly-line workers. However, the unity of work was lost along with the satisfaction that followed from being able to execute a wide number of different tasks with some degree of skill and control. The important point to be grasped here is that with wine-growing, as with the factory, the augmentation of the division of labor was not simply an indicator of technical progress but rather was a social index of transformed social relations, social relations that were redolent of power and social inequality both in the vineyards and the factory.

The founding in 1901 of the Maraussan cooperative in Languedoc, one of two early cooperative experiments, challenged the capitalist division between viticulture and viniculture, although one could argue without intention, by collectivizing the vineyards of its members. Not only did collectivizing the vineyards undermine inequalities that potentially ensue from differences in the size of properties owned by cooperative members, but it increased the likelihood that cooperative members would become involved both in working collectively owned vineyards and in processing the harvested grapes into wine. However, the Maraussan initiative was short-lived as the members of this cooperative resumed private ownership of their vineyards in the first year of the cooperative's existence.

All French wine cooperatives are now vinification and marketing organizations exclusively. This exclusivity of function contributes manifestly, I believe, to the maintenance of the historically produced division between vinification and viticulture reproduced in their founding charters and organizational structures. Moreover, members of cooperatives everywhere in France are resolute across the political spectrum in their defense of private property and therefore have shown, as even Maraussan members quickly realized, no desire to abandon their ties to household or family production. Consequently, while cooperative members carry out the work in their own vineyards, sometimes with the assistance of hired labor, they have relatively little to do with the actual processing of harvested grapes into wine that takes place at the cooperatives and under the supervision of hired specialists. Therefore, while previous generations of small-scale winegrowers understood the process of vinification well, the present generation of winegrowers who are members of cooperatives have virtually lost this knowledge altogether.

The above observation concerning the loss of knowledge was confirmed by Raymond Frossard, one of the older members of the
St.-Estèphe cooperative, and Robert Leclerc, a wine-cellar worker at
the Sigoulès cooperative. Frossard learned vinification from his parents
and used to make very good wine in his own home, and was employed
in the *caves* of a noted Médoc château. He told me that he is one of the
few people at the St.-Estèphe cooperative who still knows how to vinify,
or in his own words: *Je viens à être comme le dernier des Mohicans, oui* ("I
have come to be like the last of the Mohicans, yes"). Likewise, Robert
comes from a family of winegrowers and so is conversant with all
aspects of winegrowing, having learned the winemaking process as an
apprentice to his parents. Robert related that although cooperative
members are sometimes reluctant to admit that they know very little
about how to vinify, for the most part they have lost a knowledge of
winemaking, especially the younger members, that was second nature
to prior generations.[6] This, he believes, leads to the vast majority of
members being disengaged from the daily affairs of the cooperative.

Without knowledge of vinification, not to mention the knowledge
demanded by marketing, it is nearly impossible for the average winegrower to play an active role in the governance and operation of the very
organization on which they are, at the very least, partially dependent
for their livelihoods. This places them, I contend, in a subordinate
position to technical experts hired by the wine cooperatives and to
larger growers who have the leisure to become involved in the daily
operation of the cooperative.[7] However, before the importance of this
development can be fully appreciated, especially in light of Braverman's
assertions concerning fragmentation and power, it is necessary to review
and evaluate both the actual structure and governmental organization
that is universal to southwest French wine cooperatives and, most importantly, the social composition of the cooperative membership.

THE SOCIAL COMPOSITION OF WINE COOPERATIVES

While there is little doubt that the membership of wine cooperatives is
composed of small and medium proprietors who have a subaltern po-

sition within the southwest French wine hierarchy, the internal class structure of cooperatives is by no means homogeneous. Moreover, it is important to comprehend the internal differentiation of wine coopera- tives in order to appreciate or critically understand how class differences influence the governmental process if not the operational structure of the cooperative itself. This is consistent with Marx's view that social relations should receive analytical priority over the technology of pro- duction and the product itself (1967).

At the Sigoulès cooperative in the Dordogne, 20 percent of its over three hundred members exploit less than a half hectare (1 hectare = 2.2 acres). Sixty percent hold less than two hectares, in spite of the somewhat puzzling impression of some members that the average hold- ings are much larger.[8] Only 12.8 percent own more than two hectares. On the other hand, there are nine cooperative members at Sigoulès, slightly more than 2.5 percent, who have holdings that range from sixteen to sixty-seven hectares. Of these larger properties, not all the land is necessarily devoted to viticulture as the Dordogne as a whole tends to be polycultural. On some of the large farms, crops such as cereals and tobacco are grown. Since Sigoulès is located in a less es- teemed winegrowing region, the size of the harvest is important for determining whether or not winegrowers will have to subsidize their winegrowing with outside employment. This is especially apparent once it is recognized that a hectare of vineyards in this region produces approximately forty-six to fifty hectoliters of wine and that this yields for the winegrower anywhere from 100 to 167 francs per hectoliter.[9] My informants from the Sigoulès cooperative led me to believe, and they are no doubt correct, that it was impossible to gain one's livelihood from winegrowing alone unless one owned from nine to twelve hectares of vineyards. Given that the average holdings are just over one hectare, a minimum of 60 percent of the Sigoulès cooperative members are obtaining their livelihood from sources outside of their own holdings. These outside sources range from working for other winegrowers who have large estates to being employed in the nearby industries of Ber- gerac, located only 12 kilometers from the village of Sigoulès.

The situation of the Listrac cooperative, like others in the Médoc, is not essentially different from what we have seen with Sigoulès. However, the primary difference, and no doubt one that is very important, is that it requires fewer hectares of vineyards in order to gain a livelihood because the financial return on Médoc wine is much higher than that of the Dordogne. For example, in 1988 members of the Listrac cooperative were paid 15,000 francs for nine hundred liters (one *tonneau*) of wine, more than nine times the amount received by the Sigoulès winegrowers (the permissible yields are approximately the same).[10]

However, at Médoc cooperatives such as Listrac, not unlike those of the Dordogne and elsewhere, it is not uncommon for members to have as little as a half hectare. This is in part due to a long history of partible inheritance. Nonetheless, even in the Médoc it is impossible to live off of the returns from a half hectare and so many of these individuals are, likewise, part-time winegrowers who gain the majority of their income from industrial jobs or they are employed by nearby elite winegrowing estates. These part-time winegrowers have little choice other than to work their vineyards in the evenings after work and on weekends. Moreover, because the Médoc, unlike the Dordogne, is monocultural, it is impossible for small growers to subsidize their income through growing other crops or raising cows and pigs.[11] Small growers simply do not have the option to augment their holdings because the price of land in elite winegrowing regions is far beyond their means.[12] In short, the fate of these smaller growers is more tied to the vicissitudes of industry, such as the closing of the Shell oil refinery at Pauillac in the late 1970s, than to the vicissitudes of the wine trade.[13] This is a testimony to their marginality to both the wine hierarchy and the cooperatives themselves.

The largest proprietors of the cooperatives are, to the contrary, less effected by the cycles of local industry than their smaller counterparts in that they have the financial resources to increase their holdings and to supplement household labor on their estates through wage labor.[14] Moreover, their attitudes toward productive resources are not all that different from the proprietors of elite estates and larger independents in that the vast majority reinvest their profits in family enterprises and thus seek to increase the size and productivity of their domains. Most of these growers, furthermore, especially in the Médoc, accept the standards of cultivation, production, and quality established by the elite vineyards and thus make an effort, as far as resources will permit, to emulate them. Such is the case with Albert Colineau of the Listrac cooperative and Pierre Besson of St.-Estèphe.

Albert Colineau's father was a founding member of the Listrac co-operative and Albert himself until recently served as vice-president. At the time of his father's death, Albert and his sister inherited their father's vineyards. However, Albert's sister, who had little interest in winegrow-ing, married a Spaniard and left the region to settle with her husband in Spain. Albert agreed to care for his sister's five hectares of vineyards, an arrangement that is common with partible inheritance, in addition to his own holdings which he has gradually sought to increase over the years. While Albert held back a modest sum of money for his efforts and investment in his sister's vineyards, he paid her a sum proportionate to the return received from the cooperative based upon the size of the harvest delivered in its entirety.[15]

In addition to the arrangement with his sister, Albert also maintains a partnership with another local winegrower, Claude Prévert—a situ-ation that is somewhat unusual by cooperative standards. Like Albert, Claude is from a winegrowing family. Likewise, his one sibling had little interest in winegrowing and thus preferred to pursue a business career with an American company in France. Albert and Claude cul-tivate thirty hectares collectively. The partnership is formalized contrac-tually and specifies details such as when a partner has to be notified of a planned vacation, even if only for four days. Albert and Claude believe that combining their resources enhances their potential for expansion while providing some mutual protection during the periodic difficulties of the wine trade. Not only does their partnership distinguish them from most growers at the Listrac cooperative but they are among a very few at the cooperative to have their wine commercialized with a château label.

Pierre Besson is, like Albert, vice-president of his cooperative. More-over, Pierre is following in the footsteps of his father, who recently retired from full-time winegrowing. Pierre and his father, Michel, are among the largest proprietors at the St.-Estèphe cooperative and like-wise have their wine bottled with a château label. However, their situ-ation is somewhat privileged by virtue of the fact that the St.-Estèphe cooperative has, along with the one at Pauillac, the most esteemed reputation in the Médoc. Consequently, a higher portion, nearly half, of the St.-Estèphe members are full-time winegrowers. In addition, the cooperative markets the wines of an unprecedented eighteen members with château labels. Nonetheless, the Bessons have managed to distinguish themselves from even such an elite group in that they recently purchased several hectares of vineyards outside of the commune of St.-Estèphe so that they can vinify their own wine at a recently constructed *cave* on their property. This does not mean that they have plans to leave the cooperative. Rather, Pierre in particular wanted to undertake the challenge of making his own wine, an option that is evidently not available to him, or for that matter others, at the St.-Estèphe cooperative. In this regard, Pierre's motives and actions are similar to those of the large independents.

Albert Colineau, his partner Claude Prévert, and Pierre Besson are not, however, typical in that they are among an elite minority of members of the Listrac and St.-Estèphe cooperatives, not to mention cooperatives as a whole, to have their wines bottled with château labels. This is accomplished by ensuring that their wines are vinified separately from other cooperative members, thus meeting the mandates of the laws that regulate the bottling and marketing of château wines. The château label gives to Albert and Claude's wines and to those of Pierre commercial advantages not available to the general cooperative membership whose wines are marketed with the cooperative labels of Grand Listrac and the Marquis de Saint-Estèphe respectively. While the cases of marketing cooperative wines with château labels are in the minority, it thus illustrates how the social or class differentiation of the cooperative membership is reproduced commercially and corresponds with the general social differentiation that separates members of cooperatives from the large proprietors of elite wines.

THE SOCIAL ORGANIZATION AND STRUCTURE OF WINE COOPERATIVES

The Médoc and Dordogne wine cooperatives where I conducted field research were governed in an essentially similar manner, as should be evident from the sample charter (Table 6.1). All the cooperatives have an *assemblée générale*, "General Assembly," *conseil d'administration*, "Board of Directors," and a *président* and/or *directeur*. Since the sample charter outlines many of the specific details of the cooperative government, I limit my discussion to those characteristics which I believe to be salient and which bear especially on the issue of the reproduction of hierarchy among the members.

The General Assembly consists of the total membership of the cooperative. While this is not specifically a policy and decision-making body, most important decisions which are made by the cooperative administration, such as those related to marketing or quotas to be imposed on production, are brought to this body for support. However, all major decisions which manifestly influence the operation and future of the cooperative must be approved by a two-thirds majority of the General Assembly. The cooperative cannot, for example, be dissolved without majority approval of the General Assembly. The General Assembly is required to meet once per year, as is the case at the Pauillac cooperative, but may meet more often if circumstances should warrant. These meetings are generally held to inform members of the state of the cooperative, financial and otherwise, and to disseminate information concerning such matters as new technology and chemical treatments for the vineyards that are effective against certain maladies. However, if the General Assembly meets only a few times per year at most, it is hard to imagine how the majority of cooperative members could play an important role in policy formation and decision making. This certainly was my impression and I believe that it is not wrong to conclude that the real power at the cooperatives resides with the Board of Directors and the president.

The Board of Directors is largely responsible for making decisions concerning all the important activities that the cooperative undertakes on a daily basis, from the harvest to marketing. It is the Board of Directors, for example, that oversees quality control both in the vineyards and at the cooperative and, as specified in the charter, decides yearly when the harvest will begin. Moreover, the Board of Directors assumes the responsibility for naming a president and vice-president of the cooperative.[16] The size of the Board of Directors, all of whom must be French nationals and from a member country of the European Union,[17] varies depending upon the overall size of the cooperative membership. Some cooperatives such as St.-Saveur in the Médoc have only fifty-five members while others such as Sigoulès in the Dordogne have over three hundred members. Consequently, the Board of Directors can range in size from four individuals to more than fifteen. However, in all cases the Board of Directors is composed of individuals who are winegrowers and members of the cooperative on whose Board they serve. Board members are elected by the membership of the cooperative at large and generally for terms not to exceed three years.

Because the Board of Directors meets much more frequently than the General Assembly and works very closely with the cooperative director, president, and vice-president, Board membership is a position of considerable responsibility that is also time-consuming. Consequently, those individuals who serve on the Board are, without exception, the members of the cooperative who are full-time winegrowers. The full-time winegrowers, as noted earlier, are individuals at the cooperative who have the largest holdings. Those who have to subsidize their income through working in a factory or some other enterprise simply do not have the time to become involved in the daily affairs of the cooperative and so they never hold an elected office or assume other important duties at the cooperatives. In addition, because those growers who gain their livelihood from winegrowing alone tend to be small in number, it is these same individuals who serve from year to year on the Board of Directors. In short, the cooperative reproduces governmentally the very class structure that is a salient feature of both the larger community of winegrowers and the cooperatives themselves.

One must be careful, however, not to conclude precipitously, in spite of the example of Colineau and others like him who serve perennially on the Board of Directors and who enjoy the advantages of a château label, that the class divisions within the cooperative are identical to the class interests of the larger winegrowing world. In other words, while the cooperative reproduces the class structure and privileges of the winegrowing hierarchy in general, it does not necessarily create, or even promote, an arena where the class interests of growers are opposed.

That southwest French wine cooperatives do not necessarily reproduce class interests, at least in terms of members' intentions, is consistent with Peter Worsley's principle of cooperativism. Worsley maintains
that "cooperativism is not just a technical division of labor—it is mutual
aid, a positive orientation towards others in society, and a particular
identification with the ordinary—a collectivist orientation which implies
the limitation of self-interest and the institutionalization of altruism"
(1971:2). Worsley's understanding of "cooperativism" was confirmed
by most of the smaller growers with whom I had contact in that they
rejected a view of the cooperative as an arena of self-interest or as a
vehicle for advancing the interests of the larger growers exclusively.
Rather, they accepted the practical exigencies of the relation between
available time and service to the cooperative and were neither resentful
nor suspicious of the larger proprietors. To the contrary, they were
grateful for the sacrifices of time that they believed were made on their
behalf. Therefore, in spite of class differences and the widely recognized
advantages that followed from commanding greater resources, it was
generally believed by small and larger growers alike that the prosperity
of the cooperative benefited the entire membership and was not partial
to social class. The response of Paul Lefèvre of the Sigoulès cooperative
to my question regarding the interests of cooperative members is rather
typical of the small growers.

> **Ulin:** Do you think the cooperative serves the interest of the small
> proprietors?
> **Lefèvre:** It was created for that. It was created for that. . . . At the
> beginning especially, it was for those who did not have the means to
> equip a cellar, to vinify wine, who didn't have a sufficient volume of
> production, who regrouped to vinify and later for marketing. In fact,
> they went together, but the first idea was to produce wine correctly, and
> since they vinified together they sold together. But I think so.

Lefèvre thus asserts that all members of the cooperative, small and
large, do not have the means to vinify and commercialize wine on their
own so that, at the very minimum, the common interest is established
from necessity. This is not to say, however, that necessity or exigency
establishes total equity among growers as the wine-cooperative move-

ment has always exhibited a tension between a pragmatic ethos supported by a formal equality and objectives that have been and continue to be more political.

Apart from the Board of Directors, the other principal agencies of governance are the cooperative president and the director. The smaller cooperatives, generally those with fewer than one hundred members, tend to have a president only because they do not command the resources necessary to hire a full-time administrator. Cooperative presidents and vice-presidents are always winegrowers and generally are, to no one's surprise, among the largest proprietors at the cooperative. Moreover, it is not uncommon, as we have seen with Colineau, for presidents and vice-presidents to be the sons of those individuals who were involved in the founding of the cooperatives.[18] For example, when I asked Bertrand Leclerc, president of the Pauillac cooperative, why he chose to work at the cooperative he responded as follows: "Oh, my father founded the cooperative. Then I inherited the property through succession, obviously, and continued. That's it."

Thus custom and kinship ties to the cooperative are nearly as important—especially in terms of sentiment—as the practical circumstances and exigencies of winegrowing production and marketing that make membership in a cooperative the most likely option.

Although assisted by the vice-president and the Board of Directors, the president of the cooperative has enormous responsibilities. Marketing is paramount—the president spends considerable time seeking out new clients, an often formidable task.[19] It is often small restaurants that serve as the primary clients for wines produced by the cooperatives and so the contacts are numerous and time-consuming. In addition, cooperative presidents must constantly work against the general impression that wines vinified collectively are lacking in distinction. This was certainly the problem faced by the Listrac cooperative in that its wines had formerly been served on the French national railway and therefore are regarded as common in spite of the fact that the cooperative is presently recognized for its primary role in the creation of the distinguished Moulis-Listrac classification in 1986.

However, and here the controversy sets in, it is often believed, especially by younger members of the cooperative who have had some experience with the regional agricultural schools, that the demands of the present exceed the knowledge and expertise of those who have the time to serve. That is, while members of the cooperative may be well-equipped to handle the problems that arise in the vineyards based upon years of hands-on experience, they are often thought to be incapable of addressing problems related to marketing and the finances of the cooperative, not to mention the rapidly changing and evolving circumstances of world commerce. This is thought to be so because the president is usually from the older generation and is often a person with little more than a primary education. Many were forced to leave school at an early age to assist their parents on family farms or they had their education interrupted by the Second World War and the German occupation.[20] This was most certainly the fate of Jean Barbet, president of the Bégadan cooperative, as he recounts in the following:

I've been a winegrower since the age of, my youngest years. I can't tell you the story of my life—let's just say I lived through the war of '39–'45, my poor father was killed in the war, and besides I was a little lazy. At the age of eleven and a half, I left the local school and then went to work in winegrowing.

This is not to say, however, that cooperative presidents as a group are lacking in competency, as one must take into consideration that these individuals are also full-time winegrowers and thus it is often more a question of time management or availability, given the fact that they are not compensated, than lack of experience or vision. As for the supervision of vinification, cooperative administrators are somewhat relieved from the primary responsibility for this crucial process in that most cooperatives have contracts with local oenological centers in the Bordeaux region to oversee the most important phases of the fermentation of newly harvested grapes and the subsequent treatment and aging of the wine.

One solution to limitations of cooperative presidents has been to hire a director, a course of action pursued almost exclusively by the largest cooperatives. Of the seven cooperatives that were the foci of my field research in the Dordogne and the Médoc, only three had directors. While in most cases, the presence of a director was related to the size of the organization, size being taken as an indicator of complexity of business affairs and of available resources, the one exception was Bégadan in the Médoc.

Bégadan is one of the larger cooperatives in southwest France with 175 members and nearly six hundred hectares of vineyards cultivated—certainly noteworthy by Médoc standards. While Bégadan is unusual in not having a director, in one important aspect, Bégadan did not depart from the norm in that its president, Barbet, is one of the largest winegrowers at the cooperative. While Barbet told me that he took great pride in his leadership at the cooperative, he admitted that the time demands and responsibility were nearly overwhelming. "So I am the president, therefore I have things to do and I am very busy with the wine cooperative. I spend lots of time, not full days, but almost."

He conceded that one reason that Bégadan had not hired a director was the desire to provide maximum financial returns for the cooperative members and he believed that an unduly large administrative staff would only increase the overhead of the cooperative and thus undermine this objective. This was also the reason that he gave for why Bégadan did not join, apart from UNIMEDOC, the full range of regional marketing associations, as do some cooperatives. Moreover, the Board of Directors and president were reluctant to turn their daily affairs over to someone who was not one of them. The Médoc is known for its suspicion of outsiders, or so my informants claim, as the outside is often associated with the intrusiveness of the state.[21]

Barbet fits the stereotype of the insider precisely in that he is from a local village in the commune which the Bégadan cooperative serves. He has been, moreover, an active member of the cooperative since 1953. Prior to becoming president in 1989, he served on the Board of Directors, as treasurer, and as vice-president. There is little question, therefore, that he is regarded as ideally suited to lead the cooperative, part of this responsibility being to mediate, and ostensibly to keep at a distance, relations with the outside world.

The Monbazillac, Sigoulès, and St.-Estèphe cooperatives all have directors. These individuals, especially André Demarle from Monbazillac and Charles Fresson from Sigoulès, distinguish themselves from the average member at the cooperatives by virtue of their university education and the fact that they are not from the local area. This was most evident with Fresson who spoke a "standard" Parisian French.[22] However, I had the impression from my Sigoulès informants that Fresson did not use his education and Parisian French as a means of asserting or representing a position of superiority. To the contrary, he was thought to be unassuming and, according to the testimony of my informants, was well liked and respected by the cooperative members. Demarle, like Fresson, had an educational background in business and management and was also well liked and respected for his manner and skillful management of the Monbazillac cooperative. While both Fresson and Demarle could have worked in any number of industries given their university training, they both expressed to me a special passion and optimism for their respective cooperatives.

The background of Jacques Dumas, director of the St.-Estèphe cooperative, is somewhat different. Dumas was hired in 1988 as the cooperative director, not unlike Barbet, by being promoted internally. Prior to his assuming the position of director, he worked at the St.-Estèphe cooperative for fourteen years as the accountant. However, like Fresson and Demarle, Dumas did not come from a winegrowing family. Rather, his family had long worked for the Société des chemins de fer français (SNCF) or French national railway.[23] Dumas admitted that he did not have the educational background of some cooperative directors, certainly by university standards and most especially in management. His first profession was in customs for an importing and exporting company in Bordeaux. Nonetheless, Dumas's experience with financial matters, combined with his general knowledge of the cooperative's various functions acquired through the years, prepared him to assume the position of director. However, when cooperative affairs did not go as well as some members expected, and this happens periodically with the cycles of the wine trade, it was not uncommon, rightly or wrongly, for Dumas's lack of formal training in management to be a topic of debate.

The director's responsibilities are not unlike those of a cooperative president. The primary difference is that the directors are not winegrowers and thus can devote their attention full-time to the cooperatives. This has enabled them to enter into some extracooperative commercial ventures that transcend the energy and time that can be expected from a cooperative president. Nonetheless, both directors and presidents are responsible for all employees of the cooperative and they serve, as emphasized earlier, as the primary representative of the cooperative to the outside, especially the state. The latter is perhaps the most important in that it must be kept in mind that cooperatives were originally created as a means of controlling the quantity and quality of production among small producers and as a vehicle to modernize the viticultural sector along capitalist lines. That is, while cooperatives did not create capitalist social relations, they nonetheless provided a central medium through which to rationalize the production of small producers and better articulate their essentially household production with the exigencies of world markets and the standards of elite winegrowing.

I argued, moreover, in a 1986 publication that directors are in a position, even more so than cooperative presidents, to establish and pursue policies in a relatively autonomous manner given that the vast majority of winegrowers are largely removed from the cooperative's daily operations and have minimal specific or concrete understanding of vinification and marketing, the two principal objectives that define the cooperative (Ulin 1986).[24] I have since come to understand better the decision-making processes at the cooperatives and believe that most activities are undertaken with the consensus of the Board of Directors at the very least. In cases where a decision must be made, the director will call a meeting of the Board in order to obtain their input and when necessary to take a vote on a course of action to be pursued. In addition, the Board meets with the director at a minimum of once per month and often every other week. The decision-making process, while formally representative in that the Board of Directors is elected by the membership of the cooperative, is essentially the will and vision of the cooperative elites.

Members of the Board and cooperative presidents and directors are well aware of the privilege and distance which separates them from the majority of cooperative members. However, they tend to blame the distance not on the statute and governmental structure of cooperatives but rather on a lack of interest that to them appears to be ubiquitous among the general membership. That this detachment or lack of interest is not simply their subjective impression is confirmed by a study that was conducted in 1987 by a group from the Département Economie et Gestion of the L'École Nationale d'Ingenieurs des Travaux Agricoles de Bordeaux.

The study was conducted at the request of UNIMEDOC, a collective marketing organization that represents the cooperatives of Bégadan, Ordonnac, Prignac, and Queyrac.[25] A team of fifteen researchers from the Bordeaux school sought to obtain information from the membership of the four cooperatives related to marketing, to communication, and the finances of the cooperatives. Unlike my own participant-observation which involved working with a small group of informants in the social round of their daily activities, the method that was employed by the team of researchers involved the use of surveys or questionnaires. The study was of particular interest to me because it surveyed the opinions and compiled the data from a sufficiently large sample of cooperative members, seventy-five in all, to be of some value in understanding the attitudes of winegrowers toward the cooperative system, especially in light of what I knew from my informants. The research team was careful to select a sample of winegrowers that was sufficiently broad to cover the age spectrum. This was an important strategy, as I noted previously, in that the perceptions of younger and older winegrowers often diverge because of different educational backgrounds and life experiences.

The researchers concluded, as I have above, that the administrators of the cooperative are extremely important in the dissemination of information to the membership as a whole. This is attributable, in large part, to older members who prefer to obtain their information on winegrowing through meetings or personal contact. For example, the researchers discovered that only 62 percent of cooperative members prefer to learn about new winegrowing techniques through agricultural journals and newsletters. If, however, one considers members between the ages of thirty-five to fifty-five, the figure increases to 81 percent. While co-op members under the age of thirty-five were found less likely to appreciate meetings, they did seem to favor, like their older cohorts, personal contact as a means of obtaining information. Most cooperative members also found television, which is popular in rural France, to be a valuable source of information.

The research team also surveyed the attitudes of cooperative members concerning the quality of wine, marketing, dates of payment, investments of the cooperative, management, results of the cooperative, date of the harvest, the ambiance at the cooperative, the nomination of the Board of Directors, and the sufficiency of information provided by the cooperative. As for quality of wine and marketing, those members between the ages of thirty-five and forty-five thought this to be more important than their older counterparts. The younger members saw the dates of payment as relatively unimportant compared to the group over thirty-five while the cooperative's investments were thought to be very important by those under the age of fifty-five. The management of the cooperative was seen to be most important by members under fifty-five while those under thirty-five saw the management and the results (e.g. profitability) to be crucial. The dates of the harvest were not of great concern. Only 17 percent of members saw the ambiance of the cooperative as important. Much to my surprise, only 14 percent of members saw the nomination of the Board of Directors as very important. Finally, the circulation of information was seen to be largely sufficient by members fifty-five years or older and lacking by at least half the members under the age of thirty-five. However, only 48 percent felt that the cooperatives had acted appropriately in informing members of the activities of their collective marketing organization, UNIMEDOC.

Members were also questioned concerning their participation in the life of the cooperative. Forty percent of those questioned claimed that it was very easy to participate in the life of the cooperative. However, when pushed further, it was clear that participating had to do with attending the meetings of the General Assembly (the meetings of the Board of Directors and special committees are not open to the general membership).[26] The members reported that only 69 percent always attended meetings of the General Assembly with a significantly higher percentage, 83 percent, for those between the ages of forty-five to fifty-four.

The researchers concluded that although the administrators did a fairly good job of communicating to their members information relevant to the daily affairs of the cooperatives, there was a manifest lack of knowledge on the part of members concerning the activities of UNIMEDOC. They seem to believe that some of this fault is attributable directly to cooperative administrators. Moreover, the researchers also concluded that both cooperative members and administrators were lacking in education. They maintained that the cooperative members rarely took advantage of opportunities for apprenticeships and knew very little about marketing, management, and finances. While this is certainly a weakness in the cooperative system, the judgment that the administrators themselves are lacking in education is especially serious given the considerable responsibilities of their posts and the degree of trust that has been invested in them by the winegrowers at large.

> The administrator is therefore very much in demand. Others delegate their decision-making powers to him, and he must be able to carry out this mission as well as possible. Since he occupies a very difficult position, the cooperative structure must grant him the means that he judges necessary to allow him to carry out his functions as well as possible. (L'École Nationale d'Ingenieurs 1987:70)

The Bordeaux researchers thus recommended that the administrators be given more education in all aspects of management and most especially in relation to improving communication with winegrower members. This does not, however, mean that the research team judged the cooperative system to be a failure nor does it support the impression that most cooperative members are dissatisfied with the cooperative system.

Although the survey conducted by the Bordeaux school is by no means exhaustive, it is nonetheless interesting to compare its conclusions concerning communication and membership participation with that of cooperative administrators. Administrators concede that participation in the daily affairs of the cooperative is less than they would like but, with few exceptions, see the fault not in their own lack of effort, or as I have argued in the structure of the cooperative system, but rather in the narrow interest of members in their vineyards and especially the issue of profitability.

Paul Roche, who is director of UNIMEDOC, the organization for whom the study was conducted, agreed in principle with the conclusions reached by the research team. He told me that the cooperatives must do more to reach out to winegrowing members and thus seek to improve communication in a manner that would be mutually beneficial.

Moreover, Roche confirmed my own conclusions regarding the loss of power on the part of cooperative members as a consequence of the cooperative's organization, although the institutionalization of the capitalist division of labor was for him a nonissue. However, as we can see from his testimony below, which was conveyed to me with intensity, he believes that the loss of control is the fault of cooperative members who only care about their vineyards. Roche resents their criticism of UNIMEDOC and believes that the independent winegrowers better understand his problems with the commercialization and finances of wine than do the members of UNIMEDOC. Although extensive, I reproduce his comments in their entirety because they convey a content and level of frustration that are not unlike those of the cooperative administrators themselves.

Clearly, clearly, a cooperative member, from the moment that he entrusts the vinification and he entrusts the marketing to another, he loses control of these two functions. Especially if it becomes more and more complex and he has to create structures, to create UNIMEDOC, because things [vinification and marketing] become more complicated. And UNIMEDOC has also created a structure or association. So there is a kind of delegation of power and you lose a little control. The member at the bottom has lost some control. On the other hand, you fight to create a situation in which the representative of the member at the bottom maintains control. So whatever association you establish, you build up a cooperative spirit and professionals, agriculturalists, and presidents will set the course to follow. Even if they consult highly competent people on the financial and commercial level, it will still be their show to run. So the Board of Directors and the president will not lose control. The members at the bottom, yes. Their calling, their reason for being, is to explain. But you know, how can you explain to people who are not in "the know," who don't experience it? And maybe based on that, on the restrictive side, that people say, ah yes, well, I don't understand all the aspects because I'm busy working in the vineyards. . . . If you are a member of a cooperative you must be willing to delegate a certain number of tasks, to sacrifice yourself for others. So it's not a criticism. It's just an observation that widens the gap and above all gives you the right to criticize without understanding. Ask a member and he'll say: I'm dissatisfied and UNIMEDOC is the problem. But he doesn't know at all, he doesn't know at all what is happening and above all why. That's the gap. The gap is in communicating and in not understanding what is going on. So when I talk to people who are not members of cooperatives [independent winegrowers], they understand all my problems, because they have them, not on the same scale, but they have them. Above all, people on the outside admire us more than our own members because outsiders know the problems, whereas the member, upon my word, believes he is up to date because he has his vineyards. On the other hand, he has his opinions and his opinions are not always justified.

While Roche accepts a disempowering of the average cooperative member as a consequence of what he believes to be a necessary organizational complexity that follows from the exigencies of international marketing and finance, he nonetheless maintains the conviction that cooperatives are democratically representative institutions. Moreover, he believes that institutions such as UNIMEDOC must be established in such a manner as to empower the elected representatives of the cooperatives. From what I could observe, there is no reason to doubt Roche's efforts to fully include these representatives from the cooperatives in the decision-making process, although it is clear that their considerable responsibilities to their own cooperatives means that they must entrust the director of UNIMEDOC and his technical advisors with the daily operation, or better yet complexities, of this marketing society.[27]

However, Roche exhibits complicity with what has become known popularly as "blaming the victim." That is, it is no fault of their own that the average grower at the cooperative does not assume a larger role in the cooperative's governance and daily affairs for, as I have argued, the cooperative is class stratified. Many if not most of these individuals are occupied by full-time subsistence pursuits outside of winegrowing or they work as wage laborers for the large winegrowing estates. While it is no doubt true, as Roche asserts, that the majority of these growers know little of the activities of UNIMEDOC, not to mention the activities of their own cooperatives, their complaints should be understood with respect to their own anxieties concerning subsistence and the marginality of their social position. Moreover, the historical mission of the cooperatives to modernize (to disseminate capitalist production and social relations), is not even considered by Roche in rightly concluding that the average cooperative grower has lost or given up power.

Roche is not alone however in attributing the blame for the seeming indifference and ignorance of the average cooperative grower to the individual. To the contrary, many cooperative administrators pointed out to me that they had done everything possible to improve communication with the cooperative membership. At Sigoulès and Monbazillac, for example, newsletters were established as a medium of communicating matters of importance both related to the cooperatives and the care of vineyards. However, Fresson, the director of the Sigoulès cooperative, admitted that while many members came by the cooperative to ask questions, most of these inquiries were related to their vineyards. He conceded, moreover, that he was better prepared to answer questions related to the cooperative than problems that arise with vineyards. Ducros of the Pauillac cooperative, and a member of the Board of Directors, complained, unlike Fresson, that not enough members passed by the cooperative to learn of its activities. To encourage membership participation and interest, Pauillac placed a notebook in the cooperative office in which members could write their concerns and questions, even anonymously. However, as Ducros remarked to me, the notebook did little to augment member interest.

> **Ducros:** In the office, there is a notebook open to all the members in which they can express their views, or if they have something to say, they can write it anytime. I can show you the notebook if you wish. Except for the president, the vice-president, perhaps four members of the Board of Directors, hardly anyone else makes an entry. Therefore, it is used, but that is not indicative of a cooperative spirit.
> **Ulin:** Because there are always the new technologies, the new ideas?
> **Ducros:** Oh, no, that doesn't interest them. That doesn't interest them. That's it. That doesn't interest them. Wine is a product that they really don't care about and I think it no longer interests them. I come and I say to them, as I say to you, what interests them is the harvest, the financial returns. The rest doesn't interest them. It's true.

Like the other administrators, Ducros does not take into consideration the contribution of her own privileged position to her enthusiasm for the cooperative, or the time that she has available to devote to cooperative duties and ends.

Of all the administrators with whom I had contact, only Demarle of Monbazillac was able to cast historical light on the issue of cooperative spirit and the degree and kind of commitment that exists today. He responded as follows to my question concerning the presence or absence of a cooperative spirit at Monbazillac:

So I would answer yes, but evolving greatly, if you will, greatly in the sense that the people who founded the cooperation, that is the cooperative, were pioneers who created during a period that we lived through here, namely the war. The cooperative was formed during the war. The cooperative was formed, like many cooperatives elsewhere, because of a profound need of men who united to survive difficult times together, so there was true cooperative spirit. That was really the cooperative spirit. The new generation of cooperative members is totally different. And I don't mean that the cooperative spirit doesn't exist, but it's completely, completely different. Completely different in that the new cooperative members are people interested in exportation and people who are very committed, financially speaking, expecting something else from a cooperative. They expect greater dynamism in responding to financial needs they might have. And after all, the market is different.

It should come as no surprise that Demarle describes the current Monbazillac growers as more concerned with exports and financial resources than either their predecessors or the majority of contemporaries at other cooperatives. Monbazillac, like the Médoc, is a monocultural winegrowing region and so has more growers, given the average holdings of 9.5 hectares, who are devoted to winegrowing on a full-time basis. However, while the new generation is primarily interested in finances, Demarle does not argue that they are highly engaged with other concerns at the Monbazillac cooperative.

There are numerous other directors, presidents, and cooperative administrators who could be cited in support of the minimal interest shown in cooperative affairs by the vast majority of winegrowing members. It is evident, however, that the problem of disengagement is understood, with few exceptions, as a lack of individual initiative. This is consistent with the emphasis placed on individualism in southwest France, perhaps most specifically in the Médoc, but as a form of analysis it lacks historical perspective, especially the articulation of the cooperative's objectives with the greater interest of the French state in agricultural modernization along capitalist lines. That the cooperatives have embraced agricultural modernization has a great deal to do with their reproduction of the winegrowing hierarchy and culture of winegrowing in both their founding charters and organizational structure.

I have argued that southwest French wine cooperatives through retaining privately owned vineyards and by institutionalizing a capitalist division of labor and social relations reproduced a winegrowing hierarchy of some historical depth. By adopting a uniform charter and organizational structure that duplicated the privileges and cultural objectives of elite growers, cooperatives relegated, albeit unintentionally, the smallest growers of their class-stratified membership to the margins of the decision-making process, thus leading to both their loss of skill and power. This is conversant with the process of fragmentation and control that Braverman has described in capitalist industry, although the degree of alienation experienced by winegrowers is much less apparent in that cooperative members maintain ownership of their own vineyards. However, rather than understanding their marginality as a reflection of class privilege, which should have been apparent given the subaltern position of cooperatives in the winegrowing hierarchy, the administrators tended to conceptualize the seeming indifference of smaller growers to cooperative affairs as a function of their individualism and narrow focus on their own vineyards.

Although there are important representational differences between Dordogne and Médoc cooperatives that are most evident with marketing, I maintain that the significant commonalities of organization and governance shared by the cooperatives of the two regions are a consequence of a uniform statute. Since the earliest days of the cooperative movement, the uniform statute was designed to mediate and control the cooperative membership by establishing production limits or quotas and by pushing small and medium winegrowers in the direction of agricultural modernization along capitalist lines. The cooperatives of both the Dordogne and Médoc have clearly pursued agricultural modernization as they have kept pace with all the latest technical innovations from steel fermentation vats that better control temperature to the selective promotion of mechanical harvesters. While this has enhanced their competitiveness with independents, it has also increased commensurately the indebtedness of the cooperatives and thus has furthered the pressure to produce classified wines in a manner consistent with the elite estates. Moreover, it has been the aggressive pursuit of new markets and marketing in general on the part of cooperative administrators that has enhanced the relation of small-scale cooperative producers to the rationality of international exchange, thus integrating household production more fully within the fold of capitalist social relations.

Although I have argued that cooperatives both afforded the French state some degree of control over small growers and reproduced the winegrowing hierarchy of southwest France, it is also important to acknowledge the considerable advantages over small-scale independents that have followed from membership in a cooperative. Most small-scale independent growers do not have the resources to vinify their wines and so they usually sell their entire harvest to large merchants who then blend the grapes with those of other growers. While there may be years in which independents are paid more than what one can earn from a cooperative, it is the merchants and not the growers that set the price yearly for their harvested grapes. Standing alone, one is more vulnerable to the fluctuations in market prices.

However, this is not to say that cooperative members are never critical of the financial returns received from the marketing of cooperative wines. Fresson confirmed that there was always skepticism among the Sigoulès membership because of concern that the overhead of the cooperative reduces the financial returns to members. However, not only does Fresson claim that cooperative members live as well as independent growers and are gradually coming to recognize this as the case, but he also points to the obvious advantages of cooperation in reducing the cost of production, leaving larger profits to be distributed among the members. In short, although the cooperative is a class-stratified institution that does not bestow privilege equally, it nonetheless has done much to preserve the livelihoods of those small and medium growers willing to comply with the national objectives of agricultural modernization. This is a testimony, moreover, to the wine cooperative's ambiguity—reflected in my own view and argument—and the necessary accommodation that small growers have had to make to the changing conditions of capitalist wine production.

WINE COOPERATIVES AND MARKETING: PROCESS AND ORGANIZATION | 7 |

For wine cooperatives, marketing entails much more than the individual efforts of cooperative administrators to manage the flow of commodities or the generation of strategies to place their wines successfully on established local and national markets. Rather, as we have seen in earlier chapters, the context in which the marketing of southwest French wine developed and continues today relates the particularity of winegrowing regions to a geographical domain that ever since the twelfth century has been international in scope. Moreover, the potential to market wines beyond the local horizon was not only dependent on the political diplomacy of nation-states and the articulation of winegrowing regions with international markets but also on the relations between producers who have long been stratified and highly differentiated. Marketing is thus an activity that is subject to power constraints that emerged historically from a world system of political economy.

The articulation of regional production with an emerging world market had much to do with particular vine stocks. The Médoc, for example, was planted nearly exclusively in vine stocks that are used to produce red wines because of the long-standing English preference for claret. The Monbazillac region of the Dordogne was planted in the sixteenth century with muscadelle and later on with the sémillon stock to meet the preference of northern Europeans for sweet white wines. The development of the *grands crus* themselves followed, furthermore, from international competition and the saturation of French markets during the seventeenth and eighteenth centuries with less expensive

Spanish, Portuguese, and Italian wines. The *grands crus* not only transformed the nature of viticultural labor and remade the southwest French winegrowing hierarchy but they also transformed the Médoc and other parts of the Bordeaux region into areas where winegrowing was pursued exclusively.[1] The political economy of wine and the international nature of marketing thus contributed to the identification of particular regions with a hierarchy of wines that has profoundly shaped the character of southwest French wines and the relations between growers.

The political economy of wine does not exhaust, however, the social terrain that is significant to the marketing of southwest French wines in general and those of the cooperatives in particular. As I argued previously, wine is not a "natural" product but is profoundly symbolic and cultural, having been invented or constituted historically through the efforts of elites during the eighteenth and nineteenth centuries to distinguish themselves and their wines culturally from the peasant masses. Moreover, the cultural distinction between elite and peasant wines would gradually assume formal legitimacy through the national legislation of the early twentieth century that was designed to reflect and elaborate reputed "natural" differences.[2] Winegrowing regions thus came to be distinguished not only by types of vine stocks cultivated and the character of their agricultural pursuits but also by the symbolic associations between their wine commodities and the culture and social position of those who were the proprietors and producers. In fact, it was the interrelation between an emerging worldwide political economy of wine and the cultural and symbolic construction and mediation of wine and winegrowers that was responsible for the establishment of the southwest French winegrowing hierarchy in the middle of the nineteenth century. This hierarchy persists today largely unchanged and has the practical consequence of affecting the ease with which wines are marketed and the return that producers will realize from the sale of their commodity.

The difference between the return that can be realized from elite wines and those which are deemed less noteworthy by oenologists, connoisseurs, and the general French winegrowing establishment should not be underemphasized as it not only distinguishes one region from another, the Médoc and the Dordogne, but it cuts across individual regions as well. One merely needs to recall the comments of Ducros (see Chapter 2) concerning the neighboring vineyards of Château La-tour with prices nearly thirty times those of her own as a case in point. The price at which wine can be sold is not therefore arbitrary or established autonomously but is largely dependent on a hierarchical sys-tem that is both comparative and comprehensive. This same system establishes a market value for Sigoulès cooperative wines and others of the Dordogne at a fraction of that produced by virtually all Médoc cooperatives.

While there are marked differences in the marketing potentials of elite wines and those of cooperatives as a result of the political economy and cultural associations of wine, it would be wrong to conclude that elite growers and other independents were unaffected historically by hege-monic marketing relations. To the contrary, it was powerful merchant families among a differentiated elite, some of whom, like Fernand Gi-nestet or Désiré Cordier, owned large Bordeaux marketing firms of some antiquity, who had the capital to purchase château estates in the Médoc that had fallen upon hard times, especially after the phylloxera blight (Penning-Rowsell 1969:166–67).[3] These merchant families not only played a significant role in restoring some of the southwest's most esteemed vineyards but they also shaped the course of marketing in the first decades of the twentieth century through their influence on the French parliament and larger winegrowing public.[4]

However, apart from their potential to acquire elite estates, the pri-mary impact of family-owned merchant firms was experienced by large and small growers alike through the previously described contractual system. That is, producers and merchants would agree in advance on a price that would be paid for the totality of wine coming from the yearly harvest. This was a system that worked to the advantage of merchants during crisis periods when winegrowers had difficulty selling their wines. What is noteworthy about this system was the potential of the merchants to dictate unusually low prices for elite wines. During the First World War, for example, merchants purchased elite wines under contract at a price (1,650 francs for a barrel of Château Lafite) that nearly equaled what they paid (1,000 francs per barrel) for peasant wines. The contract system illustrates that even those growers who controlled significant resources as proprietors of elite estates were not immune from the influences of powerful merchant houses, who could condition or shape the course of their marketing.

While there was some similarity in the conditions of marketing faced by elite and smaller growers, the latter controlled fewer resources and thus were more vulnerable to the exploits of merchants, a condition that the wine-cooperative movement would only partially alleviate. Prior to the creation of wine cooperatives, many small growers continued to harvest, press, and process their wines through the first fermentation (Loubère 1990:138).[5] However, Loubère remarks that there were levels of intermediaries that stood between the producers and consumers and thus limited, as we shall see shortly, the autonomy of producers (1990:178). Perhaps most familiar to the growers was the *courtier* or middleman. The *courtier* was a local broker who knew all the winegrowers and who would arrange for the sale of wine to a wholesaler. In return, the *courtier* would receive a commission of 2 to 3 percent. The *courtiers* were licensed and served furthermore as the agents who would guarantee the authenticity of the wine.[6] Loubère states that some of the *courtiers* specialized in ordinary wines while others focused on wines of greater renown. However, in spite of their personal and potentially convivial ties to producers, Nicole Ducros interprets the activities of the *courtiers* as simply exploitative of small producers.

Let's say that the middlemen did well there and that we small producers couldn't since we had to sell our wine for practically nothing. And besides, we were broke. So what we wanted to get rid of were the merchants who would buy at any price, well, at any low price, and who knew that if we did not sell today, we would sell tomorrow, because we needed room to take the grapes coming in. Therefore we had to sell. So they took advantage of the situation. It was exploitation, you see, exploitation of producers by the brokers (*courtiers*). Thus, I think it was exploitation.

According to Ducros, small growers were at the mercy of middlemen-*courtiers* prior to the appearance of wine cooperatives and thus dependent economically on their services and resources for both the purchasing of grapes and the marketing of wine.

Loubère argues that in spite of the manifest influence of the *courtiers* on producers it was the wholesalers who were actually the most important economically and professionally (1990). These merchants would purchase new wines through the *courtiers* and then store this wine in their cellars. Eventually the wine was blended and marketed under the merchants' own labels. While estate bottling at the châteaus changed the relation between these wholesalers and the elite proprietors, they continued to be the primary marketers for small producers of peasant or ordinary wines.

Small and medium producers, although able to process their own harvested grapes into wine, nevertheless found themselves dependent on middlemen and merchants who would dictate the price and conditions under which their wines would be marketed. Given the international extent of the wine trade, the constraints that it imposed, and the periodic crises in the wine trade faced by all French growers, it was nearly impossible for those with minimal resources to compete on local, national, and international markets. Moreover, the penetration and saturation of local markets by foreign wine, which has only increased since the nineteenth century, meant that local markets themselves were competitive and international and thus were not a safe haven for marketing peasant wines. While there were a plurality of motives that informed the founding of wine cooperatives in the early twentieth century both from the sides of the French state and those growers who would join, it was clear that wine cooperatives offered, as Ducros suggests, small and medium growers some degree of leverage in establishing their wines competitively on markets of more than local extent. Cooperatives also provided some degree of protection from declining prices and the potential of merchants to dictate the condition of exchange. As Loubère has argued, the goal of cooperatives was "independence from the burdens of increasing costs and independence from *négociants-éleveurs*" (1990:139).

MARKETING ORGANIZATION: THE SMALL SCALE

The primary objectives of every cooperative are, especially from the perspective of cooperative administrators, to improve the quality of wine produced, to assure that regional and national standards are met both in vinification and in the vineyards, and to make every effort possible to successfully market their wines with as a high a profit margin as possible. The marketing process at many of the largest co-operatives is overseen by a director while most of the smaller coopera-tives, with some exceptions such as Bégadan, rely upon the efforts of the cooperative president and the *conseil d'administration.*

There are currently so many inexpensive wines produced in France, not to mention the large number of imports, that marketing remains a formidable task for cooperatives and other small producers. Moreover, most middle- and working-class consumers in France and elsewhere are price-conscious, and competitive pricing is often a decisive component of successful marketing. While the system of pricing is hierarchical and comparative, cooperatives may set their own prices within this circum-scribed context. This was certainly the view of Jacques Dumas, director of the St.-Estèphe cooperative.

> **Ulin:** And it is here [the cooperative] that you set the price of wine each year?
>
> **Dumas:** Yes, the Board of Directors decides the basic sale price. Since the first marketing level begins with the barrel, for us the unit of sale is the barrel. I don't know if it was always like that . . . but the barrel contains 900 liters and the unit of measure is 900 liters, that's the price that is set and which is sold according to quality, taking into account increases. . . . It can vary, it can vary from 8800 to 15,000 francs per barrel for simply generic St.-Estèphe, and a little more expensive with the name of a château, because we can also make several château wines at the cooperative. That's the basic element. And then after the wine has matured, when it's set and bottled, then the price of a bottle is a function of the base price plus all the costs that we have expended for curing, manual labor etc., and the equipment especially, certainly with a margin, since if you want to make money you do have to have a profit margin. Then that sort of determines the price of the bottle fourteen months, twelve, fourteen, or eighteen months later, depending on when you place that vintage on the market.

While Dumas emphasizes the cooperative's autonomy in pricing, Ber-trand Leclerc, president of the Listrac cooperative, presents pricing as a more collaborative process.

Ulin: What is the system for establishing the price of wine each year?
Leclerc: Well anyway we go to meetings, hearings, inquiries, and these meetings are meetings of the Médoc-Graves group that I'm a member of, and we study things together and we see what we can do with respect to pricing. After these meetings, you have an idea of the prices you can charge.

Although Dumas is no doubt correct in emphasizing the role of the cooperative's Board of Directors in setting the price of each vintage, his explanation, unlike that of Leclerc, ignores the larger context in which prices are negotiated and then established. No matter how good the vintage, the cooperative wines will always be priced relative to the most esteemed Bordeaux wines. Moreover, it is the proprietors of these estates, merchants, and the various winegrower associations, such as Médoc-Graves, that meet each year to establish the general parameters for pricing all Bordeaux wines and so pricing at the cooperatives should be regarded as autonomous only in the most qualified sense.

Although the process of pricing and concern for profit margins are extremely important, they are not the only marketing challenges faced by cooperative administrators. The wines produced by France's over one thousand cooperatives do not have an especially favorable reputation among wine enthusiasts and restaurateurs who are potential clients for cooperative wines. Moreover, reputation can affect, in turn, the prices that cooperatives can charge and thus their profit margins. However, the problem with reputation has less to do with actual quality and taste, no matter how variable, and more to do with the cultural associations of cooperative wines with mass production. This was certainly the problem confronted by the Listrac cooperative in the Médoc because Listrac wine was once the wine for the French national railroad or SNCF. Some restaurant owners believe, especially those from large cities, that only a common or mass wine would be sold through concession and they therefore sought to dissociate their cuisine with anything vaguely representative of the common. However, the Listrac cooperative has made some progress in dissociating itself from the stigma of its railroad past by taking the lead in the recent creation of the Moulis-Listrac appellation. Moulis has in particular a number of renowned wineries and thus the new appellation has through a symbolic contiguity contributed positively to the esteem of all Listrac wines.[7]

The task of the director or cooperative president in marketing is to cultivate as many clients as possible—which can provide the cooperative with some independence from the large Bordeaux marketing firms. Michel Lebrun's comments—he is president of the Pauillac cooperative—are in response to my question concerning the most positive and negative changes at the cooperative.

> That's not an easy question. The best thing, so to speak, is that over the past few years we have developed a special clientele which allows us a certain autonomy vis à vis the large merchant. That is to say, we now sell to particular clients half of our harvest. Therefore we only have the other half to sell to the merchants. We are not obligated to say, okay to the buyer at whatever price. He knows that if he wants any, let him buy, because if he waits there will be none left.

Most of the cooperatives have been successful locally, as Lebrun's comments suggest, and one can usually find a cooperative wine available at small restaurants and *auberges* throughout the French countryside.[8] In local restaurants, most customers are keenly interested in sampling regional wines. Cooperative directors also have found clever, if not ingenious, means to promote their wines outside their locality.

The directors of the Sigoulès and Monbazillac cooperatives, Charles Fresson and André Demarle respectively, have collaborated with independent growers in the vicinity of Bergerac to promote their wines collectively. This is somewhat unusual in that while cooperatives often do collaborate with one another, it is much more unusual to form alliances with independent growers. Monbazillac has many more full-time growers and a much more esteemed reputation for its wines than Sigoulès. Nonetheless, the two cooperatives and independents believe that there is something to be gained through pooling their resources to promote wines of a region that is famous for its tourism and countryside cuisine. The advertising campaign to promote the wines of the region is directed at the large Parisian market and draws upon the general French familiarity with and popular appeal of Edmond Rostand's nineteenth-century play, *Cyrano de Bergerac*. Essentially, the campaign involved a large poster with an alluring portrait of Cyrano that captures his eccentricity and a caption that encourages the onlooker to try the wines of Bergerac. These posters were placed in the Paris metro and have been successful in generating interest in the wines produced in the Bergerac vicinity, especially on the part of those middle-class consumers who drink wine on a daily basis yet cannot afford the more esteemed southwest wines. Most importantly, the campaign illustrates the necessity of individual cooperatives to form as broad alliances as possible, even with producers who are independents.

In addition to the poster, the Sigoulès cooperative circulated a small stick-on label with a bottle of Sigoulès wine pictured and a caption that read "drink wine because water is polluted." As with the poster of Cyrano, it was common to use humor and popular appeal as a means of promoting name recognition for wine producers. The Sigoulès cooperative would also stock and market the wines and even cognac of esteemed producers in the general vicinity and adjoining regions, a strategy not unlike that of the larger cooperative marketing organizations. Potential clients, especially restaurateurs, would thus be lured to the cooperative by the esteemed wines but would also be given a sample tasting of various Sigoulès cooperative wines. It was then hoped, and this has proven to be the case, that clients would place an order that would include cooperative wines.

The Sigoulès cooperative has also recently undertaken the marketing of grape juice. While this is not common for most cooperatives, and no doubt unthinkable in celebrated regions like the Médoc, it is an idea that has served the interests of Sigoulès very well. Since Sigoulès produces a wine that is best consumed young and is thought to be ordinary by most consumers, there is no risk to the reputation of the cooperative in producing grape juice.[9] In fact, the cooperative is able to use its reputation as a winery to convince consumers that wine producers truly know how to process grapes and thus can produce a high-quality grape juice. There is much less involved in the production of grape juice than with wine and so it is a way to obtain a good return on a product that requires less investment of time and capital, while permitting the cooperative to make use of substandard grapes that would otherwise be discarded.

Although there are significant differences in the size of cooperatives and the resources they have to receive visitors, the reception of visitors is an important way to promote their wines. Both the Médoc and the Dordogne are resplendent with tourist attractions and so summer days in particular bring visitors from all over the world interested in sampling and purchasing regional wines.[10] Many of the château vineyards have very restricted hours for visitors, no doubt a means of preserving their exclusivity, and so this works to the advantage of the more accommodating cooperatives.[11]

Summer is also a time for regional festivals and the cooperatives take advantage of these large gatherings of tourists and locals to have their wines sampled. For example, each year the merchants of Sigoulès and Bergerac work cooperatively to plan a wine festival that is held annually in the village of Sigoulès during the third week of July. Merchants and winegrowers alike exhibit their wares in booths and the village square is alive with music, entertainment, and "invented" traditions.[12] Similarly, the annual St.-Estèphe festival of onions and garlic provides an opportunity to feature local wines with the added attraction of celebrities and politicians and a feast that is renowned for its cuisine and the continuous flow of diverse local wines. Most important for the wine producers, the festivals are an occasion for the judging of wines in local competitions where the medals garnered are used to promote and thus better market the wines of cooperatives and independents.

The strategies described above whether in the form of posters or grape juice may appear unremarkable in light of the earlier discussion of a world system of political economy and the cultural invention and representation of wine. However, it should be kept in mind that the strategies pursued by cooperative presidents and directors are contextual and in order to be effective must take account of how the cooperative is represented in the larger winegrowing hierarchy and what constraints and opportunities emerge in the shifting grounds of international markets and their mediation of the local. That marketing is not an autonomous activity and is subject to the constraints of representation is perhaps best exhibited through the controversy concerning the château label.

In spite of the popular association of châteaus with the houses of the nobility, the majority of château vineyards have houses which are sur-

prisingly ordinary. Although the houses of château vineyards have come
to symbolize the nobility for the general public, château wines need not
be accompanied by such material embodiments or evidence of a reputedly illustrious and distinct past. Rather, the laws in France regarding
the right to market wine under a château label, as I noted in Chapter
2, simply mandate that the bottled wines must have come from the
grapes of a single proprietor within a legally defined winegrowing
region. For the most part, this precludes cooperative wines which are
largely made from all the grapes from the membership. However, virtually every cooperative has some members whose wines are marketed
with a château label, and whose grapes are vinified separately.

There are advantages to marketing château wines as consumers
worldwide have come to identify the château label with quality. There
are, however, some surprisingly poor wines marketed with a château
label by both independent growers and merchants. Some of the largest
marketing firms, for example, buy grapes from numerous growers and,
like the cooperatives, vinify the grapes separately. Although the consumer
may imagine the wine to be "noble," many of these wines are not much
better than table wines yet they sell for a significantly higher price.

The proprietors of the esteemed château estates initially fought the
right of cooperatives to market wines under a château label through the
French courts. While the marketing of cooperative wines under a château label has currently had little impact on the celebrated vineyards, it
was nonetheless challenged by these proprietors in order to protect the
cultural capital associated with the château. Elite proprietors were concerned that the potential ubiquity of châteaus would eventually undermine associations of distinction that they have long cultivated. To date,
the courts have continued to uphold the right of cooperatives and other
small proprietors to market château wines provided that they continue
to follow the mandates of the law.[13]

The example of château labels illustrates, in spite of the apparent
equity of the court decision, that there is a structure of power that
informs the social relations upon which marketing is based, a point that
is made further evident through my conversation with Raymond Frossard of the St.-Estèphe cooperative.

Ulin: Are social classes important in the marketing of wine?
Frossard: Yes, yes. Oh you know, at St.-Estèphe it's a slapping match and we are not far from closed fists (*c'est la lutte à mains plates et on n'est pas loin des poings fermés*). . . . But I don't think at St.-Estèphe there's really a war. Because originally they criticized us, the large domains, because we sold our wines in supermarkets, this one and that one. Just go into a supermarket now and you'll see that the large domains have their wines on the shelf.
Ulin: And what do you think of organizations like the Fédération and SOVICOP and the others [for marketing]?
Frossard: Well, if you make wine, you need someone. The large monopolies at Bordeaux, the Calvets etc., have practically disappeared.[14] You have to organize, to make calls to sell your wine. Because if you don't advance, you'll quickly be set back.
Ulin: Is there a hierarchy for the marketing of wine?
Frossard: Of course. You have people who can pay 400 francs per bottle and you have people who can pay 40 francs. And when I say 400 francs, that's low, because there are some people at Pauillac and places like that who pay 5,000 or 6,000 francs or even more. Not everyone can. I can't afford a bottle of Château Margaux. So you see.

Frossard's comments make evident that there are real tensions between classes of growers, especially over how cooperatives have handled their marketing. However, it is Frossard's view that cooperation is essential for small producers and that the cooperatives must be aggressive in advancing their marketing interests. In addition, he suggests that southwest French wine cooperatives would not have nearly the success that they have enjoyed with marketing had they worked alone. While there is some prospect that the cooperatives would succeed regionally, given their personal contacts with local clients, this in itself would be insufficient to sustain the costs incurred by both vinification and marketing.

Moreover, as I have argued, the saturation of local markets with foreign wines has literally transformed local markets into international ones. This is most perceptible through the ubiquity of supermarkets where most French people now purchase wines. Initially, as Frossard remarks, the elite growers of the Médoc were critical of Médoc wine cooperatives for marketing wines through supermarkets because they believe that it would undermine the symbolic superiority of the regional appellation. However, the supermarket shelves today are stocked with wines from around the world and of all qualities and prices. Consequently, it is important that cooperatives have some success on international markets as a means of preserving ones that are local or regional. Even though Sigoulès produces only ordinary wine, this cooperative like others in the southwest has been successful, albeit on a small scale, in marketing its wines in Europe but to date has not found the means to access potentially lucrative American markets. For the majority of wine cooperatives, the potential success of exports depends on a multiplicity of marketing organizations in which the vast majority of cooperatives participate. It is thus to these large-scale organizations that we presently turn.

MARKETING ORGANIZATION: THE LARGE SCALE

The administrators of individual wine cooperatives in southwest France have come to understand the practical yet far-reaching constraints of the winegrowing hierarchy and the competitiveness of marketing that is international in scale. Most administrators have found it obligatory, therefore, to affiliate with, or even create, large-scale organizations that have done much to advance their commercial and sometimes even political interests. In the Dordogne and the Médoc, there are four principal organizations that serve this explicit purpose and with which I had various degrees of personal contact.[15] These organizations are La Fédération des Caves Coopératives de la Gironde et du Sud-Ouest de la France, the group Union Centrale Coopérative Vinicole (UCCV, which includes SOVICOP-PRODUCTA), the Union des Coopératives de la Dordogne (UNIDOR), and UNIMEDOC. However, it is the Fédération, founded in 1935, which is the largest and most influential of these organizations and, in my view, the one that is the most political in its objectives.

The first director of the Fédération was the charismatic and legendary Pierre Martin, who was especially active in organizing winegrowers in the Graves region east of Bordeaux. He brought his remarkable skills and political acumen to the leadership of this important winegrowing organization.[16] The Fédération, like the wine cooperatives, was founded during a period of crisis and extreme hardship for winegrowers. While the Fédération was modest in size at its outset, it was not long after its creation that it grew to include the wine cooperatives of the Dordogne, and then eventually Lot-et-Garonne in 1976, and the Pyrénées Atlantiques as recently as 1980. Altogether, there are presently eighty-four wine cooperatives that are members of the Fédération.

While the Fédération does not pursue direct economic objectives (the mandate of its charter is defined administratively), it nevertheless generates a wide range of initiatives that touch on the economic interests of the wine cooperatives and its various associations. The Fédération assumes, moreover, the defense of all cooperative programs by serving as a center of information on judicial, social, and economic questions—a point of view that is emphasized by the president of the Listrac cooperative, Bertrand Leclerc. "In any case, we have a federation, and it is the Fédération that is supposed to help us, to advise us, to pass on all the information that they can collect and to defend our interests."

Because the Fédération serves as a resource of information and a defender of cooperative rights, such as with the château label controversy, it compensates in part for some of the deficiencies of cooperative administrators, especially those who are full-time winegrowers. However, as former president of the Fédération Raymond Chandou notes, the defense of cooperative rights does not mean that "the cooperatives were an adversary of the merchant. Rather they seek to be the equal of the merchant" (Pijassou 1980:1056).[17] Consequently, it can be argued that the Fédération protects the rights of cooperatives by seeking to better accommodate to the existing system of wine production and marketing.

Most important, however, the Fédération provides education for cooperative administrators on commercial and public issues and thus constitutes the vital link between the wine cooperatives and various national professional organizations, a point that has become especially germane to the continuously evolving policies and affairs of the European Union.[18] The Fédération thus offers the individual cooperatives some connection to numerous levels of public power without which they would simply be limited to less effective regional and departmental channels.

At the level of marketing, it is the UCCV-SOVICOP-PRODUCTA, UNIDOR, and UNIMEDOC which are most directly involved with and thus important to the commercial exploits and potential success of southwest French cooperatives. UCCV-SOVICOP-PRODUCTA is the largest of these three organizations and is currently presided over by Pierre Chauvet, who is also secretary general of the Fédération and president of UNIMEDOC. Moreover, UCCV-SOVICOP-PRO-DUCTA is the umbrella organization for UNIDOR and UNIME-DOC, both of which are regionally specific and thus largely oriented toward resolving the marketing problems of their respective member cooperatives. Presently, UCCV-SOVICOP-PRODUCTA includes thirty-nine cooperatives located in the Dordogne, Gironde, and Lot-et-Garonne and encompasses a total of 6,500 members. The members cultivate an impressive 20,000 hectares of vineyards with an average annual harvest of 950,000 hectoliters.[19] Because of the regional diversity of member cooperatives, the group UCCV markets thirty different classified appellations of red, white, and rosé wines.

Chauvet believes, not unlike Frossard, that it is necessary to have an organization of the magnitude of UCCV especially if cooperatives are to have any hope of exporting their wines.

Because we feel and have felt for a long time that production was easy, but that wine cooperatives more and more had to preoccupy themselves with sell-ing. And it seemed more and more important to go with the current, toward the consumer, and under the circumstances to take responsibility for present-ing a finished product and for distributing and marketing that product. And it is also clear that a single cooperative does not have the means, does not have the scope, the breadth, the diversity that we represent together, and that un-der these conditions we could together, thirty-nine wine cooperatives, have impressive commercial services, go notably into exporting, and given the ever more exacting question of distribution, have a better bargaining position and make more attractive offers.

Although Chauvet summarizes well the advantages of cooperative mar-keting on a large scale, he merely alludes to the UCCV's special chal-lenge of advancing the marketing interests of cooperatives within a process of distribution that has become progressively concentrated as fewer but larger organizations handle the marketing of wine. That distribution or marketing has become more concentrated is confirmed by Pijassou who asserts that even the older family-owned marketing firms such as Barton and Guestier and Alex Lichine have been acquired by immense international corporations such as Seagrams (Canadian) and Harveys of Bristol (English) (1980:1054). While the process of corporate concentration in distribution or marketing may appear specific to southwest France, we shall see in the concluding chapter that the consequences are commensurate with those in other world regions.[20] Corporations like Seagrams, Harveys of Bristol, and more recently Santori of Japan not only have the resources to profoundly influence the marketing of southwest French wine, thus exhibiting the penetration and dominance of foreign capital, but their ability to acquire vineyards at vastly inflated prices threatens the process of succession itself among growers and consequently the future of winegrowing on both a small-scale and family basis.

The majority of French people now purchase their wines in supermarkets which in southwest France are increasingly chain stores such as Carrefour and Casino that sell wine and other products less expensively than local grocery stores.[21] These chains buy their wines directly from large distributors or marketing firms that provide the supermarkets with a wide variety of wines purchased in vast quantities and a smaller range of select wines as well. It is necessary for wine cooperatives to have a large and influential organization to represent them in the market to ensure their commercial competitiveness, if not simple accommodation to a system that they have no prospects of controlling. Furthermore, these same large-scale marketing firms or conglomerates control the exporting and importing of wine and so if cooperatives wish to sell their wines abroad, particularly given the bureaucracy and diplomacy that envelops international trade both inside and outside of the European Union, it is usually necessary to be connected with an organization of some critical mass.

The UCCV group is also composed of SOVICOP and PRODUCTA. As Chauvet's assistant Robert Cardon explains:

So the wine cooperatives produce wine from the grapes that are brought by the winegrowing members. That's all they do. After that, the commercial side is taken over by a certain number of commercial organizations. And you have five or six different organizations, but I think it necessary to concentrate on two of them, SOVICOP whose foundation in 1959 you heard about earlier, and PRODUCTA, I believe, which was founded a little earlier, also in the 1950s, each one of which serves two very different functions. As far as SOVICOP is concerned, it is an organization that is charged with the responsibility of marketing wine in bulk—what one calls *en vrac,* by which I mean not sold in bottles, for a clientele that is mainly composed, nearly 80 percent, of Bordeaux merchants. Along with this organization, there is another one called PRODUCTA that specializes in the distribution of bottled wine. You see on the chart below four bottling associations, which are really bottling factories, and always for wine that comes from the wine cooperatives. Then this product is processed, bottled, and marketed by this structure called PRODUCTA, and here distribution is essentially what in France we call mass marketing, that is modern marketing in big stores.

For wine sold *en vrac,* it is clear that the majority continues to pass through the marketing channels of the large Bordeaux firms—also true for cooperatives that pursue marketing on their own. This means that even at the level of large cooperative structures, there is no absolute autonomy or independence from the large merchant firms and multinationals, whether French or foreign. However, the size of SOVICOP in terms of simple volume of wine provides this cooperative organization with some degree of leverage in terms of negotiating the price to be paid for cooperative wines. The cooperatives are seeking to increase the percentage of wine that will be bottled and marketed through PRODUCTA, a consequence of which would be a somewhat reduced reliance on Bordeaux merchants as primary marketers for cooperative wines. Already PRODUCTA of Bergerac markets through some seventy French agents nearly nine million bottles of cooperative wines under Médoc, Bergerac, St.-Émillion, generic Bordeaux, and Entre-Deux-Mers appellations (Pijassou 1980:1056).

UNIMEDOC and UNIDOR as members of the UCCV group operate in a manner that is essentially similar to what I have described above. That is, both organizations bottle and market cooperative wines with the addition that UNIDOR, unlike UNIMEDOC, also sells wines to merchants *en vrac.* Both of these organizations were created after SOVICOP-PRODUCTA and their regional base gives them a somewhat different relation to cooperative problems and interests than

the larger UCCV, as expressed below by Albert Durafour, the technical
director of UNIDOR.

> UNIDOR was officially created in 1962. The member cooperatives of
> UNIDOR did not await the creation of UNIDOR to market their produc-
> tion. A certain number of wine cooperatives had their own marketing, a
> clientele of their own. And these wine cooperatives, of which Sigoulès is an
> example, retained their own clientele and marketing activities. UNIDOR
> came moreover to take charge of the volumes that were not marketed, that
> were available from the wine cooperatives. That's it. That is why there is an
> association that nevertheless markets important volumes compared to the
> small activity—small, average, or large depending on the wine cooperative—
> characteristic of the independent marketing activity on the part of wine coop-
> eratives. Okay? But there are nevertheless agreements related to the setting of
> price that are decided at an administrative level so as to avoid competition
> between the wine cooperative and the association. There is an understanding
> on pricing. There is maybe also some agreement reached on marketing sec-
> tors. It's not quite the same clientele.

While Durafour acknowledges that the member cooperatives have preserved their relations with long-time clients, he nonetheless seems to
emphasize the mutual accords reached between the administrations of
UNIDOR and those of the cooperatives. However, I was led to believe
by cooperative members (rather than administrators who had some
stake in concealing problems) that there is tension both over pricing of
wine and strategies of marketing.[22] Although UNIDOR is no doubt
closer to the concerns of the member cooperatives than the larger
UCCV, given its geographical proximity to the Sigoulès and Monbazillac cooperatives and the opportunities for regular exchange concerning marketing strategies, it is nevertheless symbolically associated with
Bordeaux by many cooperative members and thus perceived to be
distant from the daily issues they face. Perhaps most indicative of this
tension is the fact that the Sigoulès and Monbazillac cooperatives un-
dertook the previously described advertising venture with independents
without consulting UNIDOR. However, tension and the experience of
remoteness should not be taken as an indicator that cooperative administrators believe that their relation with UNIDOR is dispensable. To
the contrary, it is recognized that UNIDOR administrators do have

significant ties to Bordeaux and thus considerable commercial resources that they make available to Dordogne wine cooperatives.

UNIMEDOC, which is located in Le Gaillan in the Médoc, consists of the member cooperatives of Bégadan, Ordonnac, Prignac, and Queyrac. Unlike UNIDOR, UNIMEDOC has the privilege of the Médoc appellation which, as I have argued all along, vastly improves the prospects of marketing. However, the Médoc itself is divided into the appellations of Haut-Médoc and Médoc and the cooperatives of UNIMEDOC, unlike for example the Pauillac cooperative or St.-Estèphe, are marketed under the less prestigious Médoc appellation.[23] Nonetheless, UNIMEDOC produces nearly 50 percent of the appellation Médoc, which is a testimony to the advantage of cooperation over independent production at least for the smaller growers.

The director of UNIMEDOC, Paul Roche, believes like Chauvet that it is important to assume an active role in marketing.

There are two ways to market, the passive way and the active way. The passive way is to say: I have produced so much, I have produced seven vat fulls and I'll wait until someone is good enough to come and buy it from me. The active way is to say: I won't wait, I'll get organized, place my production on the market and guarantee it will be marketed. It is not a question of saying: well, this year I sold everything. It is a question of worrying about whether I've gotten organized to sell everything next year and the year after as well, etc., because the vineyards will continue to produce, because my cooperative members, they've borrowed, they are in debt for fifteen years, twenty years and they must have revenues for fifteen or twenty years. Therefore, UNIMEDOC is part of a marketing enterprise, namely the cooperatives sell a large amount of their wine to merchants, in barrels, and another part is bottled in the cellars of UNIMEDOC to be sold directly to consumers.

Apart from revealing that cooperative winegrowers live under a constant state of indebtedness,[24] Roche makes it apparent that organizations such as UNIMEDOC are a means to reduce the marketing dependency on merchants. Roche maintains that there is a secondary mission of UNIMEDOC.

I carry out other missions vis à vis the wine cooperatives and cooperative members. I provide services and I am there also to look out for their interests, the general interests of the wine cooperatives, the well-being of cooperative members and, if necessary, long-term planning to try and preserve the future by defending cooperation in general. . . . To be a cooperative member is not a sickness or a blemish. It's an honorable thing, it is a different conception of things, which favors the collective interest over the individual interest, it is a different state of mind. It is to see the general interest rather than one's own. So this mentality deserves to be, I would not say defended, but at least praised as much as others. So there is the reputation of cooperatives and in addition seeing that the cooperatives live on. If tomorrow there is a cooperative member who has a problem, if there are problems at the financial level, I'll try to make sure, even if I don't have all the answers, I'll try to make sure that the cooperative spirit persists and will be valid for tomorrow.

In spite of Roche's persuasive philosophizing directed at cooperation's critics, most unusual by administrator standards, he believes that the cooperative spirit should be praised but not necessarily defended. However, to his credit and that of UNIMEDOC, there is a personal concern exhibited toward the member cooperatives that is not in my experience replicated at UNIDOR or even the umbrella group of UCCV-SOVICOP-PRODUCTA. Nonetheless, the success of UNIMEDOC in marketing the bottled wines of its four member cooperatives transcends personal initiative and points to the significance of the formal connections between the cooperative's large-scale marketing organizations, the cooperatives themselves, and the important marketing firms located in Bordeaux.

The cooperatives, in short, have been innovative at both the individual and collective levels in grasping the ever-changing terrain of worldwide marketing. They have responded pragmatically with initiatives and on a scale that has in many cases made the member cooperatives leaders in their respective regional production while seeking to gradually reduce the long-standing dependency on Bordeaux's marketing firms by increasing the percentage of cooperative wines marketed directly to consumers in bottles. Moreover, they have managed to avoid some of the insensitivity that seems to accompany growing bureaucracies. There are frequent meetings between the administrators of the UCCV group and the regional marketing organizations. Although there is some risk of overcentralization by virtue of the fact that people like Chauvet serve in multiple administrative capacities, I was told repeatedly by administrators at all levels that decisions are nearly always open to debate and resolved by consensus. Most importantly, the leadership of the marketing organizations have been realistic about the power and influence of the large marketing firms, whether local or international, and have sought to establish convivial ties with these organizations without compromising their own interests or surrendering their current leverage to negotiate favorable prices for cooperative wines sold *en vrac*.

While the success of the cooperative marketing organizations discussed above are impressive and surely not lacking in individuals who recognize their resources as indispensable to the future of wine cooperatives, there are nonetheless some skeptics among the cooperatives of southwest France. For example, the Sigoulès cooperative, although still affiliated with the Fédération, is no longer a member of the UCCV group. The director Fresson and his Board of Directors decided approximately ten years ago that the Sigoulès cooperative could more effectively meet its marketing objectives on its own. The Sigoulès cooperative is not alone in this sentiment as both the Listrac and Pauillac cooperatives in the Médoc have chosen not to participate in the UCCV or any of its constituent organizations.[25]

There are somewhat compelling financial reasons why cooperatives would not participate in the larger marketing organizations, especially from the perspective of individual cooperative members. This was made evident to me by Jean Barbet, president of the Bégadan cooperative, although he is quite pleased with Bégadan's arrangement with UNIMEDOC. Each cooperative retains a portion of the harvest delivered by its members in order to cover the overhead expenses of vinification and marketing. At Bégadan this amounts to 10 percent but can be as high as 15 percent, claims Barbet. However, cooperatives that belong to marketing organizations must also pay for their overhead which can also amount to another 10 percent. From the point of view of the larger cooperative members, these expenses are often perceived as well worth the investment as they remove the burden of marketing from growers who are occupied with their vineyards full-time. However, 20 percent deducted from the returns of small growers may well be, as is often the case, judged to be an excessive and unnecessary charge.

The concern over the cost of supporting large-scale cooperative marketing organizations is further complicated by the often-experienced remoteness of such organizations from the average cooperative member. Most cooperative members, especially those who are part-time growers, know very little about the vinification and marketing activities of their respective cooperatives and, as we saw in the previous chapter, care most about their financial return. Their anxiety concerning financial return is partly warranted by the indebtedness of winegrowers and the periodic crises of winegrowing that must be endured. However, many of these growers have little time to pass at the cooperatives and so count on cooperative administrators to manage their marketing affairs and to make decisions that affect their financial well being. As Roche argued with passion in the previous chapter, these cooperative members simply do not know what is involved with marketing and resent whatever has to be sacrificed to support the general process. Consequently, at some cooperatives there is pressure placed on the directors, presidents, and boards of directors to keep overhead costs to a minimum as a means of augmenting financial returns.

The circumstances for Sigoulès's withdrawal from the UCCV has less to do, however, with pressure from its members and more with the size of the cooperative. Sigoulès is the second largest cooperative in southwest France and so with a membership of over three hundred persons has significant potential to fare well on its own, at least in terms of the French and English markets. Pauillac and Listrac, on the other hand, are somewhat different in being located in the Médoc and thus being able to draw upon the superior reputation of the region. Pauillac, in particular, is among the most famous appellations of the Médoc and thus while not having problems marketing its wines is faced with the problem of succession ensuing from the acquisition of vineyards on the part of multinationals. Listrac has been able to do well on its own because it has worked hard to cultivate a special clientele and has enjoyed the benefits of the recently created Moulis-Listrac appellation.

I am convinced, however, that the growing concentration of distribution identified by Chauvet will place greater pressure on all wine cooperatives to affiliate with one, if not several, of the large-scale cooperative marketing organizations. All of the literature on French winegrowing points to the importance of the American market, a market to date that wine cooperatives have had little success penetrating. However, as I have argued, even if the marketing interests of cooperatives are defined more in local terms, local markets have been progressively transformed into ones that are international, especially given what seems to be an irreversible trend in France to purchase wines from the large supermarket chains.

Marketing for wine cooperatives, not to mention independents, is an activity that is profoundly intertwined with a worldwide political economy. Not only does this political economy create important differences between the potentials of winegrowing countries, but in a manner reminiscent of Frank and Wallerstein's theory of core and periphery, though without sacrificing the vitality of human agency, it also establishes significant differences and inequalities that are also regional to France.[26] This is evident in the cultural capital to which Médoc cooperatives can appeal which is not available to the wines of the Dordogne and that is significant to the ease with which wines are marketed and the returns that can be realized for cooperative growers. Moreover, cultural capital also divides the wines of the Médoc themselves and coincidentally has made the most celebrated cooperative wines such as Pauillac and St.-Estèphe the first victims of multinationals that threaten the future of small-scale winegrowing itself. However, before we pursue this point further, let us turn to "winegrowing stories" so as to better appreciate what it is precisely that has been placed at risk.

WINEGROWING STORIES $\Big| 8 \Big|$

In her *Women of Praia,* Sally Cole argues that the life "histories" of her informants should be regarded as life "stories" in that she maintains that the concept of history implies a coherence or uniformity that is not consistent with the life accounts conveyed to her by her informants (1991). Rather, she asserts that life stories have necessary gaps and imagined components that she believes depart from how historians and other scholars view the process and product of historical reconstruction. Consequently, Cole elected to employ the concept of life stories in place of life histories to typify the style and content of what selected informants told her about their past lives and to ethnographically frame these accounts so as to allow her informants, as much as possible, to speak for themselves.

While it is true that memory, so central to the reconstruction of one's biography, is partial, imaginative, and often nonlinear, I believe that the contrast that Cole establishes between stories and histories is untenable.[1] As I showed in Chapter 1 through evaluating the relation of anthropology to history, historical reconstruction does not involve the simple discovery of "facts" nor does it have much to do with the efforts of scholars to uncover what took place in a reputedly fixed or invariable past. Moreover, as scholars who follow the so-called linguistic turn or discourse theory have made evident, there is no simple correspondence between the narratives of historians, or for that matter narratives in general, and states of affairs in the world, whether past or present.[2] In fact, the narratives that ensue from historical reconstruction, as Hayden

White among others has argued (1986), are rhetorical, imaginative, and even collage-like and thus much more like stories than the rationalized and uniform models that Sally Cole seems to have in mind.[3]

While Cole is mistaken in believing that historical reconstruction produces narratives that are distinct by virtue of their coherence or uniformity, she is nonetheless correct in emphasizing the selective and necessary incompleteness of informants' accounts of their pasts. That informants' recollection of their pasts can be characterized as incomplete is attributable, I believe, both to the opaqueness of their lives and the essentially dialogical nature of fieldwork encounters. No matter how perceptive the informant, the past remains symbolically embodied and mediated and thus memory conceals as much as it reveals in both its density and selectivity.

A view of informants' pasts as opaque and symbolically mediated does not necessarily mean, however, that one must embrace a psychological theory of the unconscious or depth psychology as a means of probing the concealed dimensions of their biographies. Although the anthropologist Obeyesekere has made a compelling defense of unconscious symbolic motivations along Freudian lines as a means of preserving the constitutive potential of human agency and thus avoiding the reification of collective representations through his theory of personal symbols (1990),[4] such theories ultimately eclipse the historicity of cultural meanings and social differentiations (e.g. class and gender) through their privileging of psychological categories and complexes (e.g. the Oedipus complex) thought to be universal to the species. That is, while Obeyesekere's theory of personal symbols has the merit of emphasizing human agency as formative of collective representations and the social order, ultimately this agency is presented in terms that reduce the broader sociocultural dimension of praxis to the invariable and the psychological. Moreover, with Obeyesekere, as with Freud, one is compelled to accept a priori the determinations of universally conceived psychological processes without however having to account for or even justify how these deep psychological processes themselves came into being and what shifting historic and social relations of power they may involve.

The limitations of a depth psychology or a psychological framework aside, it is nevertheless true, as Obeyesekere rightly concludes and Cole suggests, that there is "no getting to the bottom of" informants' reflections or deliberations concerning their pasts.[5] That is, the process of exploring life stories is always shifting and incomplete, reminding one of the infamous hermeneutic circle.[6] The more deeply one probes into the partiality of the past, the more one is forced to rethink the inconsistencies of the narrative that momentarily constitutes the construction of the present. The past in its multiplicity is thus in constant tension with the ever-shifting grounds of the present. The seeming opacity of one's past life is therefore a consequence of the mediative relation of past to present and the multivocality of symbols that envelop and enshroud one's biography, rather than a consequence of invariable categories of mind or unchanging psychological complexes.

The assertion that a hermeneutics of the symbolically constituted and mediated past should be privileged over depth psychology in the taking and understanding of life histories is not meant as an outright rejection of the psychology of the individual. There is little doubt that psychological models sensitive to historical and cultural contexts, rather than those that are exclusively universal, can assist the fieldworker in grasping unresolved conflicts and personal motivations that are significant to the past and present lives of informants, not to mention the relation between culture and personality important to understanding the human condition in its multiplicity. Moreover, as Paul Ricoeur has shown in his celebrated interpretation of the Freudian corpus, it is impossible to consider or evaluate deep unconscious motivations and psychological processes without considering their manifestation in language (1970). For Ricoeur, therefore, a depth psychology necessarily invokes a hermeneutic interpretation of symbols.[7]

I maintain, therefore, that the principal objective in taking life stories is to explore the fabric of social life, its constituted meanings, and social constraints broadly conceived which are not reducible to personal motivations, individual psychology, or within the historical disciplines, the cult of personality.[8] Thus in the taking of life histories, a critical hermeneutics, that is an interpretive framework that is contextual and yet sensitive to hegemonic social relations within and across societies, should be privileged over universal psychological models or those that focus on the motivations of individuals exclusively.[9]

The taking of life histories or stories is different, by virtue of the dialogical character of fieldwork, from the solitary reflections on our pasts that most of us engage in from time to time. The anthropologist and historian serve as interlocutors who through a dialectic of question and answer cofacilitate the disclosure and elaboration of significant events or circumstances of our informants' lives that have some bearing on the present. However, as argued above, even though the discussion of the past with an interlocutor may lead one to reach more penetrating or profound conclusions about the significance of life events than is possible in solitude, especially given the potential challenge and reflexivity of such encounters, this is likewise a process that is incomplete, partial, or fragmented, and constantly subject to revision. Moreover, from the point of view of a politics of fieldwork, it is possible, and even likely, that the taking of life histories or stories is imbued with power as the discourse that unfolds between informant and anthropologist is generally lacking in reciprocity and thus has something in common with the inequality of discourse that characterizes the therapeutic encounter.[10] Though important, interpersonal dynamics are, nevertheless, secondary to the larger political, economic, and cultural framework of relations between dominant and subaltern populations that locate informants concretely in a differentiated and often hegemonic social space and potentially transforms them, in Foucault's (1973) sense of disciplinary "gaze" or Fabian's (1983) more historically informed "coevalness," into objects of domination.

The manner in which life histories and stories are conceptualized theoretically and understood as a body of knowledge is, however, of no little significance in that this genre of ethnographic writing has taken on new, if not renewed, importance within the domain of cultural anthropology and likewise within the new cultural history.[11] While most authors now incorporate a chapter on the family or life histories of select informants, some anthropologists such as Marjorie Shostak have devoted entire ethnographies to single informants—as have historians such as Carlo Ginzburg. Moreover, both Shostak's (1981) and Ginzburg's

(1982) works have won much praise for, in Geertz's terms (1976), their "distance near" portrayals of !Kung San and sixteenth-century Italian societies respectively. In the case of Shostak, it is the eccentric Nisa and her forthright discussion of childhood, sexuality, and marital relations that gives the book an air of authenticity. With Ginzburg the authority of the text rests with the ostensibly first-person court confessions of the miller of Friuli, Menocchio. Both books produce the impression that the reader has come close to the life-worlds of the !Kung San and sixteenth-century Italians because the voice of authorship, and consequently its authority, appears to recede, or even abdicate, as the voices of the informants are foregrounded. This is, however, as James Clifford has argued, a rhetorical sleight of hand as the discourses with which the reader is confronted have been framed and edited by the ethnographer (1988). Consequently, the suggestion that informants speak for themselves, as if direct and unmediated, is little more than a seductive illusion.

In spite of the rhetorical persuasiveness of foregrounding the informants' voices and suppressing those of the authors, there is also some question as to the typicality of the eccentric Nisa and whether or not we can believe the court records of Menocchio's life based upon an account that was surely coerced. At issue in both books, therefore, are the rhetorical authority of the accounts and the degree to which we can generalize from life circumstances that may be particular to single informants.[12]

The discussion of limitations, especially typicality and power, of ethnographic and historical accounts that focus on a single informant should not be understood as a rebuke or rejection of this genre of writing nor should it be interpreted as a challenge to the taking and presenting of life histories or stories of multiple informants. To the contrary, the focus on the life circumstances of a few informants is, in a positive sense, rhetorically central for conveying to readers the seminal issues— political, cultural and otherwise—that cut across the range of concerns of a defined population or even a society as a whole. However, this is not to say that life accounts are exhaustive or that there should be any pretension of having "gotten inside informants' heads." The meaning of life circumstances remains just as opaque, multivocal, and shifting to the ethnographer and historian as they are to informants whose lives they only partially or incompletely convey. Moreover, life accounts do not speak for themselves and therefore must be viewed within a broader context of social, cultural, and political relations that they may in turn help to illuminate or clarify. Life stories thus stand with respect to ethnographic and historical enquiry as a necessarily fragmented, incomplete, and nonlinear complement, sometimes even a metonym, to the equally incomplete, but less fragmented, narrative of the social totality.

The collection of life histories is, moreover, fraught with obstacles, as most fieldworkers surely know, and like the life stories themselves, is nonlinear and often ad hoc.[13] In my own experience with French winegrowers I usually learned about their pasts through an initial formal interview that always took place in the neutral if not seemingly more depersonalized grounds of the wine cooperative. However, once I had the opportunity to establish more sustained contact, the conversations with informants were resplendent with materials, often merely anecdotal, concerning their personal and family histories. I discovered, furthermore, that while my informants would often discuss their lives informally and had their own fascinating stories to convey, they likewise demanded that I talk about my family history and life in America, a point that is exemplified well through the following fieldwork adventure.

As I noted previously, the Dordogne is a polycultural region and so most winegrowers pursue a plurality of agricultural activities. One Sigoulès informant with whom I worked closely, Gilles Darnaud, raised cows in addition to cultivating vineyards and asked if I wished to join him on an early-morning excursion to a regional market where he would try to sell two of his cows. I agreed to go along and was picked up at four in the morning for the nearly two-hour trip to the market, which began at dawn. After a morning punctuated with French farmers haggling over the price of cows with Italian meat merchants and learning to avoid the cows that were permitted to roam in certain areas unrestricted,[14] Gilles and I joined a group of his winegrowing friends who had also come to the market to sell their cows. It was common once the market activities were over, usually between nine and ten in the morning, to gather in front of the local concessionaire to purchase sausages and red or white wine and to mull over the morning's events.

Gilles introduced me as his anthropologist friend from New York and I found myself engaged in exchanging stories for wine. The winegrowers were especially interested in New York stories but also wanted to know about my past, what had drawn me to anthropology, and what I was up to in France. In turn, I was able to purchase rounds of wine in exchange for their stories about winegrowing.[15] This experience not only made evident to me what it is like to be subject to sustained questioning but it also pointed to the expected reciprocity of working with informants, not to mention storytelling. However, this is not to overlook or deny the lack of reciprocity or power inequalities that are often present in fieldwork encounters.[16]

In summary, the taking of life histories or stories is an important component of field research and ethnographic writing that makes use of the particular in order to raise questions about general social processes or even the social and political order, which, in turn, contributes dialectically to our understanding of the particular. However, life stories are necessarily incomplete and partial and thus are constantly, like ethnographic and historical narratives themselves, subject to revision. Moreover, the context in which life stories are taken is full of obstacles and constantly mediated by relations of power. It is for this reason, in particular, that a critical interpretive theory, rather than a psychology of the individual or universal psychology, is the appropriate framework for exploring the meaning and significance of life's multivocal reflections.

It is not the intention of this chapter to reproduce life histories exhaustively but rather to explore select features or vignettes of my informants' biographies in order to raise several principal issues that are relevant, if not of acknowledged concern, to all the cooperative winegrowers with whom I worked in southwest France. While there are numerous informants that I have come to know well and whose life stories could thus fulfill the above objective, I will limit my winegrowing stories to Nicole Ducros, Albert Colineau, and the father-son team of Michel and Pierre Besson. With Nicole Ducros we have the opportunity to learn more about the problems of female winegrowers while with Albert Colineau, Michel, and Pierre Besson we will pursue the problems of social class and succession. Nevertheless, the theoretical and practical concerns that I raised about life stories are equally applicable to the more limited use that I will make of these informants' biographies. The accounts are therefore necessarily fragmentary and make no pretensions of exhausting the importance of events and circumstances as they have been experienced by my informants. However, as we shall see in the following, the biographies of these informants are also windows on more general social processes, some of which are potentially international in scale.

NICOLE DUCROS

Paul Rabinow argues that the best informants are not only intelligent but they have an unusual capacity for reflection or criticism with respect to their own life circumstances and the customs, conditions, and social relations of their respective societies (1973). Moreover, Rabinow suggests that informants who are regarded as socially marginal are most likely to exhibit the critical sensibility essential to grasping social life objectively.[17] Although her standing at the Pauillac wine cooperative is anything but marginal, we shall see that Nicole Ducros nonetheless exhibits the salient characteristics of intelligence and critical reflection that make her, according to Rabinow's criteria, an outstanding coparticipant in social and ethnographic inquiry.

I first met Nicole Ducros at the Pauillac wine cooperative in the winter of 1989 at the commencement of the Médoc component of my field research. Although I encountered older informants who had more extensive and immediate experience with the cooperative's past, I was instantly impressed by Nicole's intelligence, passion for winegrowing and cooperative life, and her forthrightness, some of which we have encountered in previous chapters. Moreover, given the personal adversity that she has endured, Nicole exhibited a resilience and remarkable strength of character that was acknowledged by virtually every cooperative grower whom I encountered in the Pauillac vicinity. Nicole was, furthermore, only the third full-time female winegrower that I had met in the ten years of my research on southwest French wine cooperatives and for this alone her life story is well worth pursuing.[18]

Nicole was born in the Pyrénées and moved to the Médoc with her parents and four siblings just after the conclusion of the Second World War when she was only ten years old. Although she was largely raised in the Médoc, her place of birth established her technically as an outsider and therefore not a "true" Médocian.[19] However, this was not an enduring stigma as those persons, especially winegrowers, who had long lived in the Médoc were fully accepted by those native to the region.

Nicole's parents were not winegrowers but rather gained their livelihood in the Médoc, as they had in the Pyrénées, through the sharecropping of cereals, from raising cows, and fishing.[20] It was through her marriage to her Médocian husband that Nicole was introduced to winegrowing. At the time of her marriage, Nicole's husband still worked with his father, affectionately known to all as "Papi," who was one of the original founding members of the Pauillac cooperative. Nicole's father-in-law was representative, moreover, of a rapidly disappearing small grower in that he possessed considerable knowledge of vinification as a consequence of having served for several years as the wine-cellar master of the Bégadan cooperative prior to his association with Pauillac.

Nicole claims that it was her love for and devotion to her husband that attracted her to winegrowing. However, as she conveys below, she also found winegrowing and its associated activities to be interesting, a view that is not all that common given the repetitiveness of work in the winegrowing cycle.

My marriage led me to learn how to work in the vineyards and so forth. It was something I liked very much, that I really enjoyed, because if you watch the development, if you observe really well, if you observe really well, it's very interesting to follow a vine from the moment when you plant it to the moment when the grapes fall. It's very interesting and I really liked it. And with my husband we were really a team, we did that very well, we got along very well because he took care of the farm and I took care of bookkeeping and other things. And that's how I came to be at the cooperative.

There is little doubt that Nicole's pleasure and interest in winegrowing also came from shared responsibilities with her husband. The division of labor to which she alludes is common where a husband–wife team is involved, as with the Bosquets of the Sigoulès cooperative. However, as noted in Chapter 5, it is the men who assume the primary responsibility for labor in the vineyards. Nicole describes herself as helping her husband as needed with various activities in the vineyards such as pruning, yet it is she who assumes the sole responsibility for the important task of bookkeeping. It would be precipitous to conclude that the division of labor between Nicole and her husband was indicative of her subordination. To the contrary, her management of the books was an extension of her management of household finances, a significant arena in which her husband and father-in-law were dependents.

There has been a tendency in anthropology, however, especially its more orthodox marxist versions, to regard the division of labor by gender, whereby women assume primary responsibility for the private sphere of the household and men for the public sphere of work, as a historically evolved condition of female subordination. It is Engels (1972) more than Marx who bears responsibility for the origin of this assertion through attributing female subordination to the evolution of private property, the eclipsing of kinship by civil society, and the distinction between public and private that appears to follow from the development of the state. This has led, in turn, anthropologists like Anton Blok (1981), Campbell (1964), or du Boulay (1974) to conclude erroneously that the division between public and private space and coincident association of men with honor and women with shame, is a testimony to female subordination. However, this assertion has been challenged by anthropologists such as Jill Dubisch (1993) working in Greece, Sally Cole (1991) in Portugal, and Susan Rogers (1975) in France who argue that the division between public and private has been conventionally represented by most scholars in essentially static and reified terms and does not take into consideration how gender and the division of social space participates in wider social practices and processes. Dubisch maintains, for example, following Herzfeld (1987), that public and private, or inside and outside, can be extended to insiders' and outsiders' views of Greece whereby the Hellenic is associated by western Europeans with the outside, especially classical Greece, and the Romeic by Greeks themselves with the inside. Thus, she maintains that women as a symbol of the inside can represent Greece itself. According to Dubisch, "Gender becomes part of a discourse about reputation and bound-aries, and about the power and willingness to defend them" (1993:280).

Rogers suggests, on the other hand, that the division between public and private in peasant societies is largely a fiction that is supported by men and women alike to preserve power in their respective domains (1975, 1985). Although less committed to Rogers's notion of public and private as a fiction, Sally Cole nevertheless argues that women identify with work and thus in the case of the Portuguese fisherwomen she studied, they saw themselves as skillful managers of household resources and not as subordinates to their marital partners (1991:40). Cole's fe-male informants received public recognition for their managerial skills and their control of household resources gave them considerable influ-ence and power in the context of familial relations. The division there-fore between an ostensibly male public and female private or female household labor and male work performed outside the house is fluid and subject to mediation on both the local and national levels and should not be taken as a static index of domination in the context of rural European society.

Although Nicole Ducros assumed primary responsibility for the management of household resources rather than the cultivation of vine-yards, she enjoyed, like the Portuguese fisherwomen, a position of re-spect and influence within her winegrowing household. However, in spite of her relative equality, winegrowing in southwest France was nonetheless viewed by the majority of winegrowers, most of whom are male, as a predominantly male pursuit. Some of my informants attrib-uted the gender identity of winegrowing to the long-standing associa-tion of wine with the patriarchal Catholic Church while others sug-gested that some of the labor, such as pruning, was simply too difficult for women. In spite of some examples to the contrary, one informant from the Listrac cooperative, Marcel Armand, contended that: "So the Médoc is one of the rare regions, if not the only one, where women do not prune. I don't know why. But in Entre-Deux-Mers and elsewhere the women prune, but in the Médoc the women don't prune."

I suspect, however, that winegrowing, like weaving, came progres-sively under the control of men as winegrowing assumed more pro-nounced capitalist social relations, and with monocropping in particular wine became the principal source of household income. This can be seen in part, as I argued in Chapter 3, through the history of the *grands crus*. Families of workers housed on the winegrowing estates, with both men and women participating in winegrowing labor, were replaced by a more highly developed division of labor and the wage labor contract. Under these conditions, it was men who assumed the supervisory position in the vineyards of the elite winegrowing estates with a commensurate development to follow, though less rigidly defined, in the independent winegrowing households.

The specific historical reasons aside, Nicole's fortunes would take a turn for the worse when her husband died in 1980. With an aging father-in-law, she was forced to assume primary responsibility for the sizable family winegrowing estate of 12.5 hectares, 3.5 of which were share-cropped while the remainder was directly cultivated by the family. Although Nicole was thought of as very able, she had much to prove in this largely male winegrowing community of Pauillac. Moreover, Nicole had three children, two boys and a girl, one of whom was young enough to demand a fair amount of attention. The girl, who was the oldest and now a young woman, had gone to Bordeaux to pursue a career in the hotel industry. The older boy, now a young man, remained at home to provide his mother with some assistance in the vineyards, particularly in light of his grandfather's advanced age and inability to work as he had in the past. In spite of the pain and practical difficulties precipitated by the loss of her husband, Nicole was resolute and it was not long before she also gained recognition as a very capable wine-grower. To help with the work in the vineyards, she eventually hired two workers, one French and the other Portuguese, with whom she worked side by side. While she attributes much of her success to what she learned about winegrowing from her husband, her management of household and family vineyards is surely a testimony to skills of her own.

Nicole's outspokenness and devotion to the Pauillac cooperative resulted in her being the first woman to be elected to the *conseil d'admini-stration,* a not-to-be underestimated feat as Pauillac itself was the first cooperative in the Médoc to elect a woman to the Board of Directors.[21] As a member of the *conseil d'administration,* Nicole has the opportunity to meet with winegrowers from other cooperatives in any number of regional winegrowing organizations. It is here that she has met the largest resistance as a female winegrower.

> **Ulin:** Are there special problems for the female winegrowers?
> **Ducros:** Special, not really. But to begin with I say that it's hard to get along, that when a woman says certain things, it doesn't go over well. On the other hand, that's what I did at an agricultural meeting last year. A VIP, shall we say, had hurt my feelings during my first year there, because he hadn't thought I'd be there and had made some uncalled-for comments. I went back last year to this same agricultural meeting and this same person, this same VIP, reenacted the comments. So I was at one end of the table, took the floor, and some people laughed. And I spoke my mind and someone, a château owner, who was there said: "Eh well, that's the first time that a woman dared to say what she thinks." And I said: "Eh well, I'm delighted." So I defended myself because a woman must defend herself (*Alors, je me défends, parce que, une femme doit se défendre*).

As suggested above, much of the difficulty for female winegrowers is interpersonal, enduring male ridicule, although there can be more serious consequences in terms of policy if male winegrowers fail to listen to their female colleagues. Moreover, there are numerous wine cooperatives where women are not represented on the *conseil d'administration* and so there is a considerable challenge of gender inequality that remains to be addressed by the winegrowing sector as a whole. However, gender has presently little to do with the ability to obtain loans from Crédit Agricole and so female winegrowers have the same potential for expanding their vineyards as do their male counterparts.

The challenge that Nicole faces as a female winegrower is not confined to public meetings but has also manifested itself directly in her own extended household. As noted previously, Nicole's eldest son assisted her with labor in the vineyards at the time of her husband's death. However, after about six or seven years working with his mother, the son elected to take a job driving a tractor and working in the vineyards of the esteemed Château Lafite, a decision that Nicole explains to me in the following manner.

Ulin: What does your son do at Château Lafite?

Ducros: But he drives a tractor, he drives a tractor. He works in the vineyards, he does what he had done at my place.

Ulin: He prefers to work there?

Ducros: Yes, yes. Because I think there was nevertheless a problem with my son, because he's like many men; he does not feel at ease when it is a woman who owns the establishment. And I think that there are very many like that. So it was in his interest to leave.

Ulin: Maybe when you retire?

Ducros: Maybe he'll be more mature, maybe he'll appreciate the advantages of working for a boss and the advantages of working at his home. Perhaps he will maybe have thought about it. I hope so.

While Nicole's problems with her son may be particular, they are also consistent with the anxiety faced by most cooperative winegrowers about succession. In the case of Nicole, I recently learned from another informant with whom I have regular correspondence, that Nicole had given up hope in her eldest son's return and decided to sell her vineyards to one of France's largest insurance companies—an issue that will be explored further in the next chapter as it quite obviously bears on the future of southwest French wine cooperatives.

Nicole saw her devotion to the Pauillac wine cooperative as a measure of the shortcomings of many of her colleagues, especially the younger growers who in her view valued profitability over tradition. While not discrediting her enthusiasm, it should be kept in mind that the time and energy that she could commit to the cooperative, as with all members of the *conseil d'administration,* was a consequence of her class privilege in being one of the larger growers at the Pauillac cooperative. Nonetheless, she provided me with a wealth of material and critical insight on how the Pauillac cooperative operates and the relations between classes of growers both inside and outside the cooperative. However, it was her forthrightness, sharp wit, and especially her outspokenness, a characteristic celebrated when associated with men but stigmatized when associated with women, that made her respected by some but marginal to others. Nevertheless, it was her conviction that women must "*se défendre*" or defend themselves. Her particular plight as a woman and associated problem of succession makes her life story exemplary of salient issues that cut across the winegrowing sector with implications that, as we shall see, are even international in scale.

ALBERT COLINEAU

I first met Albert Colineau at the Listrac cooperative in the Médoc where he was a member and vice-president. Our first meeting consisted of a group interview with a cross-section of older and younger Listrac cooperative winegrowers. Albert was the most verbal of this group and like Nicole was able to articulate the winegrowers' concerns and to examine critically the cooperative's past and present. Because of a common interest in history and our nearly similar age, we also established a special rapport. Although I lived in a small apartment near the University of Bordeaux for the majority of time that I conducted research in the Médoc,[22] I spent the summer of 1990 in Albert's household and have been a welcome guest there on numerous other occasions. This afforded many opportunities to discuss late into the night, usually over a bottle of wine, aspects of Albert's past, the life of a cooperative winegrower, French politics, my life in America, and any number of other topical issues related to winegrowing.

Unlike Nicole Ducros, Albert comes from a family with a long history of winegrowing in the Médoc. Albert's grandfather had been a founding member of the Listrac cooperative and one of its first presidents.[23] His grandfather was, like many of the early cooperative founders, from a social class that Albert describes as *demi-bourgeois* or petit bourgeois which means essentially that he was a small independent proprietor with a sufficiently large estate to gain his livelihood from winegrowing alone, and he had the financial means to retain a few employees to assist him with work in the vineyards. However, as noted in earlier chapters, the 1930s were difficult times for winegrowers and so Albert's grandfather, like many small growers of the time, was motivated to form a cooperative out of a combination of practical concerns and exigencies and a politics that was sympathetic to small growers and the French working class. Moreover, Albert's grandfather, like his father, had to endure the difficulty of the war years and the German occupation. Although the Germans did not destroy the vineyards and were actually good consumers of Médoc wine, some of it obtained less expensively through a widespread black market, they did occupy the very same Colineau family home in which Albert lives with his wife today.

Albert's father followed in the footsteps of his own father as both a winegrower and president of the Listrac cooperative. However, while Albert's father was encouraged to pursue the family occupation of wine-grower, Albert himself was discouraged. In fact, as Albert explains below, this was quite common in winegrower families during periods marked by difficulties in marketing wine profitably, such as was characteristic of the mid to late 1960s, and so young males in particular who showed some promise in school were encouraged to follow an alternate profession.

What's also true is that during this period, when a son was young—it's a little like my situation—namely around 1965, the times were very bad. And there was no one who encouraged their children to follow the same profession. Many of them left at that time. They left to go into administration or other things, or the professorate, or no matter what. But they really had to do something else because their parents encouraged them to do something else and advised them against remaining on the farm because we lived very badly during this period.

Albert was a very good student and so his parents encouraged him to pursue his studies at the University of Bordeaux which he did with the intention of becoming a history teacher. However, Albert's fortunes would take an unexpected turn with the sudden death of his father while he was still in the midst of his studies.

I studied history. I completed a bachelor's degree in history,[24] then I began a master's degree and at that moment my father died. For a year, I did both, winegrowing and history. And finally, I did both badly and I opted to continue with the farm. I tell myself from time to time that if I had to do it again, I would do the same thing.

Albert expressed to me on several occasions that he knows few other occupations where one can meet leisurely in the afternoon with friends or even entertain the questions of an American anthropologist. However, the consequences of his choice were also familial in that Albert has only one sibling, a sister, who never entertained the thought of winegrowing while Albert's mother was only minimally involved in helping her husband in the vineyards. Like many wives in the Médoc, she would gather the discarded vines that had been pruned and assumed domestic responsibilities, such as cooking meals, for the troupe of harvesters who would descend annually in the fall. For Albert, the possibility of pursuing the teaching of history as a career left him with the emotionally charged and thus difficult option of selling vineyards that had been in the family for generations.

Although Albert eventually chose winegrowing over history, his university background had a pronounced influence on his life that made him unique among the vast majority of older growers and even set him apart from younger growers at the cooperative, few of whom had experience beyond the regional agricultural schools. Moreover, Albert married a professional woman—an unusual pattern in the Médoc, even among the younger generation. His wife, Marie Dumas-Colineau, is a dentist and she is distinguished by virtue of the fact that dentistry is largely a male profession in France. While it is difficult to establish a dentistry practice in the countryside, Marie had the good fortune of being able to purchase a practice in the village of Listrac from a colleague who was retiring. Albert is very supportive of Marie's career, which he regards as even more demanding than his own. However, it also means that Marie is not available to assist him with his work in the vineyards and most especially during the busy period of the harvest.

Marie and Albert do not have children. Their life together is much like that of any professional couple. Albert and Marie have a housekeeper who does the majority of cleaning and prepares most meals that are consumed at midday and evening. This pattern is unusual except for the most affluent winegrower households in that most meals are prepared and the housekeeping done by the winegrower's wife, even if she is employed outside the household. Albert thus comes in this regard very close to what Soon Young Song Yoon referred to as the "gentleman farmer," to be distinguished from both a peasant and common farmer, although this is not an identity to which he would appeal to describe himself (1973).

Albert conveyed to me one evening in a conversation that went on late into the night that he detests snobs and especially people who believe that they are superior by virtue of their social class and education, a characteristic that he associates most particularly with the bourgeoisie. While he acknowledges the petit-bourgeois background of his own family and the significance of his university education, he contends that he, like his father, identifies with and thus considers himself to be only a *paysan* or farmer. Albert desires to identify with the common farmer who, like himself, works the land or labors in the vineyards rather than the more "executive-like" owners and managers who have come to typify the Médoc's elite estates and who have sought historically to distinguish themselves culturally from the masses.

Albert likewise conveyed that his politics, like the Colineau men of the past, is *radical de gauche*. Albert explained, however, that *radical de gauche* is more of a philosophy than a political party in that it promotes a general humanism and support for worker's rights but is not anti-capitalist. In spite of his humble sentiments and identification with *paysans* that some may find admirable, it should be understood that Albert, like Nicole Ducros, is one of the larger growers at the Listrac cooperative and therefore enjoys certain privileges, not least of which is a standard of living that is beyond the means of the majority of cooperative winegrowers. Hence, Albert's identity as *paysan* should be viewed more as a cultural challenge to the elites than one of social class.

Albert does not work his vineyards alone, a situation that surely arises from not having children or a sibling with whom he could collaborate. Albert thus took the somewhat unusual measure within cooperative circles of forming a partnership with another Listrac grower who comes from a family with many generations of winegrowers. Albert and his partner, Claude Prévert, presently cultivate thirty hectares collectively of which a small part belongs to Albert's sister, who is married and lives in Spain, while a commensurately small portion belongs to

Claude's brother who also lives abroad. Both Albert and Claude allo-
cate a portion of their collective financial return to their respective
siblings, holding back a small percentage to compensate their labor and
overhead costs.

Albert and Claude are employers as well as proprietors, like their
family predecessors. They presently have four employees with whom
they work side by side, which enables Albert to fulfill his responsibilities
as vice-president of the Listrac cooperative. Albert and Claude have
been members of the Listrac cooperative since the early 1980s and have
their wine vinified and marketed with a château label. To reduce the
costs of tending their vineyards, they have joined a machinery cooperative that gives them access to such expensive equipment as a mechanical harvester. Thus there is considerable evidence to suggest that both
Albert and Claude understand and appreciate the considerable benefits
of cooperation.

However, upon my return to southwest France in the summer of
1992, I learned from Albert and Claude that they had decided to leave
the Listrac cooperative. While their 1992 harvest would be taken as
usual in its entirety to the Listrac cooperative, they would have to vinify
the 1993 harvest on their own. I was surprised by their decision because
I had never heard from either one of them any expression of discontent
concerning their relation to the Listrac cooperative. In fact, Albert had
led me to believe that the cooperative met his needs and those of other
growers superbly. He added, moreover, that requests for cooperative
membership vastly exceeded their capacity for accommodation, a testimony to the cooperative's success, and that very few growers had left
the cooperative in the past several years.[25] There are, furthermore,
considerable financial risks that discourage small and medium growers
from setting out on their own.

This is not to say, however, that the Listrac cooperative, like others,
does not have its skeptics and detractors. Approximately 30 percent of
the small and medium growers in the commune are not members—
preferring for the most part to sell their harvested grapes directly to the
large merchant-vinifiers. There is, furthermore, a new Syndicat Artisinale, with the appellation Artisan, that is presently composed of

twenty-one smaller growers from all the communes of the Médoc who essentially feel that they can make better wine than that produced by cooperatives.

I came to understand from Albert and Claude that it is not the quality of wine produced by the Listrac cooperative that defines their problem and thus they have no desire to join an organization like the Syndicat Artisinale. In fact, they have many friends at the Listrac cooperative and continue to have confidence in its management and prospects for a successful future. Rather, their problem ensued from what they perceive to be an inflexibility in the payment schedule that is intrinsic to the wine-cooperative system. Virtually all cooperatives pay their members on an annual quarterly basis from revenues received from the sale of wine. However, it is often the case that the revenues and financial resources of the cooperative will vary with the vicissitudes of the wine market. Consequently, both Albert and Claude felt that the cooperative could not keep pace with their need for capital in order to expand their vineyards. While this is no doubt true, the current price of vineyards (see Chapter 9) precludes expansion for all but the largest growers. In my estimation, the size of Albert and Claude's winegrowing enterprise had merely outgrown the conventional winegrower needs that the cooperative was originally designed to meet.

With the decision to leave the cooperative, the responsibility for vinification will be assumed by Albert and Claude. They therefore obtained a loan from Crédit Agricole and began construction in the summer of 1992, with an expected date of completion in late autumn, of a wine cellar large enough to vinify the harvest from their expanding vineyards and yet with sufficient space to receive the many tourists who pass their summer vacations in the Médoc. While this may in the long run prove to be a prudent decision for Albert and Claude, it most certainly compounds the problems of wine cooperatives during a period when many growers are faced with the problem of succession and thus find the prospect of selling their vineyards to a large multinational corporation or insurance company all the more appealing.

In spite of Albert's identification with the average winegrower or common person of the countryside, there is much about his life that is particular to his background and family history and thus distinguishes him from the average cooperative member. His university education and marriage to a professional alone are rare in a region that sees itself as "tradition bound" and slow to change. Moreover, like Nicole Ducros, his life story and involvement with winegrowing illustrate the class stratification of the winegrowing sector. Although he himself works in the vineyards and regards this as important, his marketing of wine with a château label and plans for expansion are thoroughly consistent with the mode of representation and objectives of the Médoc's most esteemed winegrowers. However, the very qualities that make Albert different from most cooperative growers, although in the long run taking him away from the world of the Listrac cooperative, have nonetheless contributed to his ability to analyze critically and sympathetically the history and complexity of the cooperative system.

MICHEL AND PIERRE BESSON

Michel Besson and his son, Pierre, were one of the few father-and-son winegrowing teams that I encountered during my research in both the Médoc and the Dordogne regions. This is largely attributable, as we saw in the previous section, to the difficulties in marketing experienced by independents and cooperatives alike during the mid to late 1960s which due to ensuing hardships made the life of a winegrower unappealing. Therefore, Pierre, like Albert, was not initially encouraged by his parents to become a winegrower and so he too went off to the University of Bordeaux. Upon receiving his university degree, Pierre decided to pursue a career in business and was offered a position as a *cadre* or executive for a firm that manufactured vacuum cleaners. The firm was not located in the immediate vicinity of Bordeaux and so Pierre had to enter into a commuter marriage with his wife, Mireille. However, before we can explore Pierre's life situation further, it is important to learn more about the life story of the elder Besson, Michel.

   Michel Besson, like Gilles Darnaud of the Sigoulès cooperative, married into a family of winegrowers. Michel was born in the Vendée, an area of France that is familiar to many scholars through the celebrated work of Charles Tilly who examines thoughtfully this region's counterrevolutionary support of the monarchy and persistent political conservatism (1964). Michel remarked that in addition to its political conservatism, the Vendée is also known for large families (both his parents came from families with ten to eleven children). However, as Michel recounts below, the Vendée custom of matrilocal residence led to discord when his father moved into his mother's extended family household.

We come from the north, the Vendée, the woodlands of the Vendée. And there were very large families of ten or eleven children. And custom dictated that the son-in-law, my father, come to live with my mother's family, come to work in my mother's family. But there were eleven children there. So my parents didn't like that. They came to work here in this domain. And he spent his life here at a St.-Estèphe château. Well, a part here and a part a little further away in Listrac.

Rather than endure a living situation that was for them intolerable, Michel's parents moved with their children to the Médoc and found employment as wage workers in the vineyards of a nearby château. They did not, however, have a large family of their own as Michel only has one sibling, a sister, who in turn has married a winegrower.

Michel would eventually follow his parent's profession of winegrowing, although his course of progression was somewhat indirect. Michel married into a family from St.-Estèphe, and like his father he followed, out of opportunity rather than custom, a postmarital residence rule that was matrilocal. Michel's in-laws were winegrowers although on a modest scale. At the time, however, Michel worked in a bakery but he discovered winegrowing to be irresistible, much as did Nicole Ducros.

I was a worker in a bakery, and as I married into a home where there was already a hectare of vineyards, I saw that my in-laws were getting old and that I should learn how to prune in order to be able to continue that, because after all it was interesting. We drank a bottle of the best from time to time. That created a bond. I learned to prune vines like that, a little every day, while going to work at night, in the day I would learn to prune vines. And since then I've expanded—two hectares, three hectares, etc.

Michel expresses a passion for winegrowing which he saw much more as an art tied to practical experience and tradition than as a science.

However, in spite of his good fortunes, his career as a winegrower was not always easy.

Michel, like Albert's father and many others, had his life disrupted by the war. Michel was taken as a prisoner of war and spent two and a half years in a prison camp in Germany, although he concedes that he was lucky in being treated well by the Germans. This period was hard on French winegrowers in general as many of the vineyards were left unworked and thus were in serious need of attention after the war. Michel remarks that the wine cooperatives were of immense assistance to small growers in the rebuilding that took place after the war. However, for most cooperative winegrowers, life in the countryside was not easy.[26] In addition to the periodic yet persistent crises in the wine sector, it was not until the late 1950s that many French villages had electricity, indoor toilets, and running water. More specifically to winegrowing, Michel remarks that the hours were long and the working conditions harsh, even for those who owned their own vineyards. This would only begin to change with the introduction of tractors and other labor-saving technologies that were not widespread among small growers until the middle to late 1960s.

However, the theme that Michel emphasized most often was that of the problem of succession. While he acknowledged, as we have seen in the case of Colineau, that hard times for growers was often the reason that parents discouraged their children from pursuing winegrowing, he believes that there are other important factors as well. For example, he explained that young growers who have just joined a cooperative must wait three years before they received their first remuneration. This is the case because in the Médoc, unlike the Dordogne where wine is less often aged, it is in cycles of three years that harvested grapes are vinified, aged in bottles, and then made ready for sale. For younger growers, this waiting period is simply more than they can financially endure. On the other hand, Michel spoke extensively of inflated prices of vineyards precipitated by the arrival of large multinationals able to purchase vineyards for enormous sums of money. With the inflated prices comes the inability of winegrowers to expand their own holdings, thus further discouraging the children of winegrowers from following the family tradition.

While Michel initially discouraged his son Pierre from becoming a winegrower, it is clear from his remarks that he is pleased by his son's choice to return to the family estate. "So now my son has just taken over the succession. He left industry, he was an executive (*un cadre*) in industry, he left industry to come. . . . That's very rare, you don't see that often. He was an executive. He left industry to come take over the succession."

Although Michel worked the vineyards with his wife Isabelle—she did everything except pruning—he is now secure in the future of the family estate as he himself prepares for retirement. This is no small matter. His friend and neighbor, Yvês Diouf, also a member of the cooperative and an informant with whom I had some contact, has two daughters and hopes one of them will either marry a man with an interest in winegrowing or be willing to assume this profession herself, the former being the more likely scenario.

The Besson family homestead is also somewhat unusual in that not only do father and son work together but they live in immediate proximity. The arrangement of houses reminded me of what the French refer to as a *hameau*, "hamlet" or small cluster of houses. At the time that I met the Bessons, the original family home was occupied by Michel's ninety-year-old mother-in-law Anne, his father-in-law long having been deceased. Anne was remarkably able and still could outwork and outdance persons many years younger, something I witnessed during the evening festivities of the harvest. However, in the winter of 1992, Anne died quite unexpectedly. In spite of her advanced age, she was rarely ill. At the time of my last visit in 1992 her house was still vacant. Michel and his wife Isabelle live in a house of their own approximately one hundred feet down the road from where they raised their son Pierre. An independent domicile provided some privacy and autonomy from Michel's in-laws. In like manner, shortly after their marriage, Pierre and his wife Mireille constructed a house of their own on the other side of the road from Pierre's parents, which assured their mutual privacy. However, the family takes all the noontime meals together which in the French countryside is the largest and most important of the day. For the most part, Pierre and Mireille dine separately in the evenings while the grandmother, when she was alive, customarily dined with her daughter and son-in-law.

Since returning to work with his father, Pierre has gained considerable respect as a winegrower. Pierre is now the vice-president of the St.-Estèphe cooperative and has taken on new managerial responsibilities with the retirement of the director, Dumas, in 1992. The *conseil d'administration* of the cooperative believed that Pierre and the president could assume Dumas's duties, perhaps even more skillfully, and also thought that not replacing the director was a way to avoid the costs of an administrative salary. However, their decision is also illustrative of the potential tension, and sometimes lack of confidence, that exists between nongrower administrators and the larger body of cooperative members. Nonetheless, Pierre now spends more time at the cooperative. From what he has conveyed to me it is a challenge that he welcomes. Moreover, his background in industry combined with his experience as vice-president makes him especially well suited to managing the cooperative's financial affairs and marketing, especially when compared to the generally limited experience of the vast majority of cooperative growers.

Over the past couple of years, most of the heavy work in the vineyards has been assumed by Pierre as Michel approaches retirement. Moreover, Pierre's mother no longer works in the vineyards nor does his wife Mireille. Rather, Mireille works full-time in the office of one of the most esteemed estates of St.-Estèphe, Mouton-Rothschild. To help with the work in the vineyards, the Bessons have taken on an apprentice from a nearby agricultural school. The apprentice is provided with room and board and a small salary in exchange for the opportunity to learn from experienced growers.

As I noted previously, Pierre is, like Albert Colineau, very ambitious and still eager to learn. Consequently, he and Michel have purchased several hectares of vineyards in a neighboring commune with the intention of vinifying the harvest themselves. When I last visited them in the summer of 1992, they had already completed the construction of a wine cellar and were in the process of vinifying their first harvest. The initiative for this undertaking comes from the fact that all cooperative growers must deliver their entire harvest to the cooperatives where the vinification takes place under the supervision of hired experts. Most growers are content with this arrangement and, as I have argued, have actually as a group lost the knowledge associated with vinification. This situation was not satisfying for Pierre who sought to continually challenge his existing knowledge and skills. Whether or not his success with vinification will result in his leaving the cooperative remains to be seen.

Pierre's lifestyle is, moreover, very typical of the younger generation of full-time winegrowers. Unlike the older generation, including his father, Pierre drives a sports car, likes to dine out in Bordeaux, and takes vacations through Club Mediterranean. Although there is variation among this younger generation in terms of their lifestyle preferences, gone is the pastoralism that one typically associates with the *paysan*-winegrowers of the past.

The Besson father and son are representative of a family-based working relation that has become progressively more imperiled. The difference in identity between father and son, and perhaps values that are generationally distinct, are secondary, as Michel makes evident, to a process of capital consolidation and corporate concentration that has made succession increasingly more problematic and even rare in areas of the Médoc. While there will always be differences in terms of life experiences and values that no doubt contribute to the tensions of parents working with their children, as we saw with Nicole Ducros, this seems nearly insignificant compared to the insidious threat to the livelihood of cooperative growers that is being precipitated by the purchase of vineyards at greatly inflated prices on the part of large insurance combines and multinational corporations.

The life stories presented in the previous three sections are necessarily partial, fragmented, and largely nonlinear and therefore make no pretensions of getting to the bottom of my informants' lives and intentions, whether viewed phenomenologically, psychologically, or otherwise. In fact, as we should already know from the contemporary hermeneutics of Gadamer (1975, 1976) and Ricoeur (1971, 1974), there is no "bottom." Life histories or biographies are constantly shifting as the symbolically embodied and thus multivocal past is taken up and mediated by social relations in the present. This is not to say, however, that the past or life histories are totally impenetrable or opaque and thus have nothing to disclose to us in the present. To the contrary, no matter how partial, necessarily ambiguous, or incomplete, life stories are vital links between what is contextual or concrete and more general social processes to which they are related dialectically. However, one must be careful not to take informants' life stories in their ethnographic fashioning as speaking for themselves—as if they were some sort of ethnographic version of Adam Smith's "invisible hand." Rather, the process of taking and ethnographic fashioning of informants' stories, no matter how persuasive rhetorically, is itself mediated by relations of power and thus conjointly reflective of the politics of fieldwork and representation.

The life stories or vignettes that I have presented here are therefore both specific to the individual biographies examined and also windows through which we can better envision and grasp critically the political economy and culture of southwest French winegrowers and the wine-cooperative system. With Nicole Ducros, for example, we encounter a woman who at first may seem unremarkable and actually rather conventional in attributing all that she has learned about winegrowing to her relationship with her husband. However, Nicole is a very able and self-assured winegrower whose life story points to the struggles of female winegrowers and the gender of winegrowing work.

There is little doubt that both men and women recognize that winegrowing work, most particularly pruning, is seen as largely male, especially in regions such as the Médoc renowned for quality wines. Although the view of winegrowing labor as male has never prevented women from working in the vineyards, it has, however, assigned them a secondary role on the large estates where they are remunerated less and rarely assume the management of other workers. Much the same holds for the smaller estates except for what is necessitated by a household or family organization of production. However, here again, in the elite regions women less often prune the vines.

The challenge to the gender division of labor comes primarily from problems of succession. If Nicole's husband had lived, it is likely that she would have continued with the management of household resources, leaving the management of the vineyards to her husband. It cannot be overemphasized, however, that this was not indicative of her subservience. In fact, her succession to the family estate was an extension of her managerial responsibilities and skills. For younger growers, the situation is somewhat different. Many of the younger generation, as noted, have been discouraged from winegrowing. However, there is a sizable generation of aging winegrowers who would welcome a child, whether male or female, to take control of the family estate. While Yvês Diouf may hope for a future husband of one of his two daughters to join him in the occupation of winegrower, I suspect that he would welcome his daughters rather than face the end of a family winegrowing tradition that has endured for generations. In the long run, such inheritance will challenge much of what is seen in exclusively male terms in winegrowing.

The fact that two women already serve on the *conseil d'administration* of the Pauillac cooperative is a testimony to change as the Pauillac region is among the most traditional and conservative in the Médoc. However, Nicole Ducros is not simply being swept along by the tides of change. Rather, she describes her own growing awareness of identity as a female winegrower and believes that it is important for all women to challenge their male counterparts who do not take them seriously. In this respect, Nicole should not be regarded simply as victim of discrimination and domination but rather as an agent engaged with others in the constitution of the contested world of winegrower. Nicole's life story thus stands as specific but also as generalizable to broader questions of gender and self-identity.

The life stories of Albert Colineau and the Bessons, while distinct in terms of particulars, likewise raise more general questions concerning social class, identity, and succession. With Albert Colineau, we have seen that a long family association with the Listrac cooperative did not compensate for the inability of the cooperative to advance him funds necessary for increasing the hectares of vineyards that he and Claude cultivate collectively. This is no special fault of the cooperative in that as a system it was mainly designed to assist small and medium growers in improving the quality of their wines and adjusting to conditions of marketing that at times were severe and intensely competitive. Nonetheless, the Listrac cooperative, like all of those that I studied in the

Médoc and the Dordogne, reproduces the general class structure of the larger winegrowing sector, especially through catering to full-time growers by bottling and marketing their wines with a château label. Consequently, it is likely that without the cooperative, it would never have been possible for Albert and Claude to reach the point where leaving was an option.

Albert is also representative of a new generation of winegrower whose schooling is a central part of their background. Among the older growers, many of whom left school early on to work on family farms, schooling is looked upon with a great deal of skepticism. They believe that there is no substitute for learning in the vineyards, valuing practical over theoretical knowledge. However, it was not an agricultural school that Albert attended but rather the University of Bordeaux. In this regard, his training is similar to cooperative directors such as Roche at UNIMEDOC or Fresson at Sigoulès. However, Albert disclaims the privilege of his university education and to some degree his *demi-bourgeois* family background in identifying with the *paysan*. While this may have little practical significance for Albert's life story apart from the family politics described previously, it is nevertheless symbolically important with respect to the social hierarchy and rapidly changing social terrain of the Médoc.

Absentee landlordism is nothing new to the Médoc in that with the development of elite wines in the late eighteenth and early nineteenth centuries it became increasingly common for proprietors to live in Bordeaux while their estates were managed by pruners or others specifically retained for this purpose. However, more recently, Médoc estates of all sizes have been purchased by corporations of such scale that decisions concerning their development and fate are being made in places far removed from southwest France. Although these estates are still managed locally, the management has become progressively more rationalized and removed from those who actually work in the vineyards. Therefore, the concept of *paysan* has taken on a new sense of winegrowing *sur place*. Albert's identity, therefore, with the common winegrowing farmer should be understood as illustrative of his resolve, in spite of having employees of his own, to maintain an intimate working relation with the vineyards and a tradition that one senses is on the wane.

The symbolic ambiguities of *paysan* can thus be construed as a challenge, albeit limited, to the cultural hegemony of the winegrowing elite.

The Besson family is likewise viewed by Michel himself as somewhat analogous to an endangered species. While Pierre exhibits considerable enthusiasm for his work as a winegrower and shows little hesitancy to take on new challenges such as the vinifying of his own wine, the future of the Besson estate is nonetheless in doubt. Practically speaking, this is a consequence of Pierre and Mireille not having children. However, the real challenge, as Michel relates, results from the tremendous inflation in the cost of purchasing vineyards which makes expansion way beyond the average winegrower's means. Apart from whatever consequence this may have for the Besson family, the potential effect for wine cooperatives is ominous.

The vast majority of members of cooperatives are small growers who do not gain their principal livelihoods from winegrowing. As the price of vineyards become inflated, many of these growers are tempted to sell. However, it is not to other small growers that the vineyards are sold but rather to the large corporations, insurance combines, or less frequently the château proprietors who easily command the financial resources to compete for vineyards that they covet. If the Bessons should have a problem with succession, which presently seems to be the case with Pierre and Mireille, then they will likely sell their vineyards. In the long run, this threatens the future of cooperatives, a problem of immense importance to which we now turn.

PROSPECTS AND FUTURES 9

Although it appears that southwest French wine cooperatives have adjusted well to the exigencies of the capitalist production and circulation of wine and have likewise endured the periodic winegrowing crises of the twentieth century, there are nevertheless numerous problems that they presently face and are likely to confront in the near future. Some of these problems are idiosyncratic to the membership and administration of particular cooperatives, while others are intrinsic to the cooperative system in its relation to a global economy. Of all the problems discussed with cooperative administrators and members, there were two general problems that were regarded as salient. First, much of the conversation focused on the crisis ensuing from the purchase of vineyards by global alcohol corporations and financial groups at vastly inflated prices. Second, there was considerable discussion concerning the prospect that the less constrained flow of commodities throughout the European Union (EU) that commenced in 1992 will eventually pose a new challenge to wine cooperatives. However, we shall see that the current problem with large corporations and those that are on the horizon with the EU will be experienced differentially in the two winegrowing regions of the Médoc and the Dordogne that were the foci of my ethnographic research and even within the Médoc itself. Consequently, as counterstrategies are developed by wine cooperatives and the various winegrowing associations that represent cooperatives in both the national and international arenas, they must be attentive to the particularity of region or place. The concluding section of the chapter will summarize themes raised throughout as they bear most particularly on the prospects and futures of the cooperative system.

THE "DESCENT" OF FOREIGN CAPITAL

Most of my winegrowing informants expressed significant concern and anxiety about the acquisition of vineyards in southwest France by large-scale foreign corporations, financial groups, and insurance combines, some of which, like AXA, are indigenous to France. They maintain that, if left unchallenged, this process of acquisition will eventually threaten the future of cooperatives and hence small-scale winegrowing by undermining succession. While their prognosis for the future of wine cooperatives is likely correct in the absence of a counterstrategy, the process of capital penetration and transformation that they associate with large corporations is not, as many believe, entirely new.

Over the past century or more the history of elite winegrowing regions such as the Médoc provides seemingly endless examples of estates having changed hands at the initiative of large-scale capitalist firms and merchant houses, many of which were foreign owned. For example, during the nineteenth century, the elite vineyards of Château Lafite, Château Margaux, and the less esteemed but still noteworthy Château Loudenne were purchased by merchants and financiers of English, French, and Dutch origin (Pijassou 1980:545; Unwin 1991:334).[1] Not only were there financial consequences to the sale of elite Médoc vineyards but often social ones as well in that the new owners were generally absentee landlords who hired a *regisseur* to manage the estate. In the long run, the new system of management would precipitate, as I argued in Chapter 3, a more rationalized division of labor that replaced families of workers housed on the estate with those who were retained seasonally on a wage basis.

However, the sale of château vineyards not only followed from periods of economic crisis and decline but also from the consequences of natural disasters such as phylloxera and mildew. Given that the Médoc was, unlike the Dordogne, a region of winegrowing only, proprietors' options were generally circumscribed to replanting or selling the vineyards altogether. As suggested above, it was often the foreign-owned merchant houses of Bordeaux that had the capital to purchase the elite estates and to restore vineyards that had been severely damaged.

Pijassou remarks that between 1889 and 1901 twenty-one Médoc estates were sold, with another twenty changing hands between 1918 and 1920 (1980:815). During the problematic years of the 1930s, Château Haut-Brion of Pessac, one of only four first growths according to the 1855 Bordeaux classification, was purchased by the Dillon Read corporation, an important American financial group (Pijassou 1980:933).

Although I maintain that there is significant continuity between the history of foreign capital in the Médoc and what some informants may currently experience as novel, this is not to say that the form that large-scale capital has assumed today and its present consequences for small growers are merely identical with conditions and circumstances of the past. To the contrary, the national capitalist firms and merchant houses of the nineteenth century, though powerful and influential politically within an already global economy, are a mere shadow of the corporate concentration and diversity of holdings that have come to typify the multinationals or global alcohol corporations.[2] Not only is there a difference in size and the potential to command greater resources but, as Tim Unwin notes with the wine trade and the English firm of Grand Metropolitan that serves as his model, the large global corporations have the capacity to profoundly influence, if not control, both production and distribution through acquiring ownership of vineyards and by purchasing distribution outlets such as supermarkets where a vast portion of the retail trade takes place (1991:340–42). Unwin remarks that the integration of winegrowing with retail, or what he refers to as "sectoral integration," was rare in the nineteenth century and is therefore a primary reason, as Pierre Chauvet of the Fédération also confirms, why the global corporation has assumed dominance in the wine trade (1991:325).[3]

Unwin argues, however, that sectoral integration alone does not account for the distinctiveness and success of global corporations as these corporations have vastly enhanced, in comparison to their nineteenth-century predecessors, their capacity to acquire competitors either through purchase or buyouts or more recently as a consequence of mergers. In the late 1980s Grand Metropolitan, which already had purchased the Pillsbury group and its Burger King outlets, acquired the beverage giant Heublein which in turn owns several California wineries, through its wine and spirits division, IDV. Unwin adds that the multinationals have been very innovative in focusing on the production of popular brand names such as the French table wine Piat d'Or and have devoted commensurate effort to the construction and enhancement of image through massive promotion and advertising. With French wine, the latter of these two activities is central to the continued success of elite wines as culturally distinctive and has contributed as well to the enormous popularity of less distinguished wines such as Nouveau Beaujolais. Multinationals have likewise been able to identify and expand gaps or opportunities in the market through their research and development divisions and to undertake joint international ventures with different companies and financial groups (Unwin 1991:340–42). The global alcohol corporations or multinationals have, in short, distinguished themselves from the national capitalist firms of the nineteenth and early twentieth centuries by virtue of their enhanced potential to control production and distribution through sectoral integration, by their ability to utilize marketing research and advertising to great advantage, and by their sheer capacity to acquire competitors while minimizing risks through a diversity and concentration of holdings worldwide.

From the point of view of my winegrowing informants, the primary influence of the global alcohol corporations and large financial groups is the impact that they have had on the price of vineyards. Although the price of wine has always been subject to the vicissitudes of the market, the price of vineyards by comparison has tended to be more stable. However, in recent years the price for a hectare of vineyards has risen continuously and exponentially as a consequence of the intrusiveness of foreign conglomerates like Santori of Japan (in St.-Julien of the Médoc most particularly), or the American-Canadian Seagrams, while the prices for wine have remained essentially stable.[4] Consequently, the income of growers has not nearly kept pace with the cost of vineyards, a condition that both curtails the possibility for expansion among small cooperative winegrowers and affects in turn their potential for succession.

The problem with succession that has ensued from the selling of vineyards to large corporations and financial groups is not, however, uniformly experienced in the Médoc or throughout southwest France as a whole. Gilles Blanchard, president of the Listrac cooperative, observed

> And that is a problem for this region [e.g. Listrac], for this region [e.g. Médoc] only. Next there are problems of succession and the small holding. Actually the price of a hectare being very elevated, we are worried, I am worried about the succession of small family holdings, because succession being what it is, the proprietors are tempted to sell their vineyards to châteaus that have very significant financial means. That would mean for the cooperative a significant loss of hectares. It is also our anxiety.

As Blanchard suggests but does not specifically elaborate, the problem of succession has been experienced most intensively in communes, such as Listrac, St.-Estèphe, and Pauillac, where there are significant concentrations of elite château vineyards. The Pauillac cooperative, for example, has already lost nearly one-third of its hectarage due to problems of succession precipitated mostly by large-scale capital. However, in areas of the Médoc such as Bégadan or in the Dordogne, where we find the Sigoulès and Monbazillac cooperatives, the prices of vineyards have remained essentially stable.[5]

In 1990, a hectare of vineyards was selling at one million francs in St.-Estèphe, slightly higher in Pauillac, and for nearly half a million francs in the less esteemed but still highly reputable commune of Listrac. Although the figures reported in Table 9.1 are specific to St.-Estèphe, they are nonetheless representative of a more general trend of inflation that has been experienced at Listrac, Pauillac, and virtually every other commune with a concentration of elite vineyards.

While the progressive augmentation in the value of vineyards has been welcomed and even celebrated by an increasing number of individual growers, for the majority of cooperatives in elite winegrowing regions of southwest France the unprecedented inflation in the price of vineyards threatens the future of cooperative growing itself, as Marie

**TABLE 9.1 PRICE OF LAND IN
ST.-ESTÈPHE COMMUNE**

Year	Average price per hectare (in francs)
1983	140,000
1985	250,000
1986	450,000
1987	500,000
1988	700,000
1990	1,000,000

Source: Dumas of the St.-Estèphe cooperative.

Lescot of the Pauillac cooperative conveyed to me in a conversation concerning those who leave the cooperative. Although her comments and sentiments resonate with those of Blanchard, they also present the problem somewhat more comprehensively.

> **Ulin:** Is it a problem for the cooperative if there are many people who quit?
>
> **Lescot:** If one quits? Certainly, it is a problem. The more members one has, the more one is backed up and the more one is strong. If we remain not very large, we will be weaker. But at this moment the large problem, it is precisely the large châteaus who would like to absolutely devour us and who offer fantastic sums for our hectares of vineyards. The price has tripled or quadrupled in the space of two or three years. Therefore they are many cooperative members with small holdings who are attracted by money and to whom one proposes and sells. There—that is the problem of the moment, of now. In the past, at least twelve years ago, there wasn't this problem. The vineyards were always valued at nearly the same price. You see, people handed down vineyards from father to son or one bought a little more, whereas now the cooperative grower can no longer buy. It is the price that exceeds our means. And to the contrary, the large châteaus have stimulated the sale because it is always of interest to make a large profit. Then it is a problem. I do not know what to say to you what will be in twenty years.

The large châteaus to which Lescot refers are in growing numbers of cases owned by global corporations such as Santori, Seagrams, and financial groups or insurance conglomerates such as AXA. It is these châteaus in particular that have exhibited the greatest interest in expanding their vineyards and that have the means to realize this objective. Due to a long history of partible inheritance in France that is nowadays most pronounced among the small wine producers, it is not uncommon for the vineyards of cooperative growers to be found in relative proximity if not actually side by side to those owned by the châteaus. However it is their reputation of being well maintained even more than their proximity that accounts for why cooperative vineyards in the Médoc are often sought by the large châteaus.[6] With their command of significant financial resources, the large châteaus can pay, as Lescot relates, fantastic sums of money that many cooperative growers find irresistible.

The cooperative growers who are most likely to sell to the large châteaus, financial groups or even wealthier independents are, as Yvês Diouf of St.-Estèphe states, those who face a problem of succession. "Now there are people who come to retire and who have no successors, who sell. But it is not the cooperative members who buy, because the vineyards [are] too expensive, it is not remunerative."

Although Diouf himself is likely to face a problem with succession, the informant who most comes to mind is Nicole Ducros. While Nicole's decision to sell her vineyards is especially surprising in light of her expressed resolve and passionate devotion to the cooperative system, we should recall from the previous chapter that she also faced a problem with succession given the apparent desire of her eldest son to work elsewhere. Even though her vineyards bordered directly on those of Château Latour, the very château that had previously expressed interest in acquiring her vineyards, it was to the French insurance group AXA that Nicole Ducros sold her vineyards for a sum reputedly in excess of those reported above for St.-Estèphe.[7]

Nicole Ducros's vineyards were not, however, the first to be purchased by AXA in the commune of Pauillac as this insurance group also owns several châteaus in the vicinity.[8] While AXA maintains financial control of Ducros's former vineyards and retains the right to make all important decisions, their daily care and management have been entrusted, as is typical, to a local individual, Henri Massin. In addition to being director of Château Pichon Baron of Pauillac and proprietor of Château Lynch-Bages, Massin also serves as director general of the local AXA office in Pauillac. He is thus well placed to know precisely which vineyards have been well maintained and who among cooperative growers and small independents might be prepared to sell.

It is not, however, only cooperative growers who are ready to retire or face a problem of succession who are prepared to sell but also those with a clearly identified successor. Because of the high cost of vineyards these growers find the prospects of increasing their own holdings—a great attraction to a potential successor—to be way beyond their means. Consequently many of these growers will elect to sell the family vineyards and then use the money for their own retirement and to support their children in alternate careers or endeavors.

Apart from the prohibitive cost of vineyards as an obstacle to expansion on the part of small cooperative growers, Tim Unwin also identifies France's significant inheritance taxes as another obstacle to succession (1991:353). Many families find it difficult to afford this 40 percent tax especially when vineyards are assessed at their current market value rather than at the price for which they were originally purchased or some other average figured over a number of years. Therefore, a family with as little as two hectares of vineyards in St.-Estèphe, not enough to live on as a full-time pursuit, could be assessed at 40 percent of two million francs.[9] Consequently, selling the vineyard prior to the death of its official owner is an option being pursued by many and thus as vineyards continue to increase in value the prospects of growers leaving the cooperatives remains a substantial and daunting problem.

Although there are numerous independent châteaus of renown, like Château Clarke of Listrac, presently owned and recently restored by Edmond Rothschild, that have long sought to expand their holdings during times favorable to the wine trade, the large multinationals and financial groups have by comparison looked upon southwest French vineyards almost exclusively in investment terms. This is not to claim that enormously wealthy families such as the Rothschilds with their ownership of important château vineyards, global marketing firms, and numerous other financial holdings are disinterested in investment potential or that multinationals are indifferent to maintaining the quality and reputation of vineyards that they have purchased. To the contrary, the Rothschild family used its banking fortune to purchase French vineyards in the first place and has kept pace, in a manner analogous to the multinationals, with innovative marketing and promotion through the introduction of its own Mouton Cadet and by the recent acquisition of vineyards abroad.[10] Likewise, the multinationals and financial groups with holdings in the Médoc must protect their investment by assuring that standards of quality are maintained. This is the primary reason why the management of their vineyards is left in skilled local hands. However, from the perspective of cooperative winegrowers like Albert Colineau or Pierre Besson, the Rothschilds are regarded as having maintained a much closer association to the Médoc and its growers than either multinationals or financial groups because they spend significant time actually living at their winegrowing estates. Moreover, they are directly involved in the management of their estates and likewise have elected to participate in the Bordeaux region's many winegrowing associations. In turn, Colineau credits Edmond Rothschild and Château Clarke for enhancing the general reputation of Listrac wines and thus indirectly assisting the commercial vitality of those wines produced by the cooperative.

The suspicion or distrust that cooperative growers exhibit toward foreign capital and the multinationals is therefore not generalizable to château proprietors as a group even though many cooperative growers, especially the administrators, realize that there is little difference between elite independents and multinationals in their overall financial motivations and business practices.[11] However, and here we have the principal distinction, there is a general expectation on the part of cooperative growers and long-term residents of the Médoc that winegrowing proprietors demonstrate their commitment to the region and the resolving of its problems by participating in its numerous professional organizations, winegrowing associations, and local celebrations and festivities. Consequently proprietors like the Rothschilds are regarded as "of the Médoc" and their winegrowing estates, as we saw with Château Margaux, have likewise come to stand symbolically for the Médoc itself. On the other hand, the global alcohol corporations and financial groups are stigmatized as outsiders and regarded as intrusive and even carnivorous for their remoteness and singularity of financial purpose—even if, like AXA, they are indigenous to France.

That Médoc vineyards are an object of sheer financial speculation and interest is also illustrated by advertisements that appear frequently in the weekly newspapers that are circulated for free to the households in the Bordeaux region. These newspapers are generally utilized to advertise items for sale, apartments for rent, and may even contain personals. Several informants brought to my attention advertisements that called for potential investors interested in purchasing shares in companies whose primary objective was to purchase Bordeaux vineyards or winegrowing estates. The advertisers usually identified themselves as a group of foreign investors, often from England and Holland, and generally listed a foreign address for those interested in acquiring more information. I was assured by informants that these advertisements were not a scam but rather a legitimate means by which financial groups raised money through potential investors so as to be able to purchase Médoc vineyards. Like the more established financial groups and corporations, these groups had the capacity to purchase vineyards at greatly inflated prices and contributed to the growing problem of cooperative succession.

While the purchasing of vineyards at inflated prices was the primary threat to the future of cooperatives identified by my informants, Raymond Frossard of the St.-Estèphe cooperative also saw the banks in equally nefarious terms.

> **Ulin:** The people at the Fédération told me that the largest problem was the large multinational enterprises, American and English, with lots of money, etc.
> **Frossard:** Yes, it is a matter of capital. It is like that here. There are certain banks who invest in châteaus here and there, but when they have seen that does not yield sufficiently, not at St.-Estèphe specially, they sell the property. You see the bankers, they have a cold heart.

Because the banks also command significant financial resources they are likewise in position to invest in vineyards directly or through making loans that permit proprietors to expand. As Frossard relates, if they believe that the financial returns are inadequate, they are in a position to force the sale of the property. However, at the cooperatives, the risk of foreclosure is only likely to affect the very few larger growers who elect to borrow for vineyard expansion in a financial climate where the market in vineyards is volatile.

Although the inflated price of vineyards presents a serious problem for the future of wine cooperatives in areas with a concentration of elite châteaus, few cooperatives to date have been quick to establish counterstrategies. Of the five cooperatives with which I conducted ethnographic research in the Médoc—the Dordogne to date does not have this problem—St.-Estèphe has devoted the most effort and imagination to resolving the problem of succession ensuing from the intrusion of large-scale capital. Since the cooperative combines the resources of individual growers, it does command capital of its own that can be used to purchase vineyards. This is precisely what the St.-Estèphe cooperative has done in purchasing vineyards located in proximity to the cooperative itself. These vineyards are cared for by the cooperative members and the profits that come from the yields are then part of the collective resources to be utilized for future projects. This can only be accomplished through the consensus of the members, who must be prepared to sacrifice potential returns of their own in order to serve the "collective good" or, as Lescot emphasized earlier, to provide mutual support. However, St.-Estèphe members generally recognize the necessity of supporting the cooperative's present strategy as they know that on their own they are much more financially vulnerable.

Before his retirement in early 1992, Jacques Dumas, the director of the St.-Estèphe cooperative, discussed with me the strategy of purchasing vineyards collectively. In addition, he thought that it might be possible for the cooperative to lend money for members to purchase vineyards on their own, the lack of which led to Albert Colineau's seemingly precipitous departure from the Listrac cooperative. Nonetheless, Dumas admitted that the prospect of being paid large sums of money for their vineyards was perhaps a greater influence on part-time growers than any sense of collective good or loyalty to the cooperative system.

The hierarchical system of growers and classifications that are reproduced culturally, the worldwide markets or global economy to which winegrowers are tied inextricably, the predominance of monocropping in elite winegrowing regions, and seasonal wage labor all owe their origins to the merchant-proprietors and large international trading houses of the late eighteenth and nineteenth centuries—perhaps even earlier if one considers the formative potentials of long-distance trade between southwest France and northern Europe. The multinationals have largely built upon and deepened capitalist social relations already long established and thus have not, as they have in the Third World, contributed to the ascendancy of capitalist social relations and the formation of an agricultural proletariat.

Even though it is not capital accumulation and proletarianization that have marked the presence of global corporations in southwest France, there is nonetheless some prospect of outcomes similar to those of the Third World as a general result of cooperative growers' ties to a global economy of which multinationals are themselves both a recent product and agent of change. That is, as multinationals intervene directly in the agricultural sector, there is a tendency worldwide for family farming to give way to farming carried out on a very large and even industrial scale. While the association of elite winegrowing with artisanship and the distinctiveness of aristocratic tradition, referred to in Chapter 2 as cultural capital, may provide indirectly some degree of protection for Médoc cooperative growers from winegrowing on what some may regard as a vulgar industrial scale, it is, nonetheless, small growers and the future of family winegrowing that have been, as in the Third World, placed most at peril.[12] It is precisely this sense of scale or corporate concentration, although seen more narrowly by cooperative growers in terms of vineyard prices, that has led my informants to identify the potential consequences of large-scale foreign capital, or what they regard as its descent, to be novel.

While the St.-Estèphe cooperative has responded with innovation to the exploits of multinationals and large investment groups, it is likely that other cooperatives will eventually follow their lead or face the possibility of a highly precarious if not dismal future. This requires a new capacity to accommodate to economic and social conditions of capitalist development that wine cooperatives have neither created nor do they have much hope of controlling. Yet accommodation to changing economic circumstances has proven to be the historical strength and legacy of the cooperative system. Cooperatives were not only created to improve the quality of wine produced and to discipline the small growers, but to enable growers at the economic and social margins to compete with large capitalist firms while assuring some degree of independence. Therefore, as the capitalist system or global economy continues to evolve and change in scale, wine cooperatives and their representative organizations must be prepared as in the past to keep pace. Nonetheless, there is no certainty that efforts to accommodate will secure a future for cooperative winegrowing in regions where elite châteaus predominate and thus where the presence of large-scale foreign capital is seemingly permanent.

THE EUROPEAN UNION AND
COOPERATIVE WINEGROWING

The other salient issue that engaged cooperative growers during my 1989–90 field research, and continues to do so, was the change that many expected to come with the new liberal trading regulations and broader political and social agenda of the European Union (EU) that commenced in 1992.[13] However, unlike the crisis of cooperative succession precipitated by the global corporations, much of the discussion and planning around what to expect from 1992 and thereafter is largely regarded as speculative. Consequently, I focus on what cooperative winegrowers anticipate from more thoroughly integrated European markets and what if any plans are in the making to prepare for its potential influences.

   Although the crisis of vineyard inflation has an immediacy for cooperative growers that supersedes whatever anxiety and concern that have become associated with the new European Union, there is nonetheless some similarity between how these two distinct problems are articulated that, in turn, may suggest a connection at a more profound level. For example, it became apparent to me that any problems that will potentially develop as a consequence of a more liberalized movement of goods, services, and people across European borders and a commensurate reduction in tariffs would likely be experienced differentially, as we saw with the vineyard crisis described above, between the two winegrowing regions of my research and perhaps even among the different classes of growers in the Médoc itself. This largely follows from the historical background that sets these two regions apart and most especially from the different relations of classes of winegrowers to European markets and the global economy. Similarly, I maintain that the potential problems for winegrowers of 1992 and its aftermath emerges from the wine cooperative's relation to a changing European economy in particular and to the global economy more generally. However, this is best recognized by looking beyond the immediate horizon of southwest France and toward the external conditions and circumstances that have encouraged and shaped European economic integration in the first place.

According to Loukas Tsoukalis, the establishment of European economic integration was largely facilitated, if not made necessary, through the tremendous physical destruction of European economies that occurred as a consequence of the Second World War (1991). He adds, for example, that production levels were so disrupted by the war that they did not return to normal until 1949. Tsoukalis maintains, moreover, that the foundations for regional economic cooperation evolved during the period of reconstruction and mainly at the initiative of the Americans who provided the money for rebuilding in the form of the Marshall Plan. The money provided through the Marshall Plan was contingent on cooperation between European governments and their willingness to pursue a policy of "progressive liberalization of intra-European trade and payments" (Tsoukalis 1991:13).

The integration of European economies proceeded at best with caution and even at times with outright resistance. Apart from age-old conflicts and distrust that haunted the European panorama—such as those between England, France, and Germany in particular—and acknowledged differences in the strength and productivity of economies that threatened the viability of trade agreements, there were periodic complications introduced from questions of maintaining national or cultural autonomy. This was apparent not only in urban centers such as Paris but in the countryside as well. Like Parisians, country dwellers expressed dismay that English had replaced French as the language of commerce and were worried that efforts to make EU regulations uniform would threaten long-standing French customs such as the length of the hunting and fishing seasons.[14] The French were not alone in their anxiety. The Germans also fought tenaciously to maintain a beermaking tradition of reputedly long duration that prohibits the use of chemical additives. The potential threat posed symbolically, if not practically, by 1992 with its ambitions of integrated economies, mobility of populations, single currency, and the possibility, even if remote, of a uniform language contributed a cultural stigma to unification that coincided with those that were already politically motivated and historically rooted.

In spite of the cultural and historical obstacles to European economic integration, the exigencies of a global economy pushed the members of the EEC toward greater cooperation. As Tsoukalis argues, the 1970s were marked by extreme financial woes that renewed interest and discussion in, at the very least, the potential benefits of enhanced European economic cooperation. Tsoukalis remarks, for example, that European economies of the 1970s were characterized by rising unemployment, inflation, the deceleration of economic growth, declining rates of investment, and perhaps most important for those who supported increased European cooperation, the inability to compete on global markets with Japan and the United States in particular (1991:34). Moreover, the economic woes of the 1970s also furthered the disparities between the member countries which persisted into the early years of the 1980s and which to date continue to be a problem without an evident solution. However, by the mid-1980s European economies had recovered some of their former vitality and so the issue of regional integration was advanced, as Tsoukalis claims, as a means of sustaining economic growth and enhancing the potential to compete internationally.

Although the middle 1980s was the period in which the plans for European integration and union were renewed and elaborated with increasing vigor and resolve, French winegrowers had already had sufficient experience with liberalized trading regulations of the EEC that made them look toward 1992 and beyond with some degree of skepticism and anxiety. As we may recall, France has among the strictest regulations for wine production that are designed to control quality and quantity. However, as the president of the Pauillac cooperative Michel Lebrun asserts, the standards of recordkeeping are far from uniform in the EEC and thus potentially present a serious problem for French cooperative winegrowers and independents alike. Because Lebrun articulates well the principal concerns of most cooperative administrators regarding 1992, I reproduce his somewhat lengthy comments in their entirety.

> **Ulin:** Will there be problems with 1992?
> **Lebrun:** Certain. There will be certainly. Well, we think of it, we try to adapt to it. Actually we are in the process of making a revision of the statutes to enable us to adapt to the new system that will be applicable certainly in '92. Me, I know that personally, and that is a feeling I have, I wonder what will be with our wine. I am a little afraid, this exchange of '92. You know that it is not easy to knock down all the borders. It is not easy to find something that will be truly homogeneous everywhere. Let me explain. In France, at the fiscal level, at the cadastral level, at the level of organization, we have something that is solid and that is practical and on which we can rely. We no longer have the problems of the past, to know that there were people who apparently cultivated in writing five hectares of vineyards; in reality there were only three. You see what I want to say. And there are still countries that go about it differently. There are countries where I have heard in passing, Italy for example, that cadastral records do not exist. We in France, we are nearly 100 hectares, nearly to the square meter. And besides here every year we make what one calls a declaration of the vine stock. If there is an error, that the administration fails to recognize, it comes back against us. It is necessary to be rigorously exact. . . . We see some laws in France that are no longer applied with difficulty, because we have the means. How will they do it in other countries? It is there that I fear is the problem. The common market, good, it is not perfect. I am not against it. Me, I would like it to work well, it is a good thing. But if Europe does not manage to do something equal for everyone, that is the problem. And I fear that we will have to suffer the consequences.

The reservations that Lebrun expresses look specifically to the past and present as a means of anticipating what will be the likely problems with which the wine cooperatives will be faced in the near future. While he supports European economic cooperation in principle, he believes that the EEC has not been sufficiently vigilant in establishing standards that would apply uniformly and equitably to all the member states and thus he worries that the cooperatives will be forced to face consequences that are potentially unfavorable. Nonetheless, he does not want the cooperative to be unprepared and so he indicated that changes in the cooperative statute were presently being negotiated.[15]

However, as Tim Unwin argues, cadastral records and the accuracy of declarations are only part of a larger problem that has been exacerbated with Spain and Portugal's accession to the EEC in 1986 (1991:321–23). Not only are there problems with nomenclature (especially in relation to sherry), the practice of chaptalization as legal in France and illegal in Italy, and subsidies given for planting new vineyards in Italy while they are discouraged in France, but most seriously for French growers the prospect of cheaper Spanish and Italian wines flooding the market. If the past is any indicator, this would likely result in a drastic decline in wine prices, which Unwin maintains would also precipitate a commensurate decline in the price of vineyards. In part, the challenge of cheap foreign wines flooding the French market has been addressed directly through the activism of southern growers from Languedoc who have simply poured the wine into the streets or blocked its entry into the country altogether. While the response of Languedoc winegrowers may seem extreme by Bordeaux standards, it also illustrates the differential relation of the classes of growers to European and global markets.

Most of the elite winegrowers in southwest France have exhibited far less concern over the prospect of cheap wines flooding the French market even though they have likewise pushed for standards at the level of the EEC that are essentially uniform. However, we should recollect that the issue of cheaper wines appearing in French markets is not exactly new. It was after all this very problem, as Enjalbert argues, that initially led southwest French growers to develop the *grands crus* (1953). That is, when this very problem of saturated markets first appeared in the late eighteenth century, some French winegrowers opted to improve the quality of their wines rather than emulate their competitors in the production of less expensive mass wines. The choice in favor of quality continues to have repercussions today in that the proprietors of elite southwest wines strictly limit quantity and thus have generally avoided problems of overproduction. Moreover, elite wines have a clientele that is distinctive and thus do not compete directly with producers of mass wines, whether French or foreign. It is, therefore, less likely that they will be affected by the prospect of augmented European competition than French growers who are producing wines of lesser esteem. However, because the consequences of 1992 are yet to be realized in any manifest form, it remains to be seen whether or not Médoc wine cooperatives will be adversely effected by less expensive wines of the EEC. There is some prospect that their association with an elite winegrowing region and their modest price will secure them a future. On the other hand, there is good reason for the wine cooperatives of Languedoc and also those of the Dordogne to be concerned.

Unwin believes, however, that in spite of the possible problems that some French winegrowers potentially face with 1992 and beyond, the European Economic Community Regulation 24 of April 1962 actually provided early on a suitable foundation for a common market in wine. According to Unwin, Regulation 24 established four provisions that required that each country to: "establish a vineyard register, that annual production levels be notified to a central authority, that strict rules be established concerning quality wines produced in specified regions, and that future estimates of resources and requirements be compiled annually" (1991:321–22). Nonetheless, as Unwin argues, European legislation failed to address the problem of overproduction. Even the establishment of a new European regulation (1163/76) that banned new plantings of vineyards and provided subsidies for converting vineyards to other crops did not curtail the problem of overproduction. Consequently, the emphasis shifted to the distillation of wine surpluses which Unwin believes is an expensive alternative and does not confront the probable necessity to reduce the surface area in Europe devoted to the cultivation of vineyards. With winegrowing in Europe accounting for nearly 60 percent of the world's production and 10 percent of the agricultural labor force in Europe itself, this is not a likely course to be pursued (Unwin 1991:321).

It is not only the individual cooperatives that have made preparations for 1992 and beyond but the larger organizations that market their wines such as UNIMEDOC. That preparations should be taken seriously is emphasized by UNIMEDOC's director Paul Roche.

You know, 1992 is a little comic (*la tarte à la crème*). Now, all that one does well, one says that it is for 1992 and all that one does not do well, one says that it is for '92 also. Ninety-two will not be like that, so there, '92 we change. In '91, the 31st of December 1991 we were different and the 1st of January we are still different. No, to get ready, it is work. That which is sure, it is that, yet more in '92 than in '91, yet more in '91 than in '90, in '90 than in '89, it will be necessary to be very, very, very well organized. Therefore the cooperatives, UNIMEDOC in particular, I hope that we will have our part in this genre of evolution. Then the one who is all alone, who makes some bottles of wine in his corner, if he wants to develop, if he does not want to be consumed, crunched, he cannot resist all the exterior pressure. There is the imperative. That's it. And I say that '92, perhaps it will not be UNIMEDOC all alone; it will be Uni . . . Uni all the southwest.

While Roche suggests that 1992 has become somewhat of a blanket explanation for the successes and failures of winegrowers, he believes that organization and hard work are essential preparation for the changes likely to come through the European Union. Anyone who thinks that they can take on what is likely to be intensified competition will simply be crushed and therefore Roche hopes that the wine cooperatives will have something to say about the organization for 1992 as he believes that the consequences will surely affect all of southwest France and not just UNIMEDOC. However, Roche fails to consider that UNIMEDOC markets cooperative wines with an appellation that is generic to the Médoc and therefore not as distinct as the communal appellations of Listrac, Pauillac, and St.-Estèphe. Consequently, the potential exists that the competition with foreign wines from the European Union will be experienced more intensely by French cooperatives with generic classifications than by those with communal classifications.

Once again, it is St.-Estèphe and its director Dumas who has assumed leadership in preparing for 1992 and thus ostensibly fulfilling Roche's plea that cooperatives take an active role in the organizational preparation for 1992. Dumas attended a meeting in the spring of 1990 with wine-cooperative administrators from France, Italy, Spain, Germany, Greece, and Portugal, the member countries of the EEC with wine cooperatives. At the first meeting they formed a confederation, drew up a charter, and decided that the confederation will be known under the German acronym INTERVINUM. According to Dumas, this initial meeting was complicated because although it was held to establish mutual cooperation across borders, it was also evident that special interests of the national variety were paramount. Dumas left the meeting somewhat discouraged because he feared that special interests would counter if not sabotage the efforts of European wine cooperatives to enter into mutual projects, a vital necessity with 1992 on the horizon. Since Dumas's retirement, INTERVINUM has continued to meet without accomplishing much that is concrete. At the very least, however, a formal organizational network exists for advancing European wine-cooperative interests and concerns and I am told by my informant-administrators that there is still hope that the participants will have a vision broader than protecting their particular interests.

It is not the wine cooperatives of the Médoc that are likely to experience the most difficulty with the consequences of 1992 and the expectation of increased European competition but rather those such as Sigoulès in the Dordogne, or even more so the cooperatives of Languedoc that are engaged in the production of low-cost wines. However, Sigoulès has some protection by virtue of its size and the fact that it carries the communal appellation of Bergerac.[16] Sigoulès is the second-largest cooperative in southwest France with over three hundred members and has not to date suffered from loss of members or surface area. Even though Sigoulès withdrew from the Fédération some years ago, it has actively sought to participate in cooperative marketing ventures with other wine cooperatives, such as Monbazillac, and with independents. Nonetheless, the Sigoulès administration has been attentive to the prospects of 1992 and has watched very carefully the measures being taken by INTERVINUM and some of the larger cooperative organizations. Perhaps most important, though, Sigoulès has diversified its own production through the introduction of grape juice. Unlike Médoc cooperatives, Sigoulès produces locally recognized red, white, and rosé wines.

The Monbazillac cooperative, on the other hand, is renowned for its production of sweet white wines that sell at a fraction of the cost of the celebrated wines of Chateau d'Yquem and other noted wines of the Sauterne region.[17] French consumers as well as those elsewhere in Europe who cannot afford an expensive Sauterne will often look to a Monbazillac as a suitable alternative. It is thus diversity, quality, and the cultivation of a special clientele that have proven to be the best strategies by which wine cooperatives have competed on national and international markets in the past and they are likely to be central to any success in the future.

Southwest French winegrowers have been, in short, sometimes reluctant participants in European plans for integrated trade and the establishment of markets less subject to national restrictions. As I have indicated, the primary opposition comes from a sense that the strict regulations regarding the production of French wine will not be uniformly applied to the other wine-producing countries of the European Union. This is an objection that is not merely technical but is profoundly linked to the French winegrowing tradition as it has taken form culturally and legally throughout the late nineteenth and well into the twentieth century. Reluctant or not, the cooperative winegrowers have had little choice but to organize and prepare for the consequences of 1992 as French politicians have often been those who have worked hardest to advance the interests of the Union. However, beyond the purview of European markets, Europe itself has been pushed forward toward greater cooperation, political, economic, and otherwise, both as a means of balancing economic and social inequities internal to the EEC itself, and as Tsoukalis has argued, as a strategy of securing the well-being of European economies within an arena that is manifestly global. However, perhaps Roche has said it best when he suggested that lack of preparation and the desire to confront the forces of European integration alone will merely lead to economic defeat if not outright disaster. With this in mind, most cooperatives have worked hard to diversify their offerings, to develop a special clientele, to improve the quality of their wines, and to make some effort to establish vital links to both French cooperative organizations and those that are more international so that their voices will be advanced along with the many competing interests of the European Union. While such linkages enhance the competitive potential of cooperatives, they by no means assure the future of cooperative winegrowing.

The southwest French wine-cooperative movement arose in the crisis years of the 1930s when winegrowers of all social classes found it progressively more difficult to market their wines. The crisis was precipitated, as we have seen, by several poor harvests, a worldwide economic crisis, a declining demand for wine among France's traditionally best clients including the United States, Canada, England, and the Soviet Union, and the hostilities of the Second World War which exacerbated the problem of circulating wine altogether. By collectivizing the resources of vinification and marketing, and yet maintaining conventional patterns of private ownership of vineyards and family succession, the wine cooperatives enabled the small and medium growers who primarily constituted their membership to endure years of hardship and to emerge from the postwar era with good prospects.

The survival of years of hardship and the adjustments to the global marketing of wine were not made, however, without some sacrifices on the part of those growers who elected to join wine cooperatives. The wine-cooperative legislation mandated stricter controls on the quantity of production and a commensurate commitment to agricultural modernization. This had the dual consequence of marginalizing and eventually eliminating most small growers unwilling to modernize and in the long run reduced the skill of future generations of growers who abdicated the knowledge and process of vinification to experts hired by the cooperatives. On the other hand, modernization has not completely destroyed the artisan quality of viticulture and has, according to my informants, positively reduced the hardships and time-consuming nature of work in the vineyards. The cooperatives thus provided a fair measure of security for small growers willing to conform to the mandates of the national cooperative legislation. Cooperatives have proved well able by virtue of their size and connection to organizations such as the Fédération, UNIMEDOC, and UNIDOR to keep pace with the changing scale and vicissitudes of capitalist wine production.

Wine cooperatives presently face, however, a challenge that is both profoundly connected to the past and yet immeasurably greater in scope. While wine cooperatives have fared reasonably well in the arena of global marketing and have pursued a special French clientele with vigor, they have been caught somewhat off guard by changing conditions of distribution and by the potential of multinational corporations and large financial groups to purchase vineyards at vastly inflated prices. As I have argued, the cooperative marketing organizations to date are managing to accommodate to the concentration in distribution through keeping prices competitive, aggressive advertising of their own, and in some cases by diversifying the products marketed. Cooperative wines can be found in the large supermarket chains that have assisted immeasurably in maintaining their distribution as competitive. However, this has done little to counterbalance the problem of cooperative succession as many small cooperative growers see the prospect of selling their small holdings for fabulous sums of money, even if only one to two hectares, as an unprecedented opportunity. It is therefore not clear that even strategies such as those of St.-Estèphe will do much to resolve the problem and consequences of corporate concentration to the wine cooperative's benefit.

The prospects that the new European Union will compound what is the already serious problem of corporate concentration has contributed to the anxiety presently experienced by cooperative administrators. There is no guarantee that international cooperative organizations such as INTERVINUM will definitively manage to mediate the privileging of national interests over the general welfare of wine cooperatives from all member nations. It is thus conceivable that disparities in the rules and regulations that govern wine production from one nation to the next will be maintained and that overproduction and the flooding of markets with surplus production will once again surface, as it has so many times in the past, as a serious threat to small-scale French wine-growing.

Although it is likely that the problems ensuing from multinationals and the potential for French markets to be flooded with inexpensive foreign wines will lead, as it has elsewhere agriculturally, to viticulture carried out on a more concentrated and grander scale, I believe that some southwest French growers will be better positioned than others to confront this challenge. There is little doubt, as Enjalbert has demonstrated with authority, that the choice historically early on to pursue and promote quality over quantity wine production has vastly enhanced the protection and viability of local and national markets and global competitiveness of those southwest French growers opting for quality (1953). That is, the quality growers have carved a niche in the market that so far has withstood the test of time, only periodically shaken by natural disasters, war, and worldwide economic decline. Therefore, those southwest growers who have sought to reproduce the practical and cultural standards, invented or otherwise, of the elite proprietors, at least as closely as resources will permit, are in the best position to survive the potential for enhanced competition in the European arena that surely follows from liberalized trading regulations. At the present time, it is thus Pauillac, Listrac, St.-Estèphe, and Monbazillac among the southwest French cooperatives that I studied that are most prepared for new developments in European trade, followed by Sigoulès mostly because of the diversity of its grape and wine production.

The potential for southwest French wine cooperatives to survive changing circumstances at the European and global levels is not merely, as I have argued throughout this book, a reflection of their differential position within the French winegrowing hierarchy and world system of political economy. To the contrary, I asserted, following Roudié (1985), that the construction of the southwest French winegrowing hierarchy itself was intended among other things to set elite growers and their wines apart culturally from both the product and lives of the vast majority of peasant winegrowers. The elite growers of the Médoc thus constructed homes that were small-scale replicas of the medieval châteaus and sought to market their wines, though also to protect against fraud, in bottles marked by the exclusivity of the château label. However, in seeking to differentiate their lives and wine culturally from the vast majority of southwest French growers, they also established practices which were embodied formally in classifications and legislation that set a standard for southwest wines and which many growers, including the wine cooperatives, sought to emulate. Therefore, while virtually no cooperative growers live in houses of splendor, they do aspire today to replicate as closely as possible the quality of elite wines and to play upon and benefit from their cultural associations. Thus, the position that southwest French wine cooperatives occupy presently within the French winegrowing hierarchy and their articulation with a global economic system is not the result of the logic of production and circulation or an economic rationality alone. This position has also been culturally produced, sustained, and differentiated.

However, it is equally important to recognize that cultural production and reproduction is not an autonomous activity. If discourse should serve as the metaphor for cultural invention, as it has so often in contemporary social theory, then we must be attentive to the power constraints that locate human agents or interlocutors historically and concretely within a potentially shifting social terrain. With the exception of some village elites, the majority of small producers who joined southwest French wine cooperatives were subaltern to the merchant-proprietors who owned the elite estates and who played a significant role in influencing the winegrowing legislation and classifications that have changed little to the present day. Social class in the context of a global wine economy was thus central to the inequalities that ensued in the unfolding of winegrowing discourse and culture. This does not mean that small growers who joined cooperatives were simply victims. To the contrary, as we have seen through Lescot and Bourgode, they were equally capable of making use of their common status to reinforce claims to authenticity. Nonetheless, this modest challenge to the cultural privilege and status of elite wines is secondary to the potential cultural capital and relative economic security that comes to wine cooperatives from identifying with rather than rejecting the special symbolic significance of elite wines. Thus the prospects and future of southwest French wine cooperatives will be fought out and forged on the interrelated terrains and frontiers of political economy and culture, an example that points beyond the product itself and to the struggles for self-recognition that mark more generally the lives of those who so often find themselves in the margins of history.

APPENDIX
SUMMARY OF WINE COOPERATIVES RESEARCHED

DORDOGNE

Cave Coopérative de Sigoulès
Appellations: Bergerac, Côtes de Bergerac
Founded: 1938
Number of members: 355
Area cultivated: 1,300 hectares

Cave Coopérative de Monbazillac
Appellations: Monbazillac, Bergerac Blanc Sec Sauvignon, Côtes de Bergerac liquoreux, Bergerac Rouge, Pécharment
Founded: 1941
Number of members: 150
Area cultivated: 800 hectares
Châteaus: Château Monbazillac, Château Septy, Château La Brie, Château Pion, Château Marsalet

MÉDOC

Cave Coopérative de St.-Estèphe
Appellation: Saint-Estèphe
Founded: 1934
Number of members: 188
Area cultivated: 305 hectares
Cooperative label: Marquis de Saint-Estèphe
Principal châteaus: Château Ladouys, Château Les Combes, Château Lartigue, Château La Croix de Pez, Château Tour de Pez

Cave Coopérative de Listrac
Appellation: Listrac
Founded: 1935
Number of members: 72
Area cultivated: 156 hectares
Cooperative label: Grand Listrac
Principal châteaus: Château Capdet-Clos du Fourcas, Château Vieux Moulin, Château Moulin du Bourg

Cave Coopérative de Pauillac
Appellation: Pauillac
Founded: 1933
Number of members: 122
Area cultivated: 106 hectares
Cooperative label: La Rose Pauillac
Principal châteaus: Haut-Saint-Lambert, Haut-Milon, Domaine des Gémeaux

Cave Coopérative de Bégadan
Appellation: Médoc
Founded: 1934
Number of members: 175
Area cultivated: 596 hectares
Cooperative label: Cave Saint-Jean
Principal châteaus: Château Le Bernet, Château Bessan-Ségur, Château Lassus

COOPERATIVE MEMBERS AND INDEPENDENTS

	Cooperative Members		Independents	
Area	*No. members*	*ha. cultivated*	*No. growers*	*ha. cultivated*
Gironde (Bordeaux region; 60 cooperatives)	6,646	24,205	12,747	78,771
Dordogne (9 cooperatives)	1,527	4,775	11,127	12,361
Lot-et-Garonne (8 cooperatives)	2,002	3,642	5,932	4,081
Pyrénées Atlantiques (4 cooperatives)	940	1,205	3,194	1,241

Source: La Fédération des Caves Coopératives de la Gironde et du Sud-Ouest de la France

NOTES

INTRODUCTION

1. This is not to say that wine cooperatives are totally apolitical. As I show in Chapter 4, there was a strong component of political motivation from the Left in the founding of wine cooperatives. While much of the political motivation has faded, to be replaced by motives that are largely pragmatic, there does remain some tension and ambiguity of motives between the pragmatic and the political.

2. While my use of the concept of margin certainly takes something from Derrida and his idea of textual exclusion (1974)—in my case the narrative of history—I believe that Wolf's general political contention that subaltern Europeans are often viewed without history is also germane to the southwest French wine-cooperative movement.

3. Of all three wines, Sigoulès rosés were the most respected and had on numerous occasions won medals of distinction. However, the Sigoulès rosé is not regarded with the same esteem as those of the Loire valley.

4. The Médoc is divided into two regions, Haut-Médoc and Bas-Médoc, that correspond respectively with Haut-Médoc and Médoc wine classifications. These terms have less to do with the elevation of winegrowing terrain than with the quality of the wine. According to Penning-Rowsell, the soil of the Bas-Médoc is sandier and has a higher content of clay than the Haut-Médoc which results in a larger yield at harvest (1969:174–77). It is widely accepted among experts that quality declines with higher yields and thus the lower-yielding harvests of the Haut-Médoc are believed to produce better wines. Bégadan is located in the Bas-Médoc and thus carries the generic Médoc classification. In addition to Haut-Médoc

and Médoc, the Médoc also has the communal classifications of St.-Estèphe, Pauillac, Moulis, Listrac, St.-Julien, and Margaux. It is the communal classifications that have the highest esteem in the Médoc.

5. In my original study in the Dordogne, I came across no women who were the actual working proprietors in the vineyards. However, in the Médoc the number of women proprietors working their own vineyards was on the increase and some of these women had assumed important administrative positions at the wine cooperatives.

6. Anthropologists have come to challenge the conventional view of culture as a set of beliefs and practices passed from one generation to the next. The problem with this conventional view, perhaps best represented by Tylor's "complex whole" (1873), is that culture is represented as uniform throughout a given population. What is overlooked is the degree to which culture can be an arena for conflicting or competing views, values, and social practices.

CHAPTER 1. ANTHROPOLOGY AND HISTORY

1. The concept of knowledge-constitutive interests is attributable to Jürgen Habermas (1971). Habermas uses the concept to refer to the establishment of actual and potential objects of knowledge. For Habermas, the constitution of these objects of knowledge is transcendental rather than empirical. Habermas identifies three transcendental knowledge-constitutive interests; the instrumental as reflected in work or labor, the communicative as reflected in consensus through language, and the emancipatory as reflected in reflexivity and critique. I use the concept of knowledge-constitutive interests here to refer to the social construction of objects of knowledge based upon the mediation of actual historical contexts. In this regard, my use of the concept is empirical without being empiricist.

2. My own *Understanding Cultures* discusses in detail the relationship between European colonialism, instrumental rationality, and British structural-functionalism (1984). Apart from the political implications that are evident, my critique is essentially epistemological.

3. In Marx, it is the concept of oriental despotism that Said has in mind. Said believes that this concept has the unfortunate consequence of treating widely different societies as the same.

    While there is much merit to Said's argument, he tends to treat the Occident as if it were homogeneous. I am sure that he would maintain that the East has not systematically tried to impose itself on the West in any manner equivalent to Western imperialism. However, any view that maintains that Western societies are essentially the same is a mystification.

4. I believe that Fabian's insight is very important insofar as it points to the historical formation of anthropology and the unrecognized hegemonic continuities between past and present. However, there is some question as to whether it is possible to engage informants under conditions that are mutual or reciprocal.

5. Structural-functionalism in anthropology, which predominated throughout the colonial era, is a derivative of Malinowski's functionalism and Radcliffe-Brown's structuralism. Malinowski argued that the purpose of the cultural system and its institutions is to meet the biologically derived needs of its members. For Malinowski, society was analogous to a biological organism whereby the social parts, like the parts of a cell, are interrelated in such a manner as to contribute to the maintenance of the whole.

   For Radcliffe-Brown, the principal component of a cultural system is its structure or sets of social relationships between individuals and groups of individuals. As with Malinowski, the purpose or function of social action was to maintain the integrity of the social order. Consequently, the emphasis in both Malinowski and Radcliffe-Brown on the integrative function of human activity eclipsed the transformative potentials of human actors in that change was regarded as dysfunctional. Human societies were viewed as law-like and thus continuous with the very nature from which structural-functionalism as a theoretical model was derived.

6. There was a long period in which peoples without writing were regarded as not having a history. Oral accounts were viewed with the greatest suspicion as highly subjective. It is, of course, the case today that oral history has assumed a place of importance nearly equal to that of written history.

7. I say ambivalence because clearly anyone familiar with the works of Dickens or Marx will recognize both a sense of wonderment and horror at the nascent development of industrial capitalism and the squalor that it produced. For an excellent account of nineteenth-century views of the Industrial Revolution, see Steven Marcus (1974).

8. Raymond Williams has, perhaps better than anyone, pointed out the nostalgia present in late-nineteenth-century literature for the pastoral countryside (1973). Williams reminds us, though, that capitalism had its origins in the countryside and not in the city and thus the pastoral conceals the disruptive and violent features of capital accumulation.

9. For a comprehensive overview and critique of the Anglo-American rationality debates, see my 1984 *Understanding Cultures*. In short, the Anglo-American rationality debates depart from arguments between anthropologists, sociologists, and philosophers over the nature of rationality. Evans-

Pritchard's writings on Zande witchcraft become a central focus of the debates as some participants find rationality to be contextual and thus witchcraft is rational while others believe in universal criteria and thus dismiss the rationality of witchcraft beliefs in light of modern science.

10. I have argued elsewhere that not only do anthropologists base their identities on the Third World other but also that this is reinforced by the funding of research, hiring in the discipline, and the directions of American foreign policy. This has resulted in a situation where Europeanist anthropologists are all too often marginal. For a developed version of this argument see Ulin 1991.

11. I have in mind here Hobsbawm and Ranger's *The Invention of Tradition* (1983). This book has made a major impact on how anthropologists think of tradition and will also serve as a point of evaluation of my discussion of French elite wines in Chapter 2.

12. For an excellent critique of Giddens's theory of structuration, see R. W. Connell's *Gender and Power* (1987). Connell argues that the process of structuration is static and insufficiently responsive to historical agency.

13. Marxism by no means constitutes a uniform position or school. It should be clear that Wolf and Mintz distance themselves from reductive versions of marxism, such as that of Althusser, in that they do not accept the primacy of base over superstructure. Rather, Wolf and Mintz see culture in terms of material practice and so believe that the life of symbols is necessarily tied up with productive social relations. However, it should also be clear that the primacy of the logic of production in the historical life of humankind is what the marxist tradition shares. For a discussion of the limits of this perspective, see Ulin 1984 and 1991.

14. See, for example, Emiko Ohnuki-Tierney's *Culture Through Time: Anthropological Approaches* (1990), especially the essays by Ortner and Fernandez.

15. Geertz also acknowledges quite specifically his theoretical debt to Max Weber, Gilbert Ryle, Ludwig Wittgenstein, and Kenneth Burke. The essential link between these scholars is the articulation of a communicative understanding of social life whereby the emphasis on socially constructed meaning is primary.

16. The concept "life world" is taken from Husserl and that of "lived experience" from phenomenology in general. In both cases, the emphasis is on socially constructed or constituted meanings.

17. Geertz holds a position at the Institute for Advanced Study in Princeton, New Jersey. This has enabled him to conduct a sustained intellectual exchange with the many esteemed members of the history department at Princeton University. The Princeton historians, such as Darnton and

Natalie Zemon Davis, have played a leading role in the shaping of the new cultural history.

18. It should be noted that the fourth-generation Annales historian, Roger Chartier, has criticized Geertz for overlooking the conflict and struggle that is certainly part of cultural forms and practices. This is why I have qualified my comments to refer to certain versions of cultural history as the cultural historians most certainly do not speak with one voice.

    There is always some risk to characterizing scholarly work in such sweeping terms. Geertz and Ladurie are discussed in order to illustrate certain kinds of problems that arise when human populations are regarded as undifferentiated and culture is viewed as univocal. I believe that this is much less of a problem in Darnton's work or in that of Natalie Zemon Davis.

19. I have reviewed this book for *International Studies in Philosophy* (Ulin 1995). As a whole, the essays are very stimulating and do make the important point that culture has been given insufficient attention in studies of social change. However, I find the emphasis on structure in some of the essays to be problematic, especially since the cultural continuities of the *longue durée* seem to be forced. However, there are essays, such as those by James Fernandez and Valerio Valeri, that owe much more to Bakhtin and theories of tropes than to any specific version of structuralism.

20. While I follow's Habermas's characterization of social life as communicative and his critique of the marxist concept of labor, I do not accept his theory as a totality. There are significant problems with Habermas's use of Kohlberg's developmental psychology to characterize the reflexive and critical potentials of different types of societies. For a more comprehensive summary of my objections, see Ulin 1991.

CHAPTER 2. INVENTION AS CULTURAL CAPITAL

1. For other sources that stress the invention-of-tradition theme, see Benedict Anderson (1983), Richard Handler and Jocelyn Linnekin (1984), and Allan Hanson (1990).

2. Handler and Linnekin both believe that tradition is a cultural construction, that social life in general is symbolic, and that it is objectivist to maintain a distinction between authentic and invented tradition. I do not mean to imply, however, that their views are identical. Linnekin seems to speak more directly in support of postmodernism while Handler (1986) seems to tie the issue of authenticity to our own history and "possessive individualism."

3. Linnekin is concerned that the continual challenge to social-science concepts will leave us without a vocabulary to critically engage or construct the social world. These problems are not simply epistemological but political as well.

4. It is the oenologists who are the most reductive in emphasizing natural conditions over those that are social. However, even scholars such as Dion (1977) and Lachiver (1988), both of whom have written widely cited works on French winegrowing history, make no small matter about climate and soil. Furthermore, they seem to accept the idea that there is only one standard of quality and thus of taste.

5. The historical reconstruction of southwest French wines that follows is necessarily abbreviated and is more thoroughly developed in Chapters 3 and 4.

6. It is, however, the case that Médoc wines are less subject to destructive summer storms, especially those with damaging winds and hail. This does not mean though that the essential climatic conditions on a day-to-day basis are much different.

7. Many of the elite growers assumed a position of leadership in the local or regional winegrowing associations. These associations were then used to pressure the French government to pursue legislation to counter fraud. In the late eighteenth century, many of these elites, especially in winegrowing regions like the Médoc, were also members of the Bordeaux Parliament and thus had considerable political connections. Later on, in the nineteenth and early twentieth centuries, it was owners of the large merchant houses, like Rothschild, who gained ownership of elite vineyards and assumed leadership roles in the various winegrowing associations.

8. Nobility of the robe were bourgeois who purchased aristocratic titles. This was a common practice among the bourgeoisie following the French Revolution.

   Much to the surprise of those who have come to associate wine with France, the consumption of wine by peasants and industrial workers would not occur on an extensive basis until the late nineteenth and early twentieth centuries.

9. There is little doubt that wine guides such as Robert M. Parker, Jr.'s *Bordeaux* have done much to influence the educated consumer. That the connection to cultural capital is paramount is supported by the introductory sentence to Parker's book: "There can be no question that the romance, if not downright mysticism, of opening a bottle of Bordeaux from a famous château has a grip and allure that are hard to resist" (1991:11). While Parker goes on to qualify this statement by suggesting that some châteaus have an inflated reputation, just as others are overlooked, he nonetheless

devotes much of the book to celebrating the elite châteaus and thus reproducing the allure.

CHAPTER 3. CAPITAL ACCUMULATION AND THE SOCIAL TRANSFORMATION OF WINEGROWING IN SOUTHWEST FRANCE

1. Althusserian structuralist marxism has lost its position of influence in the marxist literature with the ascendancy of poststructuralism and postmodernism. Nonetheless, theorists such as Sahlins (1985) and Giddens (1984) have made some effort to maintain its vitality, albeit in a reformulated version.

2. For a critique of the formalism of structuralism, including the Althusserian version, see my 1984 *Understanding Cultures*.

3. This is a theme that has largely been argued by anthropologists in their attempt to show that capitalism as an international system is interpreted and shaped locally. See, for example, Michael Taussig (1980) and Jean and John Comaroff (1992).

4. Pijassou maintains that the historical materials on Bordeaux wines in general are scant prior to the period of the English occupation.

5. I owe much of the historical reconstruction of the early period of Bergerac to Jacques Beauroy's excellent account of winegrowing (1976). Most of the principal works on French wine such as Dion (1977) or Lachiver (1988) are devoted, to the contrary, to accounts of the elite winegrowing regions of which Bergerac is not a part. In most cases, these sources devote only a few pages to the Bergerac region. Elsewhere (Ulin 1987), I have developed the theme of Bergerac's exclusion from the major works on French winegrowing as illustrative of the relation between historical writing and hegemony.

6. The city of Bordeaux is actually located on the Garonne River which, like the Dordogne, joins the Gironde just north of the city.

7. Eugen Weber argues that the creation of a French national identity took place between the last quarter of the nineteenth century and the First World War (1976). Prior, to this period, Weber maintains that the rural population of France had an essentially local or regional identity.

   During my fieldwork throughout the 1980s, especially in the interior, informants would periodically refer with distaste to the English occupation. I believe that this was more related to the purchasing of summer homes on the part of the English and the inflation in property values that ensued rather than a cultural memory dating to the twelfth century.

Nonetheless, it is interesting to note that the English occupation is invoked to account for social inequality.

8. There is really very little agreement among winegrowing experts as to the specific advantages of soil and climate in the Bordeaux region. For example, Pijassou begins his book on the Médoc by arguing that the soil is superior in this region directly to the north of Bordeaux (1980). However, this is countered by Roudié who argues that the topography of Bordeaux is essentially the same as that of Bergerac although he remarks that Bergerac wines have not enjoyed the same success (1988). I believe that there are minor differences in the natural conditions of both regions but monumental differences in terms of how these natural conditions have been socially and historically constructed.

9. Sweet white wines can be made from any number of white grapes. The grapes are left on the vine until they begin to rot (called the noble rot) which increases the sugar content. This is a process that demands careful attention because if the grapes rot too far they will be of no use in the making of wine. During the seventeenth century, it was the muscadelle grape from which sweet white wines, and white wines in general, were commonly made in the Bergerac region. Today, at the Monbazillac cooperative, located just outside Bergerac, muscadelle is blended with sauvignon and sémillon grapes. In fact, the largest component is sémillon which makes up approximately 80 percent of the blended wine. Sémillon grapes are excellent for making sweet white wines because they have a thin skin and so the grapes rot very quickly.

10. For an excellent account of the sugar trade that linked Europe, Africa, and the Caribbean, see Mintz 1985.

11. It can be argued that the *grands crus* were developed in the latter half of the seventeenth century. However, given that the majority of the development took place in the eighteenth and nineteenth centuries, I begin my discussion of the *grands crus* with the eighteenth century.

12. This is most evident in the long-term association of red wines with the Médoc and the association of whites, especially sweet white wines, with the Bergerac region. Their respective histories accounts for differences in plantations and different ties to northern European markets.

13. I believe that Sobul is correct in claiming that "feudal-like" social relations were not so quickly swept away in certain areas of France. In this respect, his argument supports that of Skocpol in claiming a gradual transition to capitalism. However, because the southwest of France was tied into international markets since the twelfth century, the sector of viticulture was ahead of other arenas of agriculture in terms of the transition to capitalism.

14. This was the case with Thomas Jefferson who made a trip to the Bordeaux region toward the end of the eighteenth century. At this time, he had already tasted the wines of Haut-Brion and so made a visit to this estate located just outside of the city of Bordeaux in Pessac.

15. It is important to note that other forms of labor, such as labor exchange, coexisted with wage labor.

16. In just the past year, it has been reported that there is an outbreak of phylloxera in the California vineyards. One proposed solution is to graft phylloxera-resistant French vines onto American stocks. This would no doubt be a just repayment of a long-standing debt.

17. The leaders of syndicates were well aware of the sporadic peasant rebellions that marked the history of wine production. They therefore sought to maintain the status quo by alleviating some of the most severe financial burdens on the peasantry such as the cost of resources used in vineyard cultivation and wine production.

18. *Piquettes* are made by adding sugar and water to the skins of already pressed grapes. *Piquettes* were normally consumed by workers on the large estates and sometimes these workers would hold back on the first pressing so that the *piquette* made from the second pressing would be improved.

CHAPTER 4. THE "MAKING" OF SOUTHWEST FRENCH WINE COOPERATIVES

1. Loubère, Dion, and Lachiver seem to look at the movement only in terms of its overall economic telos or the necessity of accommodating to capitalist social relations. While their assessment is not wholly incorrect, I believe it overlooks radical social movements in the countryside which affected the creation of the first wine cooperatives and the possible articulation between urban working-class movements and those of the countryside.

2. It has been Bakhtin who has had a marked influence on viewing ethnographic narratives as polyphonic or multivocal. In terms of ethnography, many anthropologists now recognize that the representation of the other is problematic and laden with power. Consequently, there has been some attempt to foreground a multiplicity of voices in the writing of ethnography, a situation that Bakhtin in other contexts referred to as heteroglossia. The foregrounding of informants' voices has been seized upon by postmodern ethnographers in their argument that ethnographies should be fragmented as this more nearly approximates the fragmentation and multiplicity of views and voices central to the fieldwork encounter. For a review and critique of postmodern ethnography see Ulin 1991.

3. It was Althusser who introduced the notion of overdetermination to marxist theory by implying that the economy in the last instance was dominant in shaping the course of social interaction. There has been a tendency in structuralist and poststructuralist theory alike to eclipse the significance of human agency, a position that is challenged by Thompson's idea of "making." See, for example, his classic *The Making of the English Working Class.*

4. While individual proprietorship may be largely sacrosanct, French agriculturalists are clearly not selfish or even self-absorbed. I witnessed on numerous occasions my informants putting aside their own work to assist their neighbors.

5. See my discussion of the invention or cultural construction of wine as a natural beverage in Chapter 2. Albert was responding to the fact that wine could be made from agricultural products such as beets and it was his desire to have wine limited to the natural fermentation of grapes. Wines made from beets and other agricultural products contributed not just to fraud but to the flooding of the market and declining prices.

6. It is interesting to note that my informants have identified the purchase of vineyards by foreign investment groups as a very recent development. While none of these informants were alive in the period described by Pijassou, foreign capital does not seem to have precipitated the same degree of social disruption as is the case today. I discuss the intrusion of foreign capital and its social consequences in Chapter 9.

7. In difficult times, it was not uncommon for winegrowers to agree on a price with merchants in advance of the harvest. This guaranteed a certain return to the grower but often at a price considerably lower than that normally obtained at market. For example, Pijassou remarks that unlike Lafite and Margaux, Latour did not renew its contract with the merchant and so received 2,650 francs per cask.

8. I owe this idea to Yvês Lebreton. He suggested to me that he knows many individuals from the city who still travel to rural areas to visit friends and parents and that these visits are often the occasion for protracted political discussions. Lebreton believes, and I agree, that there is no reason to believe that it was different in the past. I can attest, furthermore, especially from my earlier research in the Périgord, that French winegrowers were eager to discuss both local and international politics. I was always deeply impressed by their awareness of international politics and skepticism toward the national government.

9. When I commenced research on Dordogne and Médoc cooperatives, I expected to be able to work with and interview persons who had a direct involvement in the cooperative movement. While I knew that they would

likely be very advanced in age, given that the cooperatives I studied were all founded in the 1930s, none of the original founders were alive. I was therefore left with the option of interviewing surviving relatives who in most cases were an excellent source of information. Archival sources on the founding of wine cooperatives are at best meager.

10. Lenin wished to account for the fact that the middle peasantry seemed more willing to participate in political rebellion than either the upper or lower peasantries. Though the context is Russia, Lenin believed that the upper peasantry had too much to lose by participating in political rebellion while the lower peasantry was too dependent on the patronage of the elites. In the case of southwest France, we do not have three levels of peasantries, but Lenin's example does help us to understand why the most destitute and thus most dependent winegrowers were often resistant to cooperatives.

11. I will take up in the next chapter the question of whether in spite of the censuring of political discussion at the cooperatives that they still have a collective political purpose to serve.

12. Contrary to what many scholars have asserted, Rogers argues that the precapitalist family structure persisted in rural France in spite of capitalist modernization. It had been traditionally thought that a greater nucleation and isolation of the family went hand-in-hand with modernization.

13. This comment is made with full recognition of the social construction of taste and quality as argued in the previous chapter. However, when talking about French wines, it is difficult to get away from a stratified or hierarchical discourse and so I may periodically reproduce this in my own discussion of French wines.

14. My informants told me repeatedly that fraud is still perpetrated by unscrupulous merchants who buy up the harvests from numerous growers and then blend the wines in their own cellars.

CHAPTER 5. CYCLES OF LABOR

1. We will see in Chapter 6 that Braverman's discussion of the division of labor under capitalism is in fact useful for grasping the subordination of cooperative members to the administrators and elites of the wine cooperatives.

2. The largest growers at the cooperative will often hire one or two workers to help either year round in the vineyards or seasonally. This is especially so when the children of the winegrower show no interest in winegrowing as a profession. An alternative is to take on an apprentice from the local

agricultural school. The apprentice is taught by working side by side with a winegrower in exchange for room and board.

3. Sider explains that fisher families were prevented from owning land and thus they could not diversify their production. This intensified their dependency on exchange with the merchants for essential resources.

4. This is a point that I will take up in Chapter 7 when I discuss the extensive marketing capabilities that have been instituted by the wine cooperatives and the relative degree of independence from the large merchant houses that this has offered cooperative members.

5. The inhabitants of the southwest, especially uneducated farmers or *paysans,* are well aware of the ridicule to which they are subjected by Parisians.

6. In the Médoc and the Dordogne, it was common for full-time growers to compose only 5 to a maximum of 10 percent of cooperative members. Monbazillac was an exception in that the majority of cooperative members are full-time. Moreover, at Monbazillac the average vineyard size is 9.5 hectares, compared to Sigoulès where 60 percent of the members hold less than 2 hectares and 20 percent less than .5 hectares. While there is no general rule, it is nearly impossible to conduct winegrowing on a full-time basis without 9 hectares of vineyards in the Dordogne and approximately 6 in the Médoc.

7. There were other tasks that I was not permitted to perform. Much of the work in the vineyards, such as spraying, is now done by tractor and it involves much more skill and risk than simply being able to drive in a straight line. Consequently, my services were often the most mundane and least skilled labor.

8. Loubère and his coauthors have shown that the mechanization of agriculture has done much to take women out of the vineyards (1985). They argue that women in the agricultural labor force in general have declined from 44 percent in 1921 to 19 percent in 1962.

9. I was often teased by the winegrowers for my predominantly intellectual work. They argued that I must also do the heavier manual work and must have pictures of myself doing such work so that my friends back in the States would have evidence that I really labored. I complied and thus agreed to carry one of these heavy packs into which the harvested grapes were deposited. After several hours of such labor, I paid the price the next day. I could not get out of bed as I had excruciating pains and spasms in my lower back. The only relief I had for several weeks of discomfort was cortisone shots given by a French physician.

10. I refer to the driver as "he" because I did not witness, nor was I told of cases, where women perform this work. However, I see no reason apart

from the weight of tradition as to why women could not perform this type of work.

11. Bourgode knows that the loans from the French national bank were necessary for cooperatives to be created. However, he, like many growers, likes to see the winegrowers who joined the cooperative movement as self-sufficient and self-sacrificing.

12. There are oenological centers all over the southwest of France. These centers serve as advisors both to cooperatives and to the famous château estates. Most the oenologists at these centers have received their education at the University of Bordeaux and often under the celebrated Emile Peynaud.

13. Brazil is now exporting a fair amount of fine wine to the United States. Brazilian winegrowers are aging their wines in oak barrels because they believe American consumers like their wines with a slight oak flavor. They purchase the handmade oak barrels from artisans in Kentucky.

14. This assertion is potentially supported by Herzfeld, who argues with theoretical import that self-identity is not only contingent on its particular regional embodiment but also, as he has shown with rural Greece, on its symbolic and historical potential to represent metonymically the nation-state (1982).

Although it may seem like common sense that identity and work are linked inextricably, this assumption, as Baudrillard has shown, is itself contingent or historically particular (1975). I therefore wish to avoid the conclusion that my informants identified with winegrowing and nothing else.

15. This is not to say that local pride in their wines was absent. However, Sigoulès growers understood well their subordinate position in the winegrowing hierarchy, not to mention the winegrowing hierarchy's fundamental ties to elite French culture.

16. By standardized, Sigoulès cooperative members had in mind a wine that would taste the same from year to year. This is quite contrary to the attitudes of Médoc growers who expect the wine to vary in taste from year to year. For Médoc growers, a wine that is standardized is one lacking in distinction. Moreover, the Sigoulès cooperative now produces and markets grape juice which would be unthinkable to Médoc cooperatives where the reputation of wines and thus quality are paramount.

17. In France, *paysan* has actually been used in both positive and negative senses. When establishing the antiquity of French national tradition and its ties to the soil, *paysan* has been employed positively. However, within a discourse that emphasizes "modernization," and especially from the perspective of those who live in cities and identify with elite culture, *paysan*

connotes the unrefined and rude, the antithesis to progress. For a discussion of the uses of *paysan* in France, see Susan Rogers's excellent essay on this theme (1987).

18. There are a fair number of part-time growers in the Médoc who, like the growers in the Dordogne, gain their livelihoods outside viticulture. These growers are, therefore, less likely to take their identify from the activity and work of winegrowing.

19. Because Monbazillac has a better reputation than Sigoulès, the members of the Monbazillac cooperative are more likely than other growers from the Dordogne to see their own work as analogous to an art. On the whole though, there is much more mystique and sense of a hermetic tradition surrounding the labor in elite winegrowing regions than in regions where mass or table wines predominate. Consequently, maintaining an identity with winegrowing as an art places an emphasis on something that can only be learned in the vineyards, thus preserving and protecting the reputedly special character of elite growths.

    Emile Peynaud (1988) argues that most Médoc winegrowers were reluctant to accept the advice of oenologists in the early stages of this science as they saw their practice as much more akin to an art not subject to control. It was only as recently as the 1960s that oenology began to be widely accepted among growers.

20. Given the segregation of men and women in some small rural French communities, it was not always easy for me to obtain information on female contributions to winegrowing from the women themselves. However, I will discuss the case of Ducros in Chapter 8. While her particular circumstances may not be illustrative of all female winegrowers, they nonetheless show the struggle of a female winegrower to gain the respect of her predominantly male colleagues.

21. The importance of class stratification among cooperative growers is developed more fully in the next chapter on the structure and organization of wine cooperatives.

22. There is in fact considerable competition between the Bordeaux and Burgundy winegrowing regions. There is, however, no consensus as to which region produces the better wines.

CHAPTER 6. COOPERATIVE ORGANIZATION AND THE REPRODUCTION OF POWER

1. I use "ordinary" rather than the more common "table" wines because 43.4 percent of the wine produced in the Dordogne is *appellation d'origine contrôlée* (AOC). As for the Sigoulès cooperative, 80 percent of their

wines are AOC while at the Monbazillac cooperative the figure is slightly higher. The term *table wine* is misleading in that it gives the impression that the wine is unclassified. Nonetheless, even the classified wines from the Sigoulès cooperative fall far short in reputation compared to those from Médoc cooperatives.

2. In some respects, the standardized charter operates much like a standardized apartment lease that can be purchased in virtually any stationery store in the United States. These leases simplify the drawing up of a contract between a landlord and tenants, thus avoiding expensive legal costs, and may be modified to comply with local housing laws.

3. I can assert this authoritatively with respect to wine cooperatives in the Médoc and the Dordogne. However, I have been led to believe through cooperative officials and the scant published literature on cooperatives that the stratification at cooperatives is essentially ubiquitous. I use the qualifier "essentially" because it is the case that the stratification or hierarchy of growers who are members of cooperatives is somewhat more pronounced in elite winegrowing regions. Nonetheless, the consequences, as I shall show, are the same for the governance or daily operation of the cooperatives.

4. For those unfamiliar with industrial psychology, Taylor remains the founding figure based upon his contributions throughout the early part of the twentieth century. Taylor's intent was to make workers more efficient through measuring their movements and timing their activities. Such studies enabled managers and owners of factories to adjust the location of machinery and to rationalize, monitor, and thus control the movements and work habits of employees. Taylor's time-management studies have been regarded by marxists such as Braverman as part of the degradation of labor.

5. Braverman's point concerning nonalienated labor is consistent with Marx's and even Hegel's notion of identification. That is, when workers have control over both the concept and execution of their work projects they are able to see their own labor embodied in the products of their work. This is not the case when work becomes fragmented and workers lose control over the labor process. Under such conditions, the product of labor appears to take on an independent existence and thereby appears as alien to those who have produced it.

6. The division between younger and older members of the cooperatives has been exacerbated by the fact that younger members tend to be graduates of regional agricultural schools. This training is often looked down upon by the older members who have learned their trade through apprenticeship and look upon schooling as abstract theoretical knowledge. This

point will be taken up in Chapter 8 on winegrowing and the life world of winegrowers.

7. The leisure of the full-time growers was perceived to be a positive characteristic of their labor. They often remarked to me "where else can one take the time off in the afternoon to speak to an anthropologist."

8. I found at most cooperatives that the members consistently exaggerated the size of the average holding. For example, Lefèvre of the Sigoulès cooperative believed the average holding to be ten hectares.

9. The differences in price followed not so much from vicissitudes of the market, though these are important, but rather from the appellation or classification of the wine. Obviously, the higher the classification, the larger the sum received for the wine.

10. In other communes of the Médoc such as Pauillac, the permissible yields can be half of what is permitted in Listrac. It is asserted that there is an inverse relation between quality of wine and yields per hectare.

11. Monbazillac is the one exception in the Dordogne in that it is a delimited winegrowing area that is monocultural. Consequently, there is a greater emphasis, even if not always realized, on gaining one's livelihood exclusively from winegrowing.

    Gilles Blanchard, president of the Listrac cooperative, was the one exception in the Médoc. He had a large herd of cows and was assisted in their care by his son. I know of no other similar circumstances in the Médoc.

12. This is a point that I address in Chapter 9 by discussing the impact of multinationals on elite winegrowing regions and the problems this has caused for wine cooperatives.

13. With the closing of the refinery in Pauillac, many jobs were lost, resulting in an exodus to urban areas. Consequently, numerous small growers who left the Médoc sold their properties to proprietors of large estates. Although we are talking about small properties, this resulted in an important net loss for the Pauillac wine cooperative.

14. The largest proprietors generally make up no more than 2.5 percent of the membership.

15. The arrangement that Albert had with his sister was a common means through which siblings dealt with the problem of partible inheritance. Another arrangement that was somewhat less common was for one sibling to buy out his/her brothers and sisters to create a property sufficiently large to gain one's livelihood exclusively from winegrowing. This was less common because of the capital or loans required to buy out siblings.

16. This is a point that is somewhat variable. In the case of the Listrac cooperative, the president and vice-president are named by the Board of Directors, while at other cooperatives they may be elected by the membership at large. However, in all cases those named for office must be approved by the membership of the cooperative.

17. The fact that members of the Board of Directors must be of French nationality has taken on renewed significance in light of the purchasing of vineyards, especially in elite winegrowing regions, by foreign multinational corporations. This issue will be taken up in Chapter 9.

18. Unfortunately there are no daughters who have become presidents and vice-presidents of cooperatives. However, their importance to winegrowing administration is beginning to change as in the Médoc in particular one can find women serving on the Board of Directors. I address this theme in my discussion of Ducros in Chapter 8.

19. Given the importance of marketing to the cooperatives and the various forms that it takes, I will devote the next chapter exclusively to the marketing channels pursued by cooperative presidents and directors.

20. There are rare circumstances when a cooperative president will go back to school. For example, Lebrun, president of the Pauillac cooperative, decided that it would benefit the cooperative if he took an oenology course at the University of Bordeaux. He enrolled and completed the course. His actions are, however, exceptional.

21. There is some irony here as the cooperative structure is mediated by the French state and articulates well, as I have argued, with the objectives of agricultural modernization.

22. Language is an important marker of regional identity in France. In the southwest of France, apart from the patois that is spoken on some social occasions by the elderly, the French is distinct from that spoken in Paris by virtue of the fact that the ends of words are not dropped when spoken. People from the south are often ridiculed by Parisians for the way they speak French.

23. In France it is not uncommon for sons especially to follow in the footsteps of their fathers who worked for the French national railway. In this sense, Dumas was breaking with family tradition.

24. This is not to say that presidents do not have autonomy, especially in cases where there is no director. However, they must attend to their own vineyards and so cannot devote themselves full-time to the cooperatives, as a director can.

25. So as not to overcomplicate matters here, I will leave the description of UNIMEDOC and marketing in general to the next chapter.

26. I was of course curious to attend a meeting of the Board of Directors and on more than one occasion requested to do so. However, while this was a topic of some debate, I was never granted permission to attend.

27. There were times that I came to truly understand the limits of fieldwork undertaken alone. Given the number of cooperatives and informants with which I had contact, it was just not possible to spend a great deal of time with the number of marketing organizations and societies upon which some of the cooperatives relied.

CHAPTER 7. WINE COOPERATIVES AND MARKETING: PROCESS AND ORGANIZATION

1. In the eighteenth and nineteenth centuries, the Médoc was heavily forested. Forests were cut down in order to expand the plantation of vineyards as demands for Médoc wines increased worldwide. With the expansion of vineyards, polyculture essentially disappeared from the Médoc.

2. As I argued in Chapter 2, the naturalization of wine criteria was also extended to climate and soil. Thus, it is generally argued that Bordeaux wines are superior to those of the southwest interior because of a more favorable climate and soil. This conceals the sociocultural and historical foundation to such criteria.

3. The crisis of the 1930s also resulted in the sale of many elite estates to both French and foreign firms. Most of these proprietors were forced to sell due to indebtedness to the banks. Those who did survive were often faced with reducing the size of their vineyards.

4. It was these influential merchant houses that had a great deal to do with the defining of wine as a "natural" beverage thus excluding other dried fruits used to make peasant wines.

5. Evidence of the small proprietors processing their own grapes exists in the Médoc with abandoned stone buildings which I am told housed the presses of peasant proprietors. With the formation of cooperatives, those who joined relinquished the processing of harvested grapes to the cooperatives.

6. As noted in Chapter 2, the issue of fraud raised questions for consumers concerning the authenticity of wines. *Courtiers* were thus relied upon to guarantee that a wine did in fact come from a particular region and property.

7. There are of course some renowned châteaus in Listrac as well that have contributed to the overall regional reputation of Listrac. Perhaps the two most famous are Château Fourcas Hosten and Château Clarke, the latter being owned by the Rothschild family.

8. In contrast to Parisian restaurants, it is expected that local restaurants will feature local wines. This contributes to the charm of the restaurant and the nostalgia the city dwellers have for the countryside.

9. Technically speaking, Sigoulès wine has a Bergerac appellation. However, it costs only 8 francs per bottle and is therefore the sort of wine that most middle- and working-class families can consume on a daily basis.

10. The major attractions of the Médoc, apart from its vineyards, are the Atlantic beaches and campgrounds. As for the Dordogne or the Périgord, its medieval villages, country cuisine, and prehistoric caves are famous.

11. The Médoc cooperatives are in proximity to Atlantic beaches and campgrounds which are especially popular among Dutch and German tourists. I witnessed at the cooperatives on numerous occasions groups of Dutch and German tourists purchasing large quantities of wine, which was dispensed directly from the vats into plastic containers. The wine was then consumed at the campgrounds.

12. Tourists often come to small villages in search of "authentic" French culture and it is the tourist boards that play a significant role in imaginatively reconstructing what life was thought to be like in past times.

13. There are large marketing firms that also market wines under château labels. Like the cooperatives, they merely vinify separately the grapes from the many proprietors from whom they have purchased harvests.

14. Frossard is referring to the fact that some of the large Bordeaux merchant houses have disappeared and have been replaced by international capitalist firms sometimes in the form of banks and insurance companies. I will take up this issue in Chapter 9.

15. Because these organizations perform essentially similar functions, I will highlight the specific objectives of each and only summarize their general activities so as to avoid redundancy.

16. Pierre Martin, like many of the early cooperative leaders, came from an influential family and thus can hardly be considered a peasant. Nonetheless, he was a passionate advocate of the rights of small growers.

17. Chandou succeeded Martin as president of the Fédération in 1974 and retired in 1988. It is not surprising that Chandou's position would differ from that of Ducros as Chandou was obligated to work cooperatively with the large marketing firms and distributors.

18. The impact of the European Union on wine cooperatives will be by no means uniform. It is likely that the impact will be most specifically felt by cooperatives that produce table wines. However, I will take up this issue more fully in the concluding chapter.

19. Although wine cooperatives are subordinate in the winegrowing hierarchy, collectively they produce a large percentage of French wine. For

example, Loubère reports that in 1985, France's 1,158 wine cooperatives with 273,711 members accounted for 47 percent of the national production (1990:147).

20. One merely has to think of the impact of United Fruit Company in Latin America and the displacement of the peasantry through the concentration of land ownership and the control of markets.

21. These large supermarket chains are beginning to have the same impact in France that Wal-Mart has in the United States. Because they buy and sell in volume, they can outcompete local stores by selling at a much cheaper price. Consequently, local stores are beginning to give way to these supermarket giants. As one can imagine, it is important to ensure that one's wines appear on the shelves of such chains as Carrefour or Casino.

22. They could not always be frank with me for fear that their criticism would, if made public, hurt their working relations with others. I believe that their guarded attitude is perfectly appropriate.

23. While St.-Estèphe and Pauillac carry their own communal appellations, they both fall within the general domain of the Haut Médoc.

24. Money is often borrowed from the French national bank, Crédit Agricole, in order to finance the purchasing of tractors, vineyards, and other equipment used in the treatment of the plants. These loans are long term and so the cooperative members are dependent on regular returns from the sale of their wines.

25. The St.-Estèphe cooperative, to the contrary, has long been a member of the UCCV and from what I could ascertain is very pleased with the relation.

26. For the critique of Frank and Wallerstein's respective theories, see Chapter 1. The small winegrowers of southwest France were not simple victims in that they embraced the discourse of the elite wines and, in turn, used it to their advantage.

CHAPTER 8. WINEGROWING STORIES

1. While it is true that conversations concerning one's past will often begin with the early years, in most cases the linear pattern will give way to a discussion of seminal events and meaningful circumstances, tacking back and forth between multiple pasts and the present.

2. The linguistic turn, which is often attributed to the ordinary-language philosophy of the later Wittgenstein, argues against a view of language as a vehicle for plotting or mapping social reality. Although there is a good deal of theoretical variety to what presently typifies the linguistic turn, that is, Foucault's notion of discourse is not reducible to the sociolingu-

ist's speech events, there is nonetheless the shared idea that language or discourse is constitutive of social reality.

3. While the position that Hayden White takes about rhetoric and historical narratives may be extreme by the standards of some historians, it is no longer that controversial to maintain that facts are socially constructed and that historically reality is as much socially constituting as constituted. This is consistent with the new cultural historians discussed in Chapter 1 and has significant points of overlap with a Geertzian interpretive anthropology.

   In maintaining that historical narratives are not necessarily uniform, I am not arguing in support of postmodern social theory. To the contrary, I believe that it is important for social theory to seek to make connections between social phenomena and processes that have the appearance of being unrelated. For a more developed version of this argument, see Ulin 1991 on modernism and postmodernism in anthropology.

4. I find that Obeyesekere has made use of Freudian theory in a very imaginative way through his interpretation of the possession of Sri Lankan priestesses (see, for example, his 1981 *Medusa's Hair*). However, while he convincingly shows how cultural symbols are given personal meaning, the ultimate appeal to psychosexual process through Freud strikes me as contrived and ultimately undermining of the very connections that he seeks to support between the social and the personal.

5. To their credit, scholars like Obeyesekere who support a depth psychology believe that there is a density to the human mind that cannot be completely disclosed or penetrated.

6. The hermeneutic circle is sometimes regarded with misgiving because its relating of part to whole is conceived by some scholars to be nothing more than circular. This is, however, contested by Paul Ricoeur (1973).

7. In fact, much of Ricoeur's book is directed toward challenging the medical model of Freud by illustrating the dependency of depth psychology on the life of symbols and thus a hermeneutic framework. For Ricoeur, Freud's approach belongs as much, if not more, to the human sciences as to the natural sciences.

8. This is the ostensible goal of Obeyesekere in seeking to understand how the social is present in the personal. However, he is resolute in his defense of psychological complexes, which he believes to be universal, and thus he dehistoricizes the social. Consequently, his explorations of personal motivations and individual psychology seem to me to be contrived or forced.

9. This sense of critical hermeneutics departs from Ricoeur's version, which he calls a "hermeneutics of suspicion," by emphasizing the constraints of social life under which texts are produced rather than, as with Ricoeur,

the suspension of the external reference of texts in order to examine its internal order. For a more detailed critique of Ricoeur's hermeneutics of suspicion see Chapter 5 of my *Understanding Cultures*.

10. While the number of therapies are multitudinous, it is generally the case that the discourse between therapist and client is oriented exclusively to the self-disclosure of the client. Moreover, the therapist often represents authority or, as Foucault has argued, the standard of bourgeois values and discipline (1965). The analogy between fieldwork and therapy is not far-fetched as in both cases the medium of disclosure is discourse.

11. This genre of writing is not of course new to anthropology. Paul Radin made use of the biographical genre in his *Autobiography of a Winnebago Indian* as did Marcel Griaule in his celebrated *Conversations with Ogotom-mêli*.

12. For this genre of ethnographic writing Vincent Crapanzano's (1980) *Tuhami: Portrait of a Moroccan* is uncharacteristically self-conscious of the theoretical strengths and limitations of focusing an account on a single informant. Perhaps the distinguishing feature is that we learn as much about Crapanzano as we do about Tuhami, thus disclosing the reflexive dimension of the work.

13. Sociologists have become more involved in recent years in collecting life histories. The means of collecting such life histories usually consists of several formal interviews. This is quite different from the case of the anthropologist, who comes to know informants over a period of years and in contexts which are far less formal than the interview setting.

14. In naive fashion, I had failed to realize that cows are excellent fertilizer factories. So, in addition to the problem of personal safety, I was ill prepared for cow dung by my wearing of jogging shoes. So go the foibles of fieldwork.

15. I often had the impression that a test of my "manhood" was at stake as winegrowers, especially the males, will seek to establish whether or not the newcomer can hold his or her wine.

16. I generally felt a sense of privilege in my fieldwork situation by virtue of my ability to extricate myself to Paris when the burdens and loneliness of fieldwork became too hard to bear. However, more than once some informants expressed to me the privilege of their occupation and the fact that they could often take afternoons to discuss their activities and lives with me. The fact that some informants likewise control when they work does not avoid the issue of representation and power, and the fact that the ethnographer assumes the responsibility of writing about others in circumstances where the informants do not write about themselves.

17. Stanley Diamond was among the first to point out the marginality of the anthropologist and thus the critical stance of anthropology with respect to Western civilization (1974).

18. The first female winegrower that I met was Anne Bosquet who worked side by side with her husband. Both are members of the Sigoulès wine cooperative. At the Pauillac cooperative, I also met Marie Lescot who is at least twenty years younger than Nicole Ducros.

19. It is not uncommon in rural France and elsewhere in Europe that place of birth or the natal village establishes one's identity. This point is explored by Barbara Anderson in her *First Fieldwork* (1990).

20. While sharecropping is still alive in the Médoc today, the raising of cows has virtually disappeared. Practically all the available land has been converted to vineyards.

21. Since Ducros's election, the younger Lescot was also elected to Pauillac's Board of Directors. However, the election of women to the boards of directors of southwest French wine cooperatives remains an exceptional occurrence.

22. There are several reasons that I decided to live near the University of Bordeaux. First of all, I had a research affiliation at the University with the Centre d'Études et de Recherches d'Histoire institutionnelle et régionale and so wanted to have contact with the Center's historians. Second, I was also conducting research at the departmental archives and they were located in the city of Bordeaux. Moreover, my field site was spread over a rather large area and so my apartment near the University was only at most fifty minutes from the most distant cooperative location and informants.

23. I am very grateful to Albert for sharing with me his grandfather's notebooks which provide interesting background information on the cooperative's founding as well as accounts of the early meetings of the membership.

24. There is not an exact equivalent in France to the American bachelor's degree. However, the *licence,* like the bachelor's, is the first university degree. It would involve much more intensive study in history alone than is the case in the United States.

25. Requests to join the cooperative are entertained directly by the *conseil d'administration.* The Board of Directors seeks to ascertain the seriousness of the intent and the quality of the vineyards of the prospective members. However, many more are turned down than actually accepted as members.

26. Raymond Williams has been foremost in disclosing the harsh reality of the countryside in the light of its pastoral representation, especially in nineteenth-century art and literature (1973).

CHAPTER 9. PROSPECTS AND FUTURES

1. There were occasional periods of sustained economic crisis when declining prices of vineyards enabled merchants and financial groups to purchase Médoc estates at what amounts to a virtual bargain.

2. I use multinational and global alcohol corporations interchangeably because the alcohol corporations are in fact multinational and thus share the same organizational framework. However, the corporations that have had the most significant influence in the Médoc are the global alcohol corporations and not multinationals in general.

3. The merchant houses that purchased elite vineyards in the nineteenth and even early twentieth centuries had enormous influence over production and marketing but had not developed the resources to control retail as would their multinational successors.

4. Santori, Seagrams, and the insurance group AXA were pointed out to me by my informants as among the leaders in purchasing Médoc vineyards.

5. The Dordogne experienced a dramatic loss in population following the phylloxera blight. Moreover, there were large sections of the Dordogne, especially to the north, where vineyards destroyed by the phylloxera were never replaced. The potential destruction ensuing from vineyard maladies has been a discouragement in itself to sons and daughters taking up their parents' winegrowing profession.

6. Since cooperatives are concerned about the quality of wine, the administrators pay special attention to the quality of care given to the vineyards of members. Those growers who do not live up to the standards can be evicted from the cooperative altogether if they fail to correct an identified problem.

7. While I cannot speak conclusively on this issue, I know enough about the transaction to suggest that the sum being offered by AXA for Nicole Ducros's vineyards was far in excess of Château Latour's offer.

8. I thank Pierre Besson for supplying me with details concerning the fate of Nicole Ducros's estate and the activities of AXA in the Médoc.

9. While there may be ways around the inheritance tax my informants never discussed this option with me. Even if they had, I would not betray such a confidence in print.

10. Many consumers mistakenly associate Mouton Cadet with the famous Rothschild estates. However, it is a wine that is blended from the grapes purchased by the Rothschilds from growers in the Bordeaux region. However, image counts for a great deal and so the rather unremarkable Mouton Cadet has been a tremendous financial success.

11. This is not to say that there has not been conflict between cooperative growers and château proprietors; the controversy over the use of château labels stands as a case in point. However, the relations between these two groups is not univocal as there is without question some recognition on the part of cooperative growers that the châteaus have brought much in the way of worldwide esteem to the Médoc which in turn has supported the considerable financial value of Médoc wines. However, the cooperative growers do distinguish between the elite proprietors who live in the Médoc and faceless corporations that they find to be a menace because of their indifference and seemingly exclusive interest in profits.

12. This is potentially experienced as a betrayal on the part of the French government whose agricultural policies for so long had supported small-scale family farming, albeit within a context that demanded modernization.

13. The European Economic Community (EEC) became the European Union (EU) in 1992. The EU has a broader social and economic agenda than the former EEC that includes among other things plans for a common currency and even a common European language. While I make reference in this section to both the EEC and EU, the EEC is employed for the period that predates 1992 and the EU for the period of 1992 onwards.

14. Apart from this being conveyed directly by informants, I also used to listen to talk shows as I drove from field site to field site. I was amazed by the passionate distrust—and here the time is 1990—of the impending European Union. Some callers would protest the insult to the French people that English had become the international language of business and that this would only be worse if a single, albeit invented, European language was imposed. Moreover, there were callers from the Hunters and Fishers political party who claimed that they would not accept the hunting and fishing regulations of the larger European community because they went against the grain of French tradition and culture.

15. Lebrun would not be specific about what changes were being considered as he said the process of discussing changes was still ongoing among the *conseil d'administration*. Moreover, I was not permitted to attend the meetings of the Board of Directors as the conversations conducted there were regarded as confidential.

16. The Bergerac appellation does not occupy an especially elevated position in the southwest French wine hierarchy. Nonetheless, standard table wines are not classified as AOC but as *Vin Délimité de Qualité Supérieure* (VDQS) or *Vin de Pays*. Therefore, the Sigoulès wines have some status over those normally referred to as table wines. However, at 8 to 10 francs per bottle, there is little difference in price between Sigoulès wines and table wines.

17. Château d'Yquem was the only first great growth among the Sauternes included in the 1855 Bordeaux classification (Parker 1991:926). Bottles of Château d'Yquem can sell for 125 francs or more while a good Monbazillac cooperative wine can be purchased for 35 to 40 francs.

REFERENCE LIST

Anderson, Barbara
1990   *First Fieldwork*. Prospect Heights, Ill.: Waveland.
Anderson, Benedict
1983   *Imagined Communities: Reflections on the Origin and Spread of Nationalism*. London: Verso.
Appadurai, Arjun, ed.
1986   *The Social Life of Things: Commodities in Cultural Perspective*. Cambridge: Cambridge University Press.
Asad, Talal, ed.
1973   *Anthropology and the Colonial Encounter*. New York: Humanities Press.
Bakhtin, Mikhail
1986   *Speech Genres and Other Late Essays*. Translated by V. W. McGee. Austin: University of Texas Press.
Bartoli, Pierre, Daniel Boulet, Philippe Lacombe, Jean-Pierre LaPorte, Robert Lifran, and Etienne Montaigne
1987   *L'économie viticole française*. Paris: Institut de la recherche agronomique.
Baudrillard, Jean
1975   *The Mirror of Production*. St. Louis: Telos Press.
Beauroy, Jacques
1976   *Vin et societé à Bergerac: Du moyen age aux temps modernes*. Saratoga, California: Anma Libri & Co.
Benjamin, Walter
1969   *Illuminations*. Edited by Hannah Arendt. New York: Schocken Books.
Bernstein, Richard
1976   *The Restructuring of Social and Political Theory*. Philadelphia: University of Pennsylvania Press.

Biersack, Aletta
    1989   Local Knowledge, Local History: Geertz and Beyond. In *The New Cultural History,* edited by Lynn Hunt. Berkeley: University of California Press.

Blok, Anton
    1981   Rams and Billy-Goats: A Key to the Mediterranean Code of Honour. *Man* 16, no. 3:427–40.

Bourdieu, Pierre
    1977   *Outline of a Theory of Practice.* Cambridge: Cambridge University Press.

    1984   *Distinction: A Social Critique of the Judgment of Taste.* Cambridge: Harvard University Press.

Braverman, Harry
    1974   *Labor and Monopoly Capital.* New York: Monthly Review Press.

Campbell, Joseph
    1964   *Honour, Family and Patronage: A Study of Institutions and Moral Values in a Greek Mountain Community.* Oxford: Clarendon Press.

Clifford, James
    1988   *The Predicament of Culture.* Cambridge: Harvard University Press.

Clifford, James, and George E. Marcus, eds.
    1986   *Writing Culture: The Poetics and Politics of Ethnography.* Berkeley: University of California Press.

Cohn, Bernard S.
    1980   History and Anthropology: The State of Play. *Comparative Studies in Society and History* 22:199–221.

    1981   Anthropology and History in the 1980s. *Journal of Interdisciplinary History* 12, no. 2 (Autumn): 227–52.

    1987   *An Anthropologist among the Historians and Other Essays.* New Delhi: Oxford University Press.

Cole, John W.
    1977   Anthropology Comes Part-Way Home: Community Studies in Europe. *Annual Reviews in Anthropology* 6:349–78.

Cole, Sally
    1991   *Women of Praia.* Princeton: Princeton University Press.

Comaroff, Jean
    1985   *Body of Power, Spirit of Resistance.* Chicago: University of Chicago Press.

Comaroff, John, and Jean Comaroff
    1992   *Ethnography and the Historical Imagination.* Boulder: Westview Press.

Connell, R. W.
    1987   *Gender and Power.* Stanford: Stanford University Press.

Corbin, Alain
　1986　*The Foul and the Fragrant: Odor and the French Social Imagination.*
　　　　Cambridge: Harvard University Press.
Crapanzano, Vincent
　1980　*Tuhami: Portrait of a Moroccan.* Chicago: University of Chicago
　　　　Press.
Darnton, Robert
　1984　*The Great Cat Massacre and Other Episodes in French Cultural History.*
　　　　New York: Vintage Books.
Derrida, Jacques
　1974　*Of Grammatology.* Baltimore: Johns Hopkins University Press.
Diamond, Stanley
　1974　*In Search of the Primitive.* New Brunswick, N.J.: Transaction Books.
Dion, Roger
　1977　*Histoire de la vigne et du vin en France.* Paris: Flammarion.
Dubisch, Jill
　1993　"Foreign Chickens" and Other Outsiders: Gender and Community
　　　　in Greece. *American Ethnologist* 20, no. 2:272–87.
du Boulay, Juliet
　1974　*Portrait of a Greek Mountain Village.* Oxford: Clarendon Press.
Duby, Georges
　1976　*Histoire de la France rurale.* Vol 4. Paris: Seuil.
L'École Nationale d'Ingenieurs des Travaux Agricoles de Bordeaux,
　　　　Département Economie et Gestion
　1987　*La Relation Cave Coopérative-Adherent: Étude Realisée sur les Quatre
　　　　Cave Coopératives Adherentes à UNIMEDOC.* Gradignan.
Engels, Frederick
　1972　*The Origin of the Family, Private Property and the State.* New York:
　　　　International Publishers.
Enjalbert, Henri
　1953　Comment naissent les grands crus: Bordeaux, Porto, Cognac.
　　　　Annales 8:315–28, 457–74.
Enjalbert, Henri, and Bernard Enjalbert
　1987　*L'Histoire de la vigne et du vin.* Paris: Bordas S.A.
Fabian, Johannes
　1983　*Time and the Other: How Anthropology Makes Its Object.* New York:
　　　　Columbia University Press.
Foucault, Michel
　1965　*Madness and Civilization.* New York: Vintage Books.
　1973　*The Order of Things: An Archaeology of the Human Sciences.* New
　　　　York: Vintage Books.

1979   *Discipline and Punish: The Birth of the Prison.* New York: Vintage Books.

Frank, Andre Gunder

   1969   *Capitalism and Underdevelopment in Latin America.* New York: Monthly Review Press.

Friedman, Jonathan

   1991   Further Notes on the Adventures of Phallus in Blunderland. In *Constructing Knowledge: Authority and Critique in the Social Sciences,* edited by Lorraine Nencel and Peter Pels. London: Sage.

Gadamer, Hans-Georg

   1975   *Truth and Method.* New York: Seabury Press.

   1976   *Philosophical Hermeneutics.* Berkeley: University of California Press.

Gay, Peter

   1968   *The Enlightenment: An Interpretation.* New York: Random House.

Geertz, Clifford

   1973   *The Interpretation of Cultures.* New York: Basic Books.

   1976   From the Native's Point of View: On the Nature of Anthropological Understanding. In *Meaning and Anthropology,* edited by Keith Basso and Henry Selby. Albuquerque: University of New Mexico Press.

Giddens, Anthony

   1984   *The Constitution of Society.* Berkeley: University of California Press.

Ginzburg, Carlo

   1982   *The Cheese and the Worms.* New York: Penquin Books.

Gramsci, Antonio

   1971   *Selections from the Prison Notebooks.* London: Lawrence and Wishart.

   1975   *The Modern Prince and Other Writings.* New York: International Publishers.

Griaule, Marcel

   1965   *Conversations with Ogotommêli.* London: Oxford University Press.

Guichard, François, and Philippe Roudié

   1985   *Vins, vignerons et cooperateurs de Bordeaux et de Porto.* Vol. 1. Paris: CNRS.

Habermas, Jürgen

   1971   *Knowledge and Human Interests.* Boston: Beacon Press.

   1984   *The Theory of Communicative Action.* Vol. 1: *Reason and the Rationalization of Society.* Boston: Beacon Press.

Handler, Richard

   1986   Authenticity. *Anthropology Today* 2:2–4.

   1988   *Nationalism and the Politics of Culture in Quebec.* Madison: University of Wisconsin Press.

Handler, Richard, and Jocelyn Linnekin
   1984   Tradition, Genuine or Spurious. *Journal of American Folklore* 97, no.
         385:273–90.
Hanson, Allan
   1989   The Making of the Maori: Culture Invention and Its Logic.
         American Anthropologist 91:890–902.
Herzfeld, Michael
   1982   *Ours Once More: Folklore, Ideology and the Making of Modern Greece*.
         Austin: University of Texas Press.
   1987   *Anthropology through the Looking Glass: Critical Ethnography on the
         Margins of Europe*. Cambridge: Cambridge University Press.
Hilton, Rodney, ed.
   1978   *The Transition from Feudalism to Capitalism*. London: Verso.
Hobsbawm, Eric J., and Terence Ranger, eds.
   1983   *The Invention of Tradition*. Cambridge: Cambridge University Press.
Hunt, Lynn, ed.
   1989   *The New Cultural History*. Berkeley: University of California Press.
Hymes, Dell, ed.
   1972   *Reinventing Anthropology*. New York: Random House.
Keesing, Roger
   1992   *Custom and Confrontation: The Kwaio Struggle for Identity*. Chicago:
         University of Chicago Press.
Lachiver, Marcel
   1988   *Vins, vignes et vignerons*. Paris: Fayard.
Lass, Andrew
   1988   Romantic Documents and Political Monuments: The Meaning-
         Fulfillment of History in 19th Century Czech Nationalism.
         American Ethnologist 15, no. 3:456–71.
Ladurie, Emmanuelle Le Roy
   1979   *Montaillou: The Promised Land of Error*. New York: Vintage Books.
Lévi-Strauss, Claude
   1963   *Structural Anthropology*. New York: Basic Books.
Lévy-Bruhl, Lucien
   1965   *The Soul of the Primitive*. London: George Allen and Unwin.
Linnekin, Jocelyn
   1983   Defining Tradition: Variations on the Hawaiian Identity. *American
         Ethnologist* 10:241–52.
   1991   Cultural Invention and the Dilemma of Authenticity. *American
         Anthropologist* 93:446–49.
   1992   On the Theory and Politics of Cultural Construction in the Pacific.
         Oceania 62:249–63.

Loubère, Leo
   1978   *The Red and the White.* Albany: State University of New York Press.
   1990   *The Wine Revolution in France.* Princeton: Princeton University Press.
Loubère, Leo, Jean Sagnes, Laura Frader, and Rémy Pech
   1985   *The Vine Remembers: French Vignerons Remember Their Past.* Albany: State University of New York Press.
Malinowski, Bronislav
   1961   *Argonauts of the Western Pacific.* New York: E. P. Dutton.
Marcus, George E., and Michael M. J. Fischer
   1986   *Anthropology as Cultural Critique.* Chicago: University of Chicago Press.
Marcus, Steven
   1974   *Engels, Manchester and the Working Class.* New York: Vintage Books.
Marx, Karl
   1967   *Capital.* New York: International Publishers.
Mintz, Sidney W.
   1985   *Sweetness and Power.* New York: Penguin.
   1987   Author's Rejoinder. *Food and Foodways* 2:171–97.
Obeyesekere, Ganath
   1981   *Medusa's Hair.* Chicago: University of Chicago Press.
   1990   *The Works of Culture: Symbolic Transformation in Psychoanalysis and Anthropology.* Chicago: University of Chicago Press.
Ohnuki-Tierney, Emiko, ed.
   1990   *Culture through Time: Anthropological Approaches.* Stanford: Stanford University Press.
Ortner, Sherry
   1984   Theory in Anthropology since the Sixties. *Comparative Studies in Society and History* 26, no. 1:126–66.
   1990   Patterns of History: Cultural Schemas in the Foundings of Sherpa Religious Institutions. In *Culture through Time: Anthropological Approaches,* edited by Emiko Ohnuki-Tierney. Stanford: Stanford University Press.
Parker, Robert M., Jr.
   1991   *Bordeaux: A Comprehensive Guide to the Wines Produced from 1961–1990.* New York: Simon and Schuster.
Penning-Rowsell, Edmund
   1969   *The Wines of Bordeaux.* 6th ed. London: Penguin Books.
Peynaud, Emile
   1988   *Le Vin et les jours.* Paris: Bordas.
Pijassou, René
   1980   *Le Médoc: Un grand vignoble de qualité.* 2 vols. Paris: Tallandier.

Rabinow, Paul
1973 *Reflections on Fieldwork in Morocco.* Berkeley: University of California Press.
1989 *French Modern.* Cambridge: MIT Press.
Radcliffe-Brown, A. R.
1965 *Structure and Function in Primitive Society.* New York: Free Press.
Radin, Paul
1963 *The Autobiography of a Winnebago Indian.* New York: Dover.
Ricoeur, Paul
1970 *Freud and Philosophy.* New Haven: Yale University Press.
1971 The Model of the Text: Meaningful Action Considered as a Text. *Social Research* 38, no. 3:29–56.
1974 *The Conflict of Interpretations: Essays in Hermeneutics.* Evanston, Ill.: Northwestern University Press.
Rogers, Susan Carol
1975 Female Forms of Power and the Myth of Male Dominance: A Model of Female/Male Interaction in Peasant Societies. *American Ethnologist* 2, no. 4:727–56.
1985 Gender in Southwestern France: The Myth of Male Dominance Revisited. *Anthropology* 9, no. 1/2 (May–December): 65–86.
1991 *Shaping Modern Times in Rural France: The Transformation and Reproduction of an Aveyronnais Community.* Princeton: Princeton University Press.
Rosaldo, Renato
1986 From the Door of His Tent: The Fieldworker and the Inquisitor. In *Writing Culture: The Poetics and Politics of Ethnography,* edited by James Clifford and George Marcus. Berkeley: University of California Press.
1990 *Culture and Truth.* Boston: Beacon Press.
Roseberry, William
1989 *Anthropologies and Histories: Essays in Culture, History, and Political Economy.* New Brunswick, N.J.: Rutgers University Press.
Rosenberg, Harriet
1988 *A Negotiated World: Three Centuries of Change in a French Alpine Community.* Toronto: University of Toronto Press.
Roudié, Philippe
1988 *Vignobles et vignerons du Bordelais (1850–1980).* Paris: CNRS.
Sahlins, Marshall
1985 *Islands of History.* Chicago: University of Chicago Press.
1990 The Political Economy of Grandeur in Hawaii from 1810 to 1830. In *Culture through Time: Anthropological Approaches,* edited by Emiko Ohnuki-Tierney. Stanford: Stanford University Press.

Said, Edward
  1978   *Orientalism*. New York: Random House.
  1989   Representing the Colonized: Anthropology's Interlocutors. *Critical Inquiry* 15:205–25.
Schlumberger, Eveline
  1973   Le charme envirant de Château-Margaux. *Connaissance des Arts* (November): 101–5.
Schneider, Jane
  1978   Peacocks and Penguins: The Political Economy of European Cloth and Colors. *American Ethnologist* 5:413–47.
Shils, Edward
  1981   *Tradition*. Chicago: University of Chicago Press.
Shostak, Marjorie
  1981   *Nisa: The Life and Words of a !Kung Woman*. New York: Vintage Books.
Sider, Gerald
  1986   *Culture and Class in Anthropology and History*. Cambridge: Cambridge University Press.
Skocpol, Theda
  1977   *States and Social Revolutions: A Comparative Analysis of France, Russia and China*. Cambridge: Cambridge University Press.
Sobul, Albert
  1977   Persistence of "Feudalism" in the Rural Society of Nineteenth Century France. In *Rural Society in France*, edited by Robert Forster and Orest Ranum. Baltimore: Johns Hopkins University Press.
Taussig, Michael
  1980   *The Devil and Commodity Fetishism in South America*. Chapel Hill: University of North Carolina Press.
  1987   *Shamanism, Colonialism and the Wild Man*. Chicago: University of Chicago Press.
  1992   *Mimesis and Alterity*. New York: Routledge.
Thompson, Edward P.
  1966   *The Making of the English Working Class*. New York: Vintage.
  1978   *The Poverty of Theory and Other Essays*. New York: Monthly Review Press.
Tilly, Charles
  1975   *The Rebellious Century 1830–1930*. Cambridge: Harvard University Press.
Trevor-Roper, Hugh
  1983   The Invention of Tradition: The Highland Tradition of Scotland. In *The Invention of Tradition*, edited by Eric Hobsbawm and Terence Ranger. Cambridge: Cambridge University Press.

Tsoukalis, Loukas

1991   *The New European Economy: The Politics and Economics of Integration.*
        New York: Oxford University Press.

Tylor, Edward Burnett

1873   *Primitive Culture: Researches into the Development of Mythology,
        Philosophy, Religion, Language, Art, and Custom.* London: John
        Murray.

Ulin, Robert C.

1984   *Understanding Cultures: Perspectives in Anthropology and Social Theory.*
        Austin: University of Texas Press.

1986   Social Change through a Southwest French Wine Cooperative.
        Ethnologia Europaea 16:25–38.

1987   Writing and Power: The Recovery of Winegrowing Histories in the
        Southwest of France. *Anthropological Quarterly* 60, no. 2:77–82.

1988   Cooperation or Cooptation: A Southwest French Wine
        Cooperative. *Dialectical Anthropology* 13:253–67.

1991A   The Current Tide in American Europeanist Anthropology.
        Anthropology Today 7, no. 6:8–12.

1991B   Critical Anthropology Twenty Years Later: Modernism and
        Postmodernism in Anthropology. *Critique of Anthropology* 11, no.
        1:63–89.

1995   Review of *Culture through Time: Anthropological Approaches,* edited
        by Emiko Ohnuki-Tierney. *International Studies in Philosophy* 27, no.
        2:141–43.

Unwin, Tim

1991   *Wine and the Vine: A Historical Geography of Viticulture and the Wine
        Trade.* London: Routledge.

Vico, Giambatista

1948   *The New Science.* Ithaca: Cornell University Press.

Wagner, Roy

1975   *The Invention of Culture.* Chicago: University of Chicago Press.

Wallerstein, Immanuel

1974   *The Modern World-System: Capitalist Agriculture and the Origins of the
        European World-Economy in the Sixteenth Century.* New York:
        Academic Press.

Warner, Charles K.

1960   *The Winegrowers of France and the Government since 1875.* New York:
        Columbia University Press.

Weber, Eugen

1976   *Peasants into Frenchmen.* Stanford: Stanford University Press.

White, Hayden

1978   *Tropics of Discourse.* Baltimore: Johns Hopkins University Press.

Williams, Raymond

  1973   *The Country and the City.* Oxford: Oxford University Press.

  1977   *Marxism and Literature.* Oxford: Oxford University Press.

Wolf, Eric

  1982   *Europe and the People without History.* Berkeley: University of California Press.

Worsley, Peter, ed.

  1971   *Two Blades of Grass: Rural Coops in Agricultural Modernization.* Manchester: Manchester University Press.

Yoon, Soon Young Song

  1973   In the Final Instance: Peasant and Gentlemen Winegrowers in Provence—A Regional Class Study. Ph.D. diss., University of Michigan, Ann Arbor.

  1975   Provençal Wine Co-operatives. In *Beyond the Community: Social Process in Europe,* edited by Jeremy Boissevain and John Friedl. The Hague: Department of Education and Science of the Netherlands.

INDEX

Acrins wine cooperative, 115
agriculteur, 144
agricultural cooperation, 97–98
Albert, Marcelin, 100
Algerian wines, 49, 100
Annales school, 22, 28
Appellation contrôlée legislation, 53, 103. *See also* winegrowing legislation
apprenticeship, 122, 225, 269n
assemblée generale. See wine cooperatives, General Assembly
authenticity: and nature, 50–53; of wine, 50–51, 52, 143; social construction of, 46
AXA, 236–38

Bakhtin, Mikhail: on heteroglossia or discourse, 37, 267n
banks: investing in Médoc vineyards, 240
Baudrillard, Jean: critique of marxism, 36–37
Beauroy, Jacques, 69, 73, 80
Bégadan wine cooperative, 7, 115, 141–42, 164–65, 197–98, 259n
Bergerac wines, 10, 46, 66, 73
Bordeaux elites, 47, 54
Bordeaux merchants, 70, 74–75, 123, 179, 181, 233
Bordeaux Parliament, 54, 70
Bordeaux wines, 39, 46, 66–67, 143
Bourdieu, Pierre: on cultural capital, 39; on consumption patterns, 59; on distinction, 44, 54–55; on habitus, 37

Braverman, Harry: on capitalist degradation of labor, 121–22, 153–54, 273n

capitalism, 63, 65, 77, 82, 91, 150, 152
capitalist division of labor, 152–55, 175
capitalist markets, 72
Castillon, battle of, 47
Cessac wine cooperative, 115
Chandou, Raymond, 190
chapeau, 139
chapitalization, 50, 139
château and cultural distinction, 54, 83, 143
château label, 56, 58–59, 159, 186–87
Château Clarke, 238–39
Château Latour, 57
Château Margaux, 54–55
Classification of 1855, 48–49, 53, 83–84, 143
cleaning vineyards, 125–26
Clifford, James, 16, 205
climate and soil, 45–46, 266n
Cole, John, 17–18, 20
Cole, Sally: on history and biography, 201–2; on public, private and gender, 210–11
collaboration: with independent winegrowers, 184–85
colonialism and neocolonialism, 15
Comaroff, John and Jean, 19, 93
commodification of wine. *See* political economy
commodity fetishism, 1